Church and State in 21st Century

Church and State in 21st Century Britain

The Future of Church Establishment

Edited by

R. M. Morris
Senior Honorary Research Fellow, Constitution Unit, Department of Political Science, University College London, UK

First published 2009 by
PALGRAVE MACMILLAN

Palgrave Macmillan in the UK is an imprint of Macmillan Publishers Limited,
registered in England, company number 785998, of Houndmills, Basingstoke,
Hampshire RG21 6XS.

Palgrave Macmillan in the US is a division of St Martin's Press LLC,
175 Fifth Avenue, New York, NY 10010.

Palgrave Macmillan is the global academic imprint of the above companies
and has companies and representatives throughout the world.

Palgrave® and Macmillan® are registered trademarks in the United States,
the United Kingdom, Europe and other countries.

ISBN 978-1-349-36399-5   ISBN 978-0-230-23437-6 (eBook)
DOI 10.1007/978-0-230-23437-6

This book is printed on paper suitable for recycling and made from fully
managed and sustained forest sources. Logging, pulping and manufacturing
processes are expected to conform to the environmental regulations of the
country of origin.

A catalogue record for this book is available from the British Library.

Library of Congress Cataloging-in-Publication Data
Church and state in 21st century Britain : the future of church
    establishment / edited by R.M. Morris.
        p. cm.
    Includes bibliographical references and index.
    ISBN 978–0–230–55511–2
    1. Church of England—Establishment and disestablishment. 2.
    Established churches—Great Britain—History. 3. Great Britain—
    Church history. 4. Established churches—Scandinavia. 5.
    Scandinavia—Church history. I. Morris, R. M., 1937–
    BX5157.C478 2009
    322'.10941090511—dc22

                                                          2008052856

Contents

Tables

Preface

This study grew out of work initiated in the Constitution Unit, Department of Political Science, University College London. The first stage of the project, an examination of the origins and present meaning of establishment, was assisted by grants from the Joseph Rowntree Charitable Trust and what was then the Department for Constitutional Affairs and resulted in the publication of *Church and State: A Mapping Exercise* (2006). The unit used the material gathered during the mapping exercise together with other papers to help inform discussion at a seminar held under Chatham House rules at St Katharine's, Limehouse, in July 2006. The subsequent publication – *Church and State: Some Reflections on Church Establishment in England* (2008) – consists largely of papers circulated for the Limehouse seminar. Material from both previous publications and the seminar has been further developed for this work.

This book is, like its predecessor publications, the work of several hands. Its aim is to help inform current discussion about the future of the relationship between the two established churches in the United Kingdom and the state.

In addition to recognizing the help received most immediately from the other contributors to the present study, other acknowledgements are due. The Director of the Constitution Unit, Professor Robert Hazell, has been unfailing in his continuing support during the protracted life of the undertaking. Frank Cranmer, in addition to the material within and with which he is directly identified, has not only made his considerable knowledge of Church affairs and law unstintingly available at all times but also assisted by commenting on much material in draft. Much valued help has also been given at various times and in various ways by Mark Glover, Iain McLean, Chris Moses, Scot Peterson, Richard Pring and Vicki Spence.

It should also be noted that the authorities of the Churches of England and Scotland have at all times been open and responsive to requests for information.

I am very grateful to them all. Unless they have contributed directly, none of these sources is, however, in any way responsible for the content of what follows where, unless chapters are attributed to others, the author is myself.

R. M. Morris
Honorary Senior Research Fellow
Constitution Unit
Department of Political Science
University College London

Glossary

Anglican	Of, or pertaining to, the Church of England
Anglican Communion	Episcopal churches world wide in communion with the See of Canterbury
ASA	Archbishops' Appointments Secretary
BERR	Department for Business, Enterprise and Regulatory Reform
BSA	British Social Attitudes Survey
Canon	Church law made by extra-parliamentary procedure
CCTW	Commisssioners of Church Temporalities in Wales
Concurrent endowment	Where a government supports more than one church/religion simultaneously
CRE	Commission for Racial Equality
DCLG	Department for Communities and Local Government
DCMS	Department for Culture, Media and Sport
DfES	Department for Education and Skills
DTI	Department for Trade and Industry, precursor of BERR
EH	English Heritage
Erastian	Where the state has supremacy/control over a church in ecclesiastical as well as civil matters
EU	European Union
GLA	Greater London Authority
HC	Official Report of parliamentary proceedings – Commons
HL	Official Report of parliamentary proceedings – Lords
HLF	Heritage Lottery Fund
HO	Home Office
ICRC	Inner Cities Religious Council
LEA	Local Education Authority
Measure	Church law of statutory force made under the 'Enabling' Act 1919
MOD	Ministry of Defence
NCSR	National Centre for Social Research
NHS	National Health Service

NSO	Office for National Statistics
NSS	National Secular Society
PASC	Public Administration Select Committee of the House of Commons
PCC	Parochial Church Council
PMAS	Prime Minister's Appointments Secretary
PP	Parliamentary Papers – Sessional records of parliamentary proceedings
RC	Roman Catholic
Regium Donum	Former government payments 1690–1869 in support of Presbyterian clergy in Ireland and England
SACRE	Standing Advisory Council on Religious Education
SPCK	Society for the Propagation of Christian Knowledge
Supreme Governor	Title conferred on the sovereign as head of the Church of England
TNA	The National Archives at Kew
UCL	University College London
VAT	Value Added Tax
WH	Denotes House of Commons debate in Westminster Hall
White Paper	Firm government policy proposals
WS	Denotes Written Statement in Parliament

Contributors

Editor and author

Dr R. M. (Bob) Morris is an Honorary Senior Research Fellow, Constitution Unit, Department of Political Science, University College London, and a former Home Office career civil servant.

Other authors

Frank Cranmer – Fellow of St Chad's College, Durham; Honorary Senior Research Fellow, Constitution Unit, University College London; Honorary Research Fellow, Centre for Law and Religion, Cardiff University Law School. Formerly Clerk of Bills, House of Commons.

John Lucas is a political analyst and former member of the Constitution Unit.

The Revd Dr Marjory MacLean is Depute Clerk of the General Assembly of the Church of Scotland.

Scot Peterson is an attorney licensed to practise in the United States, and a Politics Lecturer at Balliol College, Oxford.

1
Introduction: Mapping the Issues

Despite the frenetic pace of recent constitutional change in a country renowned hitherto for its constitutional conservatism, the United Kingdom remains locked constitutionally so far as religion is concerned in the geopolitics of the late seventeenth century. According to the rhetoric of the times, a Protestant country was rescued in 1688 from popery by a foreign army led by a Dutch prince married to the daughter of the fleeing Roman Catholic king. Parliament insisted in 1689 on the Protestant character of the monarchy, and subsequently provided in 1701 for what it planned to be a perpetual royal Protestant succession. This reinforced an alliance against the Catholic powers in continental Europe by prohibiting Roman Catholic succession to the throne or even a sovereign's ability to marry a Roman Catholic, and required sovereigns to subscribe to the Church of England. On the parliamentary union with Scotland in 1707, the sovereign's obligation was extended to supporting the Presbyterian Church of Scotland – in the form of an oath still sworn by a new monarch immediately on accession to the throne. Similarly, sovereigns at their coronation swear an oath dating from 1689 to uphold the rights and privileges of the Church of England.

It is the argument of this book that it is time to look again at the relationship between the state and established religion in the United Kingdom. While the forms of establishment in Scotland and England are very different, both represent past political solutions to issues of church/state relations long overtaken by subsequent changes. Although in many respects the original character of the establishments is attenuated, both establishments persist and in more than vestigial form. The model of virtually complete separation of church and state in Scotland has allowed that Church to accommodate itself more easily perhaps to a denominational rather than a dominant status as its pre-eminence

1

declined. Things are very different in England. There, establishment took the form of a confessional state where the Church of England and the executive were joint partners in the task of governance and Parliament was the ultimate referee for both.

The treatment throughout concentrates particularly on the *constitutional* implications of the discussion. The United Kingdom is unusual in the extent to which its higher constitutional structures fuse civil government and a particular clerical Christian organization. The head of state is a Christian and Protestant monarch who is also the Supreme Governor of the Church of England, summons the Church's legislature, appoints all its most senior office holders and has direct sway over a number of churches that are free from episcopal oversight. The sovereign also approves the Church's laws whether in the form of parliamentary Measures or extra-parliamentary Canons.

The head of state as monarch of England has to be a member of the episcopal Church of England and cannot marry a Roman Catholic. As monarch of Scotland, however, there are no such requirements, though an oath has to be sworn to support the continuance of the non-episcopal and presbyterian Church of Scotland. It is therefore commonly joked that, while the monarch believes in bishops when in England, the monarch believes the opposite on crossing the border to Scotland.

Two archbishops and twenty-four bishops of the Church of England sit in the United Kingdom legislature, but there is no similar representation there for any other religious groups in England, and none at all for any religious groups in the cases of Scotland, Wales and Northern Ireland. No other sovereign legislature gives room as of right to representatives of religion.

The constitutional issues relating to Scotland on the one hand and England on the other are very different. Indeed, some commentators feel that the only reform required is that England should adopt the Scottish model where the Church of Scotland is said to be independent of the state. This typically Scottish vision does not do justice either to the extent to which the histories of the two countries differ or the degree to which state and church remain interwoven in England. In addition, as explained in Chapter 6, establishment in Scotland is less controversial (if controversial at all) because it is less visible whereas in England establishment has a much greater salience. Furthermore, as Chapter 7 explains, the common understanding of the position of the Church of Scotland may lag behind important recent changes in judicial attitudes towards the status of that Church even under the Church of Scotland Act 1921, thought to confer a very full form of legal autonomy upon it.

Consequently, much of the argument of the book concentrates on the position in England which has 85 per cent of the United Kingdom population, if conducted simultaneously with an eye to arrangements in Scotland and comparable European countries. That said, however, what follows is not a tract for or against church establishment. Polemics (Buchanan 1994; and Hobson 2003) can say a lot about authors' states of mind but are not usually designed to address remedies rather than articulate grievances. Similarly, in its defence of establishment a recent (and possibly semi-official) account of the Church of England treats the issue as either retaining all of the present arrangements or totally abolishing them (Davie, M. 2008). More solemnly, no doubt, the present book attempts to examine just what are the *range*, today, of the vital policy questions about the state's relations with organized religion, and what seem to be the *options* for responding to them.

Furthermore, it is not the argument here that establishment is necessarily incompatible with religious *liberty*. While that may once have been the case, no-one could maintain that it continues to be true (Ahdar and Leigh 2005). What is, however, more questionable is how far establishment is compatible with religious *equality*, a different question and still a live issue in the United Kingdom (Morris 2008a). Interestingly, human rights instruments have so far concentrated on the former rather than the latter, but although the two concepts are often treated as synonymous they are not. How far equality considerations should be addressed will, accordingly, be among the themes in this study.

As ever in the case of what are essentially political problems, timing is important. Normally, there are few naturally occurring stimuli to cause root-and-branch reviews of long-established and deeply entrenched mechanisms like church establishment. However, two reasons make the case for review now particularly compelling. First, incidents of high profile (if still rare and atypical) acts of Islamic terrorism spur discussion about the place of religion in the European nation state, the latter itself grappling with the effects of an increasing globalization on its vision of its own identity. Secondly, there is a purely domestic perspective: although the event is not sought and will itself be deeply regretted, the departure of the present much-respected and long-reigning monarch will expose the underlying assumptions of the British monarchy and its relations with the established churches. A review of some of the more immediate consequences from the point of view of the heir and in the context of how the monarchy may develop has been attempted elsewhere (Morris 2008b). This book, however, investigates the core issues themselves in the belief that it is imperative to order thinking on these subjects so far as possible. This is both for negative reasons – to be sure to forestall misunderstanding (and perhaps malice), and for positive reasons – to contribute to measured and shared public consideration of how change might be attempted.

The point about public discussion is important. Coronations, for example, are not just private family events of celebratory splendour where the domestic chaplain – in this case the Archbishop of Canterbury – officiates, albeit in front of the television cameras. Rather, coronations have always spoken of how we see ourselves not only in England but throughout the United Kingdom. The 1953 coronation was perhaps the last attempt at imperial glorification, and even then it was an anachronism. The world is now a different place and the United Kingdom will need to take stock of itself. A simple repeat of 1953 would be a failure of imagination and possibly an affront to parts of an unimaginably changed population.

The extent of the political, social and cultural changes do not present merely abstract problems to be glossed away by a Premier Duke's committee sitting in private to organize the coronation. The United Kingdom is no longer, in so far as it ever was, a homogenous society united by a particular form of Christian belief. Since World War II, the United Kingdom has become a place of deeper and wider plurality both as regards belief and unbelief let alone ethnicity. What are the implications of such profound changes for ancient institutions and what are the requirements for new ones? Are these matters for the state at all, or does the extent of society's secularization argue for treating religion as a purely private matter where its representative bodies fall to be regarded like any other civil, voluntary organizations? What is to be made in this context of the government's search for social cohesion, and is it best supported by resort to new forms of 'concurrent endowment' to support different religions simultaneously – precedented to some extent by the old *Regium donum*, discussed at the time of Irish disestablishment, and experimentally (ignorantly?) resurrected in some 'social cohesion' programmes?

The focus is institutional and domestic. This is not to imply that the wider Anglican Communion is not important. On the contrary, so far as the Archbishop of Canterbury is concerned, it has risen to a very high point in the hierarchy of his continuing responsibilities (Hurd 2001). However, though the Communion's difficulties appear at times intractable and often noisy, they are not related directly to the constitutional position of the Church of England in the United Kingdom. True, they may affect domestic views of the Church and its leadership, but the

Communion's affairs do not impact on the constitution. Analogies with the Commonwealth are sometimes pressed but with little relevance. In the Commonwealth's case there is some United Kingdom domestic legislation, for example, on citizenship and, in the Statute of Westminster 1931, for important mutual constitutional conventions. There is, however, no relevant domestic legislation in respect of the Communion and it falls, therefore, outside the focus of this work.

The scheme of the book

To understand how we have got to where we are, Part I of the book examines how church establishment has developed in the UK over the last two centuries and of what it now consists. Chapter 2 charts developments in England since 1800 where the longer perspective suggests that externally a gradual, if unplanned, institutional separation took place between the Church of England and the executive but not between the Church and the state more largely considered. Change of the former kind continues. Notably, the Prime Minister, Gordon Brown, signalled in 2007 that he wished to withdraw from an active role in the appointment of senior Church of England officials – a change that calls further into question the rationale of episcopal membership of the House of Lords and the position of the Crown.

Internally, the emergence (in the case of the Convocations, the *re*-emergence) of representative forms of governance can be viewed as the Church of England's counterpart response to the increasing democratization of the parliamentary franchise and the progressive dissolving of starker hierarchical styles. The gradual inclusion of the laity – ultimately into synodical form from 1969 – stemmed from the increasing implausibility of regarding Parliament as representative of the lay membership of the Church of England. That Parliament should be preferred to the General Synod as representing the laity was a position still maintained if only by a small minority of MPs in 1974 when Parliament approved the important Worship and Doctrine Measure. As society changed, so did the Church, though it continues to struggle to agree about changes in gender roles and whether practising homosexuals can validly undertake a priestly vocation. Although still a minority among stipendiary full-time priests, women are now a majority of the total ordained. Recent decisions of the Synod make it clear that women can be expected to start becoming bishops within a decade.

Chapter 2 looks also at the Church of England's involvement in education. Strictly, education is not a constitutional matter in the same way as the other topics. At the same time, the Church's role exemplifies by exception how its institutional significance in social and community care has declined as the state has moved into areas of poverty relief, healthcare and family law formerly provinces of the Church. How far religious organizations should have a role in what is in practice an almost entirely publicly funded service is at present recurrently controversial. From the point of the Church of England, however, its association with education is seen as part of its mission to society, the more understandable when its historic role is appreciated. Religious schools are an instance where religious freedom and equality have resulted in an increasing variety of religious schools as the statutory criteria have had properly to be applied impartially. The role of the 'faith' dimension in social provision has an increasing salience in contemporary discussion of religion and the public square, and is addressed in the section on 're-establishment' in Chapter 14.

Chapters 3 and 4 investigate what exactly is the current law and practice of establishment, looking accordingly at the roles respectively of the monarchy, the legislature, the executive and the judiciary. These chapters describe how establishment is articulated in the modern political system. What they describe is a minimally adjusted inheritance from a pre-modern society. Much can be accounted for by the relative absence of discontinuity in England's constitutional arrangements – no successful invasion since 1066, a religious reformation that substituted monarchical for papal headship of an existing church, a civil war that restored a limited monarchy leading to republican political realities within apparently regal forms. Because England has not experienced state failure as in, say, France, it has not been necessary to start all over again at any point and the old forms have therefore persisted with such minimum adjustment as may have been unavoidable in any particular instance – in the case of the coronation oath without actual parliamentary sanction. Their survival is not therefore the result of deliberate decision but the default outcome of the elapse of time. In that sense accidental, it does not follow that they have to be revisited root and branch. At the same time, they have but a timeworn, decaying legitimacy in modern society and, although it is often maintained that the constituent parts of establishment have to be regarded as a take-it-or-leave-it package, that view is not sustainable and does not have to be accepted. It follows that it is sensible to have in mind the possible directions and content of change in order to prepare for action as and when opportunity arises.

Chapter 5 explains the finances of establishment. A common fallacy is that the state supports the Church of England – though not perhaps the Church of Scotland – out of taxation. Not only is this not the case in Britain but it is truer as the chapter explains of certain other church/state regimes elsewhere in Europe. While there are money flows from the state to the established churches, they occur according to impartial principles that are equally available to all denominations. In practice the Church of England is the largest beneficiary: it has the more numerous public service chaplaincies and, because it possesses by far the larger share of churches that qualify for Heritage grants, it has the largest share there too. However, these flows are accompanied by some counter-flows: chaplains have to be trained for the priesthood, managing schools requires diocesan oversight and support. Moreover, the two established churches face continuing and serious financial challenges, partly because their congregations are both diminishing and getting older. This has caused the Church of Scotland to begin a review of whether it should maintain its commitment to full parochial coverage throughout Scotland. The Church of England's large historic patrimony has helped to keep the more drastic options at bay though it has done much to combine cures and reorganize its parochial network. The largest call on the patrimony is nowadays clergy pensions, a fact that has required imposing a greater burden on current parishioners who have responded gratifyingly so far, though, as in Scotland, the ageing of members of the Church of England does raise the question of longer-term viability. The most acute area of potential difficulty is the Church's ability to maintain its built inheritance. There is also the point that, the more present parishioners bear the costs, the more they will expect to determine spending priorities, and the more they may opt for policies that benefit active members of the Church rather than service to the nation as a whole. There are the seeds there of a conflict between a growing denominationalism on the one hand and an ultimate parliamentary control favouring the larger service role and being reluctant to see the Church walk away with resources originally willed for that purpose but devoted to narrower aims. This could come to a head if the Church thought of opting for disestablishment and still expected to keep all of its patrimony when the Irish and Welsh disestablishments were accompanied by measures of disendowment.

Two chapters on Scotland – 6 and 7 – consider, first, the form and content of establishment in Scotland and, secondly, the extent to which recent decisions by the courts have begun to put glosses on the Church of Scotland Act 1921, which was thought to guarantee a complete separation between that Church and the state. The 'Scottish model' is not, accordingly, what it was once thought to be. Moreover, the actions of the House of Lords in the Scottish *Percy* case appear to show the beginnings of what may be a profound change of judicial attitude. Whereas formerly the 1921 Act was held by the courts to exclude judicial intrusion, changes in the law derived from new species of European Union (EU) legislation have caused the courts to look behind the 1921 Act and limit what was formerly thought to be the operating autonomy of the Church of Scotland.

Nor are such changes confined to Scotland. Although not judicially initiated, the Church of England has also had to face up to changed state expectations of its employment practices as a result of EU law. Long-established concepts of parson's freehold and entirely clerical systems of discipline are giving way to legal codes that have sought to place all employed persons irrespective of occupation on a common basis. So far this is to be accomplished not by the direct application of the secular law but by the Church of England adapting its own law to conform to the objectives of the secular law (Church of England 2005). While this preserves the form of legal autonomy, it does not preserve its substance as the Church's code is clearly subordinate to the secular framework. It remains uncertain how far these pressures of legal standardization and harmonization will go. At the same time, the tendencies are not all in the same direction as controversies and some litigation about acceptable forms of 'religious' dress have shown. At the time of writing, whether an Employment Tribunal decision upholding a local registrar's right to refuse to officiate at same-sex civil partnerships on religious grounds will itself be upheld remains to be seen. In general, what is occurring is a process where the courts are having to pick their way in a rights environment between competing claims that cannot all be satisfied. Fear of the implied threat of rights approaches to traditional religious preferences was, of course, one of the reasons why the Church of England and others expressed serious reservations about the Human Rights Act 1998, though they had to settle for what was a wholly declaratory rather than mandatory provision in s. 13. These tendencies are one of the reasons for heightened religious sensitivities about what are increasingly seen as secular intrusions into what was regarded as justifiable religious exceptionalism and rights. Such concerns persist even where the courts have made it clear that the Church of England is not a public authority for the purposes of the 1998 Act.

Part II seeks to give some depth to policy analysis by examining not only disestablishment processes in the UK itself but also church/state relationships in Scandinavia, the group of countries in Europe whose ecclesiastical history most closely resembles our own. Chapter 8 charts the processes of the two disestablishments – Ireland 1871 and Wales

1920 – that have already occurred in the UK. It seeks to identify the significant features that led to disestablishment in each case and, by implication, how far such features may be relevant today. In hindsight, the two disestablishments appear not as models for, or precursors of, a larger disestablishment but, rather, the product of particular regional conditions at the time. Well before the 1860s it was evident (including to the House of Lords) that maintaining an Anglican church establishment in Ireland was beyond the reach of principled defence. Until Gladstone decided to remove what was a grievance for the overwhelming majority of the Irish population, disestablishment had been latterly resisted particularly because of the implications it was thought to have for continuing the establishment in England. In Wales aggressive forms of nonconformity became yoked politically to Gladstone's new Liberal coalition, one of whose principal components was the nonconformist vote, especially after franchise extensions from 1868. In that case, however, the arguments were by no means all one way, and the House of Lords felt justified in declining to pass the necessary legislation. As a result, a much-sought disestablishment could not occur at all until the House of Lords' powers were clipped in 1911 and even then did not take place until 1920. Because intervening changes had removed many of the political aims of disestablishment, the victors were perhaps privately left wondering whether the measure was indeed justifiable in the circumstances obtaining when they succeeded.

Both disestablishments included measures of disendowment whose ostensible logic was based on the contention that the successor churches, being entirely voluntary organizations, could not lay claim to monies received to support their former established missions to address whole populations. There was much confusion about disendowment during the passage of the Irish Bill, and unsuccessful moves in the House of Lords to devote the proceeds to 'concurrent endowment', that is, for the benefit of all Christian including Roman Catholic denominations. The first Welsh Act was quite clearly punitive but the intervention of World War I and subsequent changed political circumstances resulted in much ground being recovered so that the Welsh Church did not commence its new life in actual poverty.

It is difficult to envisage quite the same circumstances in either case recurring in England. Such proponents of disestablishment as exist rarely focus on endowment issues. Even the National Secular Society in the form of disestablishment it espouses does not desire to impoverish the Church of England. There is no apparent hostility to the Church on grounds of its wealth, perhaps because there is a more general appreciation that its financial condition is in fact somewhat precarious. However, if the Church itself sought disestablishment, then it is almost certain that the future of its endowments would come into contention and it may be that it is this consideration among others that will act to restrain internal proponents of the more extreme and complete forms of disengagement from the state.

Chapter 9 concentrates on developments in Scandinavia and the extent to which Protestant establishments have changed and undergone disestablishment. The experience of Scandinavia is especially relevant not only because the countries exhibit the sort of constitutional fusion seen in the UK but also because in Sweden there has been a recent disestablishment of former structures. The chapter's account emphasizes a point made implicitly throughout the book's references to practice in other countries: there is not and never has been any single model of church establishment, and each settlement has been the unique product of local political circumstance. What the chapter also shows, however, is that to some extent changes such as Swedish disestablishment that appear climactic are much less so in practice. The same could be said, for example, of disestablishment in Wales where the *civic* status of the church remained little changed and its overall position could be said to have improved. This may suggest that modern disestablishments occurring in relatively benign circumstances are more about re-presentation or, more crudely, makeovers designed to give above all the appearance (and to some extent no doubt the reality) of fundamental change. That may be less true in the Swedish case, however, where secularization had already gone a long way and almost all the accommodations had already been made.

Part III attempts the policy analysis necessary to help identify the options for change in the UK. Chapter 10 examines the state of belief (Christian and otherwise) and unbelief in the UK, and considers how best to explain the reasons for the decay in active Christian belief and the extent to which decay may be irreversible. It is often pointed out that the available data have to be approached with considerable caution. Just as Elizabeth I was loath to attempt to make windows into men's souls, so would it be wrong to be over emphatic about what the data can be held to say. It is also instructive to compare the data over time. In 1970, for example, it remained possible for the Chadwick Commission to conclude that nominal support for the Church of England ran to at least half and possibly as much as two-thirds of the adult population in England of whom more than one in four had been confirmed. At that time, one in two children was baptized and about the same proportion of all marriages took place in the Church of England (Chadwick 1970: Appendix D). As the chapter shows, all these numbers have fallen very substantially and there have also been significant increases in expressed unbelief. Whereas Chadwick had to deal with somewhat scattered data, there has been since a growth of more systematic and regular surveys, especially of the kind associated with the work of Dr Peter Brierley at Christian Research.

While these have confirmed the character and detail of decline, particularly of church attendance, no data of this kind are in themselves explanatory of *why* the decline has taken place. A survey of the literature on 'secularization' shows marked differences of opinion. On the one hand, there are those who emphasize the continuities of belief even if inactive and, on the other hand, those who interpret the evidence as indicative of a permanent decline in religious belief. Clearly, important cultural shifts have been occurring which have included an increased propensity of modern states to express moral values and expected behavioural norms in legal codes, if often strongly coincident with Christian and religiously based ethical systems. One way of understanding the changes is that, over the longer term, the expansion of state functions has progressively encroached on functions hitherto hosted within religious frameworks to the extent that churches are seen as less relevant to the lives of many people. What remains puzzling, however, is the increased *rate* of decline since the 1960s and for which it is doubtful if anyone has yet offered entirely convincing explanations. As the data show, people in Great Britain (and to a lesser extent in Northern Ireland) are now significantly less likely to resort to churches to mark life's rites of passage: baptisms, confirmations, church marriages and church funerals have all declined and appear to be continuing to decline. Constitutionally, the question is what political action seems called for as a result. Chapter 10 uses the device of offering advice to an anonymous statesman to summarize the conclusions that may be drawn and that seem most relevant to political decision making.

Chapter 11 analyses the state of opinion about church establishment, pointing out that, apart from establishment's traditional opponents, where debate occurs at all much of it takes place within the Church of England itself. That debate includes proponents who wish in practice to move the Church into a voluntary status concerned with a ministry solely for its own active members rather than to the nation as a whole. As pointed out in Chapter 5, if the financial circumstances of the Church of England continue to tighten and more of the financial burden falls on active church members, the more such voices may strengthen: why should they pay for facilities which others use free, or when services may more easily be held in local halls without the cost of shoring up expensive special buildings. However, there is no present reason to believe that such views are in the majority. Further, although traditional opponents of establishment continue to maintain their positions, it cannot be said that disestablishment is in any sense a live issue at large. Nor is establishment of concern solely to Christians: establishment is supported by members of other religions because of the recognized place it gives to religion in public life. At the same time, the constitutional discrimination against Roman Catholics continues to exercize that community and others concerned with religious equality. If their objections are not explicitly couched in terms hostile to establishment, a considerable revision of establishment would be required in order to accommodate them. Although there have been no recent tests of parliamentary opinion, it seems unlikely that Parliament would stand in the way of individual changes initiated and carefully presented by the Church of England itself. The more significant the change, however, the less confident about parliamentary reactions it is possible to be.

Finally, Part IV in Chapters 12 to 14 offers argued conclusions in respect of the range of feasible changes to establishment. Chapter 12 reviews the higher state architecture; Chapter 13 reviews the political representation of religion; and Chapter 14 moves to assess the outlines of a possible final balance. Since there are two partners to establishment, the perspectives of both have to be addressed.

A survey of just what complete disestablishment would entail is Chapter 12's initial focus. It concludes that the disturbance to the Church of England's internal structures would be very great, and likely to produce a crisis of identity and governance which it is doubtful that internal disestablishmentarians either understand or intend. Although disengaging the monarchy and at the same time abolishing the discrimination against Roman Catholics would constitute a very considerable change indeed, such steps would be less harmful to both monarchy and Church than is often maintained. If it were desired to redress Roman Catholic grievances, then there could be no halfway house. For example, it would not be practicable to repeal the ban on Roman Catholic spouses without repealing also the requirement that the monarch should be in communion with the Church of England and have the status of Supreme Governor. But it is not only the position of Roman Catholics that might call for such changes. There are quite separate and at least equally cogent arguments from the changed character of religious belief and unbelief which arguably must come first in the sense that Roman Catholic objections are now but a particular illustration of a general case. In other words, there are powerful general arguments for disengaging the monarchy from any religious tests and freeing the sovereign to have any religious beliefs or none.

Even if no such changes are made, there is a strong case for looking again at accession arrangements and the coronation. The United Kingdom is so changed a country since 1953 that repeating everything as it was done then seems unthinkable. The Church of England itself may feel that some of the language in the coronation oath prescribed in 1689 is no longer appropriate in a more ecumenical as well as more religiously plural age. But that might be only a starting point for looking anew at the whole process of accession, which would need to have imaginative regard for all the social and cultural changes that have occurred since 1953. Some suggestions are made accordingly, including as to whether the Scottish and Accession Declaration oaths should be retained and how the title *Fidei Defensor* might be regarded.

The principle and practice of political representation of religion in the legislature is analysed in Chapter 13. No other sovereign legislature has formal religious representatives whereas the United Kingdom Parliament has twenty-six Anglican bishops in the House of Lords with full membership and voting rights. The absence of political consensus on future reform of the House of Lords has made governments' approaches to continued episcopal representation cautious. They do not wish needlessly to confront or otherwise upset an entrenched group even by floating options if there is in fact no realistic chance of achieving any alterations to the existing dispensation. Accordingly, successive White Papers have avoided real discussion of principle, apart from registering the obvious point that there would be no place for bishops in a wholly elected house. In this situation, the chapter attempts to analyse the arguments of principle and practice, all of which it argues run clearly against religious representation other than on a principle of individual merit assessed as independently as possible by an independent Appointments Commission against the claims of all other applicants. How bishops might be removed from the Lords is also discussed.

As well as dealing with some lesser features of establishment, Chapter 14 attempts to look at alternative ways – 're-establishment' – of formally recognising the place of religions in, and contributions by religions to, the public commonwealth. The chapter concludes with the device again of addressing an imaginary statesman, this time with suggestions also for the Church of England itself. The argument here as elsewhere is that change is necessary to reflect the character of modern society and that, although it does not have to be climactic, change should be for the most part at least incrementally purposive. Moreover, the claim is that change can be achieved without the controversy sometimes alleged, and more often than customarily assumed on the initiative of the Church of England itself. In particular, naturally occurring opportunities such as changes of sovereign should be used to address the higher architecture. To many people, all this may seem an arcane series of subjects rightly consigned to the polite oblivion of the academy. They would be wrong. What is in fact being addressed is a vital part of how our current society constructs its modern identity in ways that make sense to all citizens. The process of change does not have to be dramatic or threatening to any of the parties. Rather, what is at issue is a further constitutional adjustment and realignment of the kind well-precedented in the long development of these islands' polity. Theory, immemorial practice and social reality have so much parted company that they need to be brought back into balance. Accordingly, it is hoped that this book will contribute to help making the choices and actions required as well informed as possible.

The last word might properly go to an Archbishop of Canterbury. On the very day of his retirement in 1974, Archbishop Michael Ramsey initiated the House of Lords debate on the Worship and Doctrine Measure. Among other things, he maintained that the Measure provided

> a way in which the link between the Church of England and the State can continue in a form which enables each to fulfil its distinctive role for the benefit of the other, with greater effectiveness in the life of the Church. (HL 14 November 1974 col. 868)

If the state has to be neutral on the last clause, the statement remains a proper ambition for the state and the Church. The problem is to find the means for the times even if the means reach well beyond anything contemplated by an archbishop in 1974.

Part I
Establishment in Great Britain now

As an essential preliminary to considering how to approach the future of establishment, this Part describes of what establishment in England and Scotland actually now consists. There are important qualitative differences between the constitutional positions of the two churches. These arise from their distinct relationships with the state. On the one hand, in England the original model was one where the Church and the state were effectively bound together in a joint enterprise. On the other hand, in Scotland the Presbyterian model was one where the spheres of Church and state were conceived as quite separate entities.

Chapters 2 and 6 trace the constitutional history of both Churches; Chapters 3 to 5 examine the detail of the English establishment; and Chapter 7 concentrates on recent judicial proceedings involving the Scottish Church. Their outcome has not only important consequences for the autonomy of the latter Church but potentially also for the Church of England too.

2
Establishment in England: Main Developments since 1800

Then and now

From the perspective of today, it is difficult to imagine the extent to which the Church of England possessed in 1800 a significance of a kind entirely distinct from now:

> [D]uring the first half of the nineteenth century the Church of England retained an institutional presence in England and Wales rivaled only by that of secular organs of government. (Burns 1999)

The contrast between that situation and the present can be illustrated by the change in the way in which commentators have located the Church constitutionally. In 1852, the editor of a compendium describing the then-constitutional arrangements entitled the work a *Handbook of Church and State*. Proceeding hierarchically, the author put ecclesiastical matters fourth out of nine gradations which were topped by the royal family, and the peerage followed by Parliament. After the Church came the judiciary, executive government, the army, the navy and, finally, the subordinate administrations in Ireland, Scotland, the Isle of Man and the Channel Islands. In addition, it was pointed out that the Archbishops of Canterbury and York came next in precedence to royal dukes (Redgrave 1852). By contrast, neither a millennium symposium (Bogdanor 2003) nor a recent academic constitutional overview (King 2008) mentioned the Church of England at all.

Nowadays the Church is commonly seen, where noticed at all, as just one of a number of Christian denominations all of which have experienced decline in the number of their worshippers. Refreshed by recent immigration from predominantly Roman Catholic countries, it is even possible that the Roman Catholic Church is the strongest of all the Christian denominations though itself still eclipsed by Protestantism as a whole. Christianity itself is no longer unchallenged as the universal religious belief system. On the one hand, immigration since World War II has brought significant numbers of Muslims and Hindus to settle and, on the other, an overall decline in religious faith has resulted in a nation where about 40 per cent are thought to have no religious beliefs at all and fewer than 7 per cent attend traditional religious services.

In 1800, matters could hardly have been more different and the comparison demonstrates the extent of the changes over the last two centuries. Although the social and economic circumstances of the countries were in many ways quite disparate, Great Britain had been joined with Ireland by the Act of Union that year. The same Act created a united Anglican establishment in England, Wales and Ireland in what in law was a single confessional state: 'the United Church of England and Ireland . . . and the Presbyterian Establishment in Scotland, were accorded exclusive endorsement as the spiritual and theological ordering of society' (Norman 1994: 277). State and Church were conceived as joint partners in the governance of the nation, active in separate spheres of public life:

> The constitution of this country is composed of two distinct establishments, the one civil, the other ecclesiastical, which are so closely interwoven together, that the destruction of either must prove alike fatal to both. (Bowles 1815: 1)

Everyone was deemed to be a member except where Parliament had made explicit provision to the contrary. The law visited civic disabilities on Roman Catholics and Protestant dissenters alike, who were not therefore accepted as full members of the political society. The sovereign could not be a Roman Catholic or marry one, and had to be in communion with the Church of England. Parliament was a wholly Protestant body and predominantly Anglican. Anglican archbishops and bishops – all appointed by the state – were ex officio members of the House of Lords. The largely Anglican Parliament legislated for secular and ecclesiastical affairs throughout the United Kingdom in a structure which in theory treated the entire population outside Scotland as a uniform entity. Unlike the position in Scotland, the Church of England had no separate legislative assembly of its own and depended on Parliament for the legislation that could alone amend its worship, doctrine and management practices. The law subjected all non-Anglicans to civic penalties designed to deny them full membership of the political society. Although from 1727 annual Acts indemnified transgressors of the penal codes, the legal position of non-Anglicans remained far from equal even if, since the late seventeenth century, the state had made limited payments, known as the 'Regium Donum', to Presbyterian ministers in England and Ireland – a limited form of concurrent endowment. While – in modern parlance – it could be argued that the state had conceded the principle of pluralism, it had certainly not done so for most purposes in practice.

The civil and ecclesiastical courts constituted a joint jurisdiction with the latter's functions controlling significant areas of family law as well as matters, such as clerical discipline, entirely of internal concern to the Church of England. Whatever the issue, all the judgements of the ecclesiastical courts were enforceable by mechanisms supported by the state. The financial support of the clergy and the fabric of the churches themselves depended on a system of local hypothecated taxation – tithe and church rates – underpinned by the state. All citizens, whatever their faith, were liable to pay these taxes. The only two universities in England were open to members of the Church of England alone.

The course of change

In retrospect, the changes from 1800 in the status of the Church of England can be viewed in a number of different ways: the result of a movement from religious toleration to a condition of religious freedom; processes of institutional intervention *and* separation in which church and state became increasingly identified as separate structures and distinct organizations; the expansion of the state into spheres, particularly of social policy, formerly regarded as provinces of the Church; and a withdrawal by the state from political involvement in the Church's affairs. The tensions involved in this expansion into social areas were particularly significant, and is why they are explored below in the case of education. The two disestablishments in Ireland and in Wales (dealt with in Chapter 8) were responses to particular regional situations: in Ireland to the massively non-Anglican character (if in different ways north and south) of the population; and in Wales to the growth of a strong majoritarian nonconformity. Both cases were shot through also with important cultural and political features hostile to a continuing English hegemony, religious and otherwise.

It is important, however, to stress that there was never any programme of deliberate overall change as such, still less one of conscious secularization or, as in France, anticlericalism. Although what follows concentrates on measures explicitly designed to address particular rubbing points, one of the most important and influential Acts had nothing on the face of it to do with religion at all. This was the Reform Act 1832 which, together with the 1828 and 1829 legislation described below, permanently altered the religious composition of the House of Commons, making it both a less Anglican institution and one more open to the arguments of non-Anglicans. The important implications of this particularly for Church finance will be further explored in Chapter 5. Here it will be sufficient to point out that, after 1821, there was no government subvention to the Church. The much-discussed possibilities of publicly financed church expansion under the Conservative government from 1841 resulted only in an 1843 Act permitting the Church to borrow £600,000 from Queen Anne's Bounty at the rate of £30,000 a year to provide for clergy stipends in new places of worship provided by the Church itself (Brown, S. J. 2001: 340–1).

Finally, it would be a mistake to assume passivity on the part of the Church. The outcomes were not determined entirely by the state: the responses of the Church itself were always significant, and increasingly so in the later period. What eventuated was the product of a complicated interplay of different factors interacting at different levels and for different purposes over an extended period, all devoid of any predetermined objectives or outcome.

From religious toleration to religious freedom

The best-remembered initiatives are the repeal of the Caroline Test and Corporation Acts in 1828 and the Roman Catholic Relief Act in 1829 which 'emancipated' Roman Catholics. The Whig Lord Holland judged the first repeal as very important because 'it explodes the real Tory doctrine *that the Church and State are indivisible'* (quoted Podmore 2005: 17). The first repeal removed the civic disabilities imposed on Protestant Nonconformists, and the second did the same for Roman Catholics. The repeals were not, however, unconditional: in both cases beneficiaries had to swear oaths designed to protect the Church of England from any influence by the enfranchized groups. Thus, Protestant nonconformists had to swear that they would never as holders of the offices now opened to them 'injure or weaken the Protestant Church, or the bishops and clergy of the said Church, in the possession of any rights or privileges to which such Church, or the said bishops and clergy, are or may be by law entitled'. For Roman Catholics the comparable oath was much longer: it required explicit acceptance of the Protestant succession and denial of Papal extraterritorial jurisdiction in addition to protection of Anglican interests. Furthermore, the protections were extended to include also the Scottish church establishment, and prevent Roman Catholics from holding the offices of Lord Chancellor, Lord Lieutenant of Ireland and the High Commissioner to the General Assembly of the Church of Scotland or exercising any Anglican ecclesiastical patronage.

Moreover, these partial emancipations were not immediately extended universally. Thus, Jews remained outside the concessions to non-Anglican Christians for some time and the end of the annual indemnity Acts could be said to have actually worsened their position. Governments were not sympathetic, the Attorney General responding to an 1830 motion by saying that the Jews

> had a peculiar character stamped upon them by their own institutions they were severed by them from all other people, they could not form a component part of any society in which they were mingled: and as our laws had not made them Jews, they could not make them Englishmen. (HC 5 April 1830, col. 1336)

It took two Acts of 1846 and 1858 to remove the remaining civil disabilities on Jews. Similarly, the religious tests at the two ancient English universities were also removed piecemeal. The admission tests were removed first at Oxford in 1854 and at Cambridge two years later. The Universities Tests Act 1871 removed the requirement of Church of England membership from all posts in Oxford, Cambridge and Durham except the Regius Divinity Chairs. Meanwhile, the government had approved the foundation of London University in 1836 as a secular institution under a Royal Charter.

Other much-contested disabilities continued. Anglican clergy could insist on conducting burial services in Church of England graveyards irrespective of the corpse's denomination, until the Burial Act 1880 conferred a general right of burial in the graveyards with or without a religious service and regardless of rite, if any, used. Bradlaugh's long campaign against religious oaths for MPs was eventually successful in the Oaths Act 1888 which permitted affirmation to be substituted for a religious declaration in all oath-taking cases, including for Parliament. Of more than merely symbolic significance was the Accession Declaration Act 1910 which substituted a brief statement of non-denominational Christian belief for the lengthy and aggressively worded declaration against transubstantiation. This had originated in the 'No Popery' panic of the 1670s and used language that George V very reasonably considered offensive to his many Roman Catholic subjects.

State withdrawal and expansion

At first sight, these contrary trends seem capable of explaining a good deal of the course of change. On the one hand, the abolition of the civil penalties of excommunication (Excommunication Act 1813) can be seen as the state declining to use its authority to support Church discipline. The Marriage and Registration Acts of 1836 saw the state stepping in to permit civil marriage and registration, both functions formerly – except for Quakers and Jews – provinces entirely of the Church. On the other hand, the 1855 Defamation and the 1857 Divorce and Matrimonial Causes Acts, because they transferred ecclesiastical jurisdictions to the civil courts, can be seen both as state withdrawal *and* expansion. The preamble to the Defamation Act put it, 'Whereas the Jurisdiction of the Ecclesiastical Courts in Suits for Defamation has ceased to be the Means of enforcing the Spiritual Discipline of the Church'. The 1857 Act not only permitted divorce other than by Private Act but also entirely removed the ecclesiastical courts' jurisdiction over marriage law and probate.

Yet movement was by no means all in one direction: after the Crimean War, attempts were made to re-Christianize the Army with paid (including Roman Catholic) chaplains from 1858, and the religious affiliations of soldiers were recorded from 1864 (McLeod 2000: 55). In 1874 the government sponsored the Public Worship Regulation Act designed to deal with disputes within the Church of England over ritual and clerical discipline. The outcomes (which included the imprisonment of ritualist priests) were not happy, and the experience almost certainly led to diminished appetites in government and Parliament for statutory intrusion in internal Church of England affairs. Indeed, looking back nearly a century later, the Chadwick Commission regarded 1874 as the year when Parliament 'finally ceased attempts to govern the Church directly' (Chadwick 1970: 22).

Institutional balance – the case of education

In practice, attempts to locate particular state behaviours on a withdrawal/expansion continuum do not work satisfactorily. The 'state' itself had no special or consistent momentum. Rather, the history of education policy shows politicians of all stripes grappling pragmatically with social problems in respect of a social policy area heavily invested by the Church. Moreover, the need to deal with denominations and even religions on a defensibly equitable basis pushed the state into a secular stance which detracted from old forms of establishment that had automatically accorded the Church of England most-favoured status.

The state began supporting the provision of elementary schooling from 1833 exclusively via two voluntary (in effect, religious) societies, one more completely Anglican than the other. This was on the basis of 'an axiomatic belief that, while local effort could be supplemented by the superior resources of government, it was never to be superseded' (Hurt 1972: 69). The state's one attempt to take an initiative of its own – to build a demonstration 'normal' school – had been frustrated by predominantly Anglican opposition in 1839. The government's attempt to give the Church of England a leading role in the education arrangements of a Factories Bill was defeated in turn by *Nonconformist* opposition in 1843. At the same time, eligibility for funding was extended to Wesleyan Methodist and Roman Catholic schools from 1847 and to Jewish schools from 1853.

The Forster Education Act 1870 was the first attempt to develop elementary educational provision nationally. It did so by incorporating the denominational schools into a dual system that preserved their status but established free-standing, single-purpose local authorities in the form of elected school boards to supply schools in areas where there were none. The school boards were empowered to precept on the relevant local authorities by means of a rate that the boards determined. It was not uncontroversial: in the Bill debates, Henry Richard, speaking on behalf of Nonconformity, alleged that the Bill was 'a measure for making the education of the people of England universally and forever denominational' (HC 20 June 1870, col. 497).

The decision to incorporate the denominational schools was entirely pragmatic:

> The chief driving force behind this [general] expansion of state power was the inability of the churches, organized on a voluntary basis in a situation of very considerable pluralism, to provide comprehensively for society's needs. (McLeod 2000: 56–7)

The denominational schools constituted four-fifths of the then elementary schools and no national system could practically contemplate their exclusion. In contrast, it was plain that Nonconformists would not accept the introduction of rate support for denominational schools. Consciences were preserved by provisions which – still in force today – permitted parental withdrawal of children from religious instruction in denominational schools, and the prohibition (via the Cowper–Temple clause) of denominational instruction in board schools – though that provision did not prevent, nor was it intended to, non-denominational Christian observance in board schools.

By the turn of the century the new boards had not only established a whole new range of non-denominational schools but also had done so to a standard that the overwhelmingly denominational schools found increasingly difficult to match. Moreover, whereas the board schools could rely on the rates more than the small fees they charged, the denominational schools felt themselves increasingly at a disadvantage when they had to raise funds by subscription from supporters and parents who also had to pay rates. This was one of the factors in the noticeable decline in their numbers which was running at a rate of 60 a year by the end of the century (Judge 2001: 48). The board schools, though non-denominational, were not secular establishments in practice: they were undoubtedly Christian establishments in the sense that, unbid, Christian – if non-denominational – assemblies and religious instruction were the norm.

By the turn of the nineteenth century the dual system had evolved into one where the denominational schools still educated the larger number of pupils (3 million as opposed to 2.6 million) but whose facilities were increasingly inferior to those of the board schools – 'the deplorable starvation of the voluntary schools', Balfour called it (HC 24 March 1902, col. 854). The government's solution in the 1902 Act was to bring all elementary schools under the wing of local authorities. This meant funding denominational schools from local taxation and, as the cry had it, leading to 'Rome on the rates'. Because Anglican schools greatly predominated, to Nonconformists the arrangement greatly advantaged the Anglican schools. Whereas the Forster Bill had received lengthy discussion in 1870, the Balfour Bill entered into a storm of Liberal opposition fury in even more prolonged debate. Nonetheless, the Balfour scheme and the new system of local education authorities was put in place, and remained proof against attempts to change it even after the Liberal electoral landslide of 1906.

Although there was other legislation after 1902, none altered the dual system, and it was addressing that system that was one of the main challenges faced in the wartime reconstruction planning that led up to the 1944 Act. Put broadly, the responsible Minister, R. A. Butler, used public money to purchase state influence within a scheme that, comprising both the elementary and secondary schools, could in principle accommodate all religious interests. It did so by requiring denominational schools to opt at different costs to them for different levels of autonomy.

Religion was accommodated, all denominations being treated equally without any special consideration being given to Anglicans.

While the religious factors remained some of the most difficult with which to deal, old inter-Protestant asperities had lost a good deal of their force. Moreover, Butler did not seek to contest Christian ambitions. The note of Butler's meeting with the Archbishop of Canterbury's Protestant ecumenical deputation of 33 worthies on 15 August 1941 records the minister saying 'he could assure the deputation of his complete sympathy with their object of securing that effective Christian teaching should be given in all schools to the children' (TNA ED136/228).

Other factors strengthened his hand, too. So far as Anglican schools were concerned, 90 per cent had been built before 1900, and the number of children at Anglican schools from 1903 to 1938 had halved. The 1944 religious settlement in the end went a long way to respond to the Archbishop's concerns of 1941. There was a statutory requirement for an act of worship in the morning assembly of all schools, and the status of religious education in schools was improved, at the same time preserving the consciences of teachers in a clause dubbed 'The Teachers' Charter'. Managerial autonomy could be preserved in aided schools where the managers assumed responsibility for half the capital costs. Where they did not, controlled status still permitted denominational influence and at no cost to the denomination. There were to be locally agreed religious knowledge syllabuses.

While since 1944 there has been much educational legislation, none has challenged the basic settlement for denominational schooling. At the same time, the requirements relating to religious education and worship have become both specified in more detail and adjusted at the margins to reflect the changed religious demography of the country.

The present position on *worship* for community and foundation schools of a non-religious character is detailed in section 70 and Schedule 20 of the School Standards and Framework Act 1998, itself largely re-enacting provisions dating from 1996 and before. The main elements are that there has to be a daily collective act of worship 'wholly or mainly of a broadly Christian character' and that it is to be deemed of that character 'if it reflects the broad traditions of Christian belief without being distinctive of any particular Christian denomination'. The requirement is further qualified by not having to be observed other than on most as opposed to all occasions. In addition it may be disapplied altogether where a standing advisory council on religious education determines that it is appropriate. In that case, for so long as the determination subsists, the collective worship may be distinctive of any particular faith.

Religious *education* in non-religious schools continues to be provided under an agreed syllabus drawn up by the local Standing Advisory Council on Religious Education (SACRE) convened by the Local Education Authority (LEA) as specified in the Education Act 1996. Membership of SACREs in England is required in all cases – the sole, explicit 'privileging' of the Church of England by reason of its universal parochial coverage – to include a representative of the Church of England, whereas representation of other religious groups depends upon the presence of their following in the LEA area. The provision prohibiting the inclusion in syllabuses of any catechism or formulary distinctive of a particular religious denomination is continued, though now with a saving to the effect that the prohibition does not extend to the *study* of such material.

The provisions for foundation and voluntary *controlled* schools with a religious character permit forms of religious education consistent with the defined ethos of the establishments but prohibit instruction of more than two periods a week. For voluntary *aided* schools with a religious character there is no such limitation.

One relatively recent development has been the extension of state support to new species of religious schools. Towards the end of the twentieth century, a number of Muslim schools had sought state aid (Parker-Jenkins, Hartas and Irving 2005: 42–50). All the applications were refused on various grounds by Education Secretaries until granted by David Blunkett in early 1998 when he extended grant-maintained status to two Muslim primary schools and one Seventh Day Adventist secondary school. It has been described as marking 'a decisive turning point in the state funding of schools in England and Wales' (Walford 2000: 1). At the same time, given the history of state support and the clear requirements of the 1944 Act, it could not be said that extension to further religions in fact raised fresh issues of principle. As one observer has put it:

> [W]e either provide equality before the law, or we dismantle existing legislation and embrace a 'common school' for all. There are compelling arguments for both cases, but we cannot have it both ways: what is required is a state policy based on consistency and equity to ensure parity of treatment. (Parker-Jenkins 2002: 273)

Subsequently, the expansion of faith schools has been encouraged by the New Labour government because it considered that religious schools were associated with higher behavioural and attainment standards: 'The established church, at one time seen as a problem for educational reform, was offered a stronger place in the state system' (Jones, K. 2003: 166–7). The Education Act 2005 was framed in part to encourage more religious schools, and the Church of England has, following the recommendations of its own 2001 Dearing Report, committed itself to form an additional 100 secondary schools. The reduction in the need now to provide only 10 per cent of capital costs – it was 50 per cent in 1944 – to qualify for aided status makes it easier for religious schools to manage start-up costs in a situation where all the running costs continue to be paid by the state. Whereas controlled status is even less costly, it requires the religious interests to be in a minority among the governing body.

That the government policy of encouraging new religious schools has not been universally supported illustrates current uncertainties about how the modern state should relate to religion. A largely secular state now contains a significantly more secular as well as more religiously diverse population. Former support for multicultural approaches has hesitated following the rise in the incidence of international terrorism associated with extreme forms of Islam. But fear of the other was not the only ground upon which reservations have been expressed. Whereas many Anglicans believe that it is a mission to the community as a whole that drives their interest in schooling, one education professional, long associated with Church of England schools, has questioned why that Church really wished to increase the number of its schools: 'What model of the Church is being held up to the nation? Are Anglicans a body of worshippers and believers who are only and essentially concerned with themselves' (Brown, A. 2003: 107). Shortly after a terrorist incident in London, the Prime Minister was, apparently to his surprise, taxed strongly by the press corps at one of his press conferences about the government's religious schools policy and remarked 'I hadn't realised that you all felt so strongly' (Blair 2005). Whether renewed Anglican interest in schools provision is to be seen as a retreat into a merely denominational self-concern reflects both some of the relational dilemmas at the heart of developments discussed below and establishment/disestablishment issues explored later in Part IV.

Institutional intervention

It is evident that withdrawal and expansion dimensions take the argument only so far. What so often engaged the state was not some self-generated agenda but, rather, a political compulsion to remedy perceived deficiency. Whereas in the past it had been enough for the state – itself a concept in modern form crystallized only in the Victorian period – to rely on voluntary social provision and regard the Church of England as the principal agency for delivery, the requirements of a vastly increased and more urbanized population made such reliance infeasible. From this perspective, the climactic moment was not the 1870 Act but the Poor Law Amendment Act 1834. This deliberately cut across the parish boundaries which had also performed duty as the basic units of local government. The new Poor Law Unions were secular authorities divorced from the former regime linked to ecclesiastical structures.

That was England: Ireland was another matter. There, the state intervened directly to remodel the Anglican Church. The Irish Church (Temporalities) Act 1833 abolished church rates (the rate levied for the support of the church fabric and divine service, and not abolished in England and Wales until 1868) in Ireland, halved the number of archbishoprics to two, reduced the number of bishoprics from eighteen to ten, and established a commission to administer the funds released by the changes. Because it was seen by some as unilateral interference by the state through a new kind of parliament that might go on to threaten the establishment in England and Wales, this Act was one of the triggers of the Tractarian movement in England which became one of the sources of Anglican renewal seeking to reaffirm the Church's identity. The government ploughed on in any case: the Irish Tithe Acts of 1833 and 1836 tried to defend the Irish tithe, the latter Act converting the Irish tithe into a charge paid by the landowner, an initiative not taken in England and Wales until 1891. The government was also responsible for the Established Church Act 1836 which set up a permanent Ecclesiastical Commission to manage and equalize the distribution of important revenues of the Church of England. It was the first in a series of initiatives – managed and led in practice by clerical commissioners – compulsorily to redistribute revenues in the interests of financing the ministry of the Church in poorer neighbourhoods. The greatest state interventions of all were, of course, the disestablishments in Ireland and Wales, both of which were accompanied by measures of disendowment.

Institutional separation

In 1800, the Church had no national institutions uniquely its own. All significant changes in the functioning of the church had to be processed through the legislature: unlike the position in Scotland, the church had no separate assembly of its own. Convocations had not met regularly since 1717 or at all since 1741 and, even when functioning, the Convocations of the two Provinces of Canterbury and York were entirely clerical bodies possessing no significant powers. They could not legislate finally for their own affairs and their power to tax the clergy had been surrendered in 1664. For all changes of organization down to parish level, for any change to doctrine, form of worship, ritual or discipline, the Church was dependent on Parliament, a body itself decreasingly Anglican during the nineteenth century. Although the bishops' membership of the House of Lords facilitated the introduction of legislation to deal with Church matters, the outcome could not be guaranteed since such legislation was by way of public general act, as open to amendment as any government Bill but without the support of the government Whips. Between 1880 and 1913, of the 217 Church of England Bills introduced into Parliament, 183 had been dropped, 1 negatived, 162 not discussed at all, and 13 of the 33 that had become law had been directly sponsored by a government minister in a situation where the other 20 successful Bills had needed some measure of government assistance to succeed (Selborne 1916: 30).

The Church itself gradually asserted a greater degree of autonomy. Some moves, such as 'the diocesan revival' (Burns 1999), grew from traditions inherent if at times dormant within the Church itself. Others can be seen as reactions to external shocks. In the Gorham judgement of 1850 the Judicial Committee of the Privy Council, the final appellate authority in ecclesiastical law but a predominantly lay body, determined a controversial doctrinal dispute concerning baptismal regeneration. It found in favour of a clergyman whom his bishop had refused on doctrinal grounds to institute into a living to which the clergyman had been presented by the Lord Chancellor exercising his ecclesiastical patronage. The case drew attention to the reality of ultimate state control over the Church of England. Shortly afterwards, the religious census of 1851 – whose methodology was much disputed among denominations – showed a considerable shortfall in the availability of places of worship for the population as a whole, and the fact that nearly half the population did not attend church at all, with the lowest rates of attendance among the poor. Denominationally, there was a slight general preponderance of dissenting numbers over those for the Church of England but with a more marked preponderance in the urban Midlands and North as well as the West country, and a four-to-one majority in Wales. Irrespective of the arguments on detail, and the differences between England and Wales, the outcome weakened the Church of England's case for privileged treatment in so far as it had rested on its continuing predominance in the population. This had implications for its exclusive control over burial grounds, for compulsory church rates, tithes, and for the remaining civil jurisdictions of the ecclesiastical courts over family law and probate.

The Local Government Acts of 1888 and 1894 can also be seen as weakening the Church's presence in civic life: the first introduced elected county councils thus curtailing the extent to which clerical magistrates had influenced the old Quarter Sessions' rule; and the latter abolished vestry parochial administration and substituted secular elected parish councils.

If slow to be given formal recognition at the highest levels, lay incorporation in Church governance (less in the Church than in Nonconformity) tended to increase as for example in the revived diocesan structures. The Convocations themselves came back to life: Canterbury in 1855 and York in 1861. Houses of Laymen became attached to the Convocations in 1886 and 1892 respectively. A Representative Church Council which combined both Convocations and their Houses of Laity was set up in 1904. It was a resolution of that body that lay behind the decision of the Archbishops to set up the (Selborne) Committee on Church and State which reported in 1916 in favour of a special legislative procedure designed to give a protected track for Church legislation through Parliament. This was given effect in the Church of England Assembly (Powers) Act 1919. However, this legislative outcome was by no means an automatic follow-on from the Selborne recommendations. As has been pointed out (Thompson 1975), the government was initially opposed to the Bill which, in its final form, gave Parliament a stronger form of veto than that originally proposed.

Known as the Enabling Act, the Act formally recognized the Church Assembly and instituted a special legislative procedure which gave the Assembly the right of initiative in proposing Measures with statutory force subject to a parliamentary veto that could reject a Measure but not amend its terms. This gave the Church of England its own legislative body and ended its complete legislative dependence on Parliament.

Interestingly, as described in Chapters 6 and 8 below and pointed out by my colleague Scot Peterson, the same Parliament in fact legislated religious settlements for all parts of Great Britain. Thus, in addition to the passage of the1919 Enabling Act, the 1919 Church in Wales (Temporalities) Act specified a date for the implementation of the suspended Welsh disestablishment Act of 1914 but mitigated its financial severity; and the 1921 Church of Scotland Act solemnly confirmed that Church's spiritual autonomy in order to pave the way for a church union in Scotland that eventually took place in 1929. This coincidence of significant provisions for each of the parts of Great Britain may therefore be seen overall as a general post-War adjustment in church/state relations. In all cases, despite appearances in one case to the contrary, the settlements were in fact all supportive of established religion.

For England, the 1919 Enabling Act also emphasized the distinctiveness of the organs of church and state. Distinctiveness is, however, not at all the same as separation. This was brought home particularly in the successive refusals by Parliament in 1927 and 1928 to endorse Measures intended to authorize a revised Prayer Book. The Archbishop of York observed that the outcome 'was a dramatic illustration of the legal right of Parliament to control the worship of the Church' (Garbett 1950: 204). The refusals provoked a strong reaction in the Church of England which had regarded the Enabling Act as securing it effective autonomy in such matters above all. Talk grew within the Church favouring disestablishment, a policy overwhelmingly espoused in the past by non-Anglicans. The immediate crisis was resolved when in 1929 the bishops of the Canterbury Convocation voted to allow clergy discretion to use the revised Prayer Book nonetheless, and for longer-term purposes the Archbishops in 1930 set up a committee under Lord Cecil of Chelwood. This committee's task was to look at church/state relations with particular reference to the Church's being able finally to determine by itself the content of its doctrines and the forms of its worship – rights which Parliament had not long before confirmed in 1921 for the Church of Scotland. Its report in 1935 was not generally thought to have identified a viable means of privileging particular species of Church legislation from parliamentary control. Overall, the experience led to continuing resentment in the Church about Parliament's remaining oversight of its affairs, and a determination to prevent it hobbling the Church's autonomy.

In what proved to become a characteristic procedural feature, the proposal for the 1919 Act had come not from a Royal Commission (the standard state-inspired initiative of the preceding period as in, for example, the commission that preceded the Clerical Subscription Act 1865) but as the result of a commission set up by the Archbishops themselves. There were two other comparable commissions in the course of the century – Moberly and Chadwick – and two (Howick and van Straubenzee) that concentrated on narrower constitutional questions – as did later initiatives like the Pilling Report in the next century. Of all these, the Chadwick Committee that reported in 1970 was the most influential. It remains the fullest, considered debate within the Church about the principle and practice of establishment, and was instrumental in paving the way for two important changes in church/state relations: the Church of England (Worship and Doctrine) Measure 1974 gave the Church full authority to determine those questions, simultaneously and tactfully nonetheless reserving to Parliament the right to make any change in the use by the Church of the 1662 Book of Common Prayer; and in

1976 the Prime Minister agreed changes to the procedures for appointing archbishops and bishops which conceded the initiative in making recommendations to the Church while reserving final choice to the Prime Minister.

Looking back it is now possible to see that the state disestablishments in Ireland from 1871 and in Wales from 1920 did not lead to the complete severance of church and state in England much agitated for by Nonconformists. The two disestablishments were also seen as emanating from a legislature that was decreasingly (especially in the Commons) an Anglican or even, in any normal sense, a body exercising legitimate religious authority – one of the issues seen as relevant in its rejection of the Church Assembly Measures in 1927 and 1928. It is from this perspective that the Public Worship Regulation Act 1874 (which attempted to legislate for ritual) is commonly viewed nowadays as the last direct legislative initiative by Parliament in relation to religious worship or doctrine.

Even so, it is necessary to pause for a moment to consider the parliamentary reception of the Worship and Doctrine Measure of 1974. The Measure passed easily through the House of Lords but proved controversial in the Commons (HC 4 December 1974, cols 1567–1698). Supporters maintained that the Measure was not a step on the road to disestablishment but simply an adjustment to an existing harmonious relationship. Rejection, in contrast, would trigger disestablishment because it would deliver a mortal blow to the mutual confidence between Church and state upon which establishment depended. Opponents accepted none of those arguments. They questioned whether Synod possessed adequate legitimacy, claiming it did not represent 'the man in the pew': moreover, acceptance of the Measure would make Synod infallible. Hugh Fraser, a senior backbench Conservative (and Roman Catholic), voiced the core of the objections: 'It is asking the House to retain the status of the Established Church while taking away from the House the power and the responsibility for its existence' (col. 1612). The House divided and the Measure passed with a substantial three-to-one majority. Such arguments have not been advanced since and the attitudes of the opponents may perhaps now be regarded as the last flicker of the sentiment that the Church of England is subject to the will of Parliament regardless of the faiths of its members. Nonetheless, the formal architecture of parliamentary control remains in place.

At the same time, the whole tenor of Church of England governance since 1919 has been, with the exception of the Tithe Act 1936 (which finally brought tithe to an end), one where the Church of England has itself taken full charge of its own affairs. In that respect, organizational change on the Church of England's own initiative has become the norm. The principal examples include the amalgamation of Queen Anne's Bounty with the Ecclesiastical Commissioners in 1947 to form the Church Commissioners, the creation of the Synod from 1970 which established full lay participation including matters such as doctrine, formerly the exclusive preserve of the clerical members, and the National Institutions Measure of 1998 which moved towards the creation of an executive which the Church Commissioners do not quite provide. Above all, a radical change like the admission of women to the priesthood, although highly controversial and carefully scrutinized in both Houses, was treated by Parliament as a matter entirely for the Church of England to initiate.

It follows that most of the ghosts of 1927/28 have been now laid for the Church at least, though later chapters will explore how far new issues may require revisiting the church/state balance nonetheless. For example, the recent decision of Prime Minister Gordon Brown to withdraw from active participation in ecclesiastical patronage has implications for the position of the Supreme Governor and the case for continued episcopal membership of the House of Lords that it will be necessary to explore. The question is how far the formal architecture should be sustained in the entirely different circumstances that now prevail and, if not, how it should be amended or brought to an end.

3
Monarchy and Legislature

This chapter sets out the position of the monarchy in relation to the Church of England and the Church's relationship with the legislature. It describes the relevant constitutional law, including the oaths taken by the sovereign on accession and at the coronation, and the position of Roman Catholics. It goes on to explain the special arrangements for Church of England legislation under the Church Assembly (Powers) Act 1919, the role of the Second Church Estates Commissioner, and the arrangements for episcopal membership of the House of Lords.

Monarchy

Constitutionally, the UK's sovereign is a parliamentary monarch: Parliament prescribes the monarch's relations with the Church of England and the rules of succession to the throne.

Although it is not formally one of the sovereign's titles, the sovereign is – as described in the preface to the Thirty-Nine Articles – 'Supreme Governor' of the Church of England and, when doing homage, new bishops are required to acknowledge that position.[1] In addition, the surviving part of the Elizabethan Act of Supremacy 1559 read with Canon A 7 makes it clear that, as spelled out in the canon, the sovereign has supreme authority 'over all persons in all causes, ecclesiastical as well as civil'. The monarch is also styled 'Defender of the Faith', a title originally bestowed by Pope Leo X on Henry VIII but subsequently appropriated permanently by the donee in circumstances very different from those of the original grant.[2]

As to the succession, the present rules have remained unchanged since the early eighteenth century and were devised from the revolution of

1688 to ensure the continuation of a Protestant succession to the exclusion particularly of Roman Catholic claimants. Thus, in addition to the monarch being qualified by primogeniture descent from a former Electress of Hanover, he or she is required by s. 3 of the Act of Settlement 1701 to 'join in communion with the Church of England as by law established'. The requirement was confirmed by the Act of Union in 1707 which repeated and thus further entrenched the anti-Roman Catholic provision first introduced in effect by the Coronation Oath Act 1688, stated explicitly in 1689 by the Bill of Rights which excluded even Protestants from the succession if they married Roman Catholics, and restated in s. 2 of the Act of Settlement.

The requirement to be 'in communion with the Church of England' does not mean that the sovereign has necessarily to be a *member* of the Church of England itself. The first two Hanoverian monarchs were, of course, Lutherans. Rather, the requirement may be satisfied wherever a successor is a baptized and communicant member of Protestant churches 'which subscribe to the doctrine of the Holy Trinity, and who are in good standing in their own Church' – the combined effect of the Church of England's Admission to Holy Communion Measure 1972 and Canon B 15A. These provisions comprehend potentially most Protestant denominations (including, of course, the Church of Scotland) but not non-Trinitarians like Unitarians or the non-eucharistic Quakers.

These provisions are variously reflected in the oaths required of the sovereign on accession. (The very first oath – dealt with below in Chapter 6 on the Church of Scotland – in the order of their being taken is in fact the Scottish oath under the Act of Union.) So far as the Church of England is concerned, these oaths are the coronation and accession oaths.

Coronation Oath

The original form of the oath as prescribed by s. 3 of the Coronation Oath Act 1688 (1 Will and Mary c 6) is as follows:

> Will you solemnly promise and swear to govern the people of this Kingdom of Great Britain and the dominions thereunto according to the statutes in Parliament agreed on, and the respective laws and customs of the same?
> I solemnly promise so to do.
> Will you to your power cause law and justice in mercy to be executed in all your Judgments?
> I will.

> Will you to the utmost of your power maintain the laws of God,
> the true profession of the Gospel and the Protestant reformed religion
> established by law? And will you maintain and preserve inviolately
> the settlement of the Church of England and Ireland and the doctrine,
> worship, discipline and government thereof as by law established,
> within the Kingdoms of England and Ireland, the dominion of Wales,
> and the town of Berwick on Tweed, and the territories thereto belong-
> ing? And will you preserve unto the bishops and clergy of England
> and to the churches there committed to their charge, all such rights
> and privileges as by law do or shall appertain unto them or any
> of them?
> All this I promise to do.

The Act requires the oath to be administered by either of the Archbishops or a bishop.

The original form of the oath was, of course, unable to anticipate subsequent political changes such as the union with Scotland and alterations
in the relationship with Ireland. The form of the oath was subsequently
amended at later coronations to accommodate such changes though
without formal parliamentary authority. The wording used in 1953 was
as follows:

> Will you solemnly promise and swear to govern the Peoples of the
> United Kingdom of Great Britain and Northern Ireland, Canada, Aus-
> tralia, New Zealand, the Union of South Africa, Pakistan and Ceylon,
> and of your Possessions and other Territories to any of them belonging
> or pertaining, according to their respective laws and customs?
> I solemnly promise so to do.
> Will you to your power cause Law and Justice, in Mercy, to be
> executed in all your judgements?
> I will.
> Will you to the utmost of your power maintain the Laws of God
> and the true profession of the Gospel? Will you to the utmost of your
> power maintain in the United Kingdom the Protestant Reformed Reli-
> gion established by law? Will you maintain and preserve inviolably
> the settlement of the Church of England, and the doctrine, worship,
> discipline, and government thereof, as by law established in England?
> And will you preserve unto the Bishops and Clergy of England, and
> the Churches there committed to their charge, all such rights and
> privileges, as by law do or shall appertain to them or any of them?
> All this I promise to do.

Accession Declaration

This is prescribed by the Accession Declaration Act 1910 as follows:

> I do solemnly and sincerely in the presence of God profess, testify and declare that I am a faithful Protestant, and that I will, according to the true intent of the enactments which secure the Protestant succession to the throne of my Realm, uphold and maintain the said enactments to the best of my powers according to law.

This oath falls to be made at the first Parliament of the new reign or at the Coronation. In recent reigns it has been taken at the State Opening of the first new Parliament of the reign rather than at the Coronation.

The former version of the oath, originating in a loyalty oath required of Parliament and Crown servants in 1678 in the hysteria of the 'Popish Plot', was extended by the Bill of Rights 1689 to the Sovereign and read as follows:

> I, A.B., do solemnly and sincerely in the presence of God, profess, testify and declare that I do believe that in the Sacrament of the Lord's Supper there is not any Transubstantiation of the Elements of Bread and Wine into the Blood and Body of Christ, at or after the consecration thereof by any person whatsoever; and that the Invocation or the Adoration of the Virgin or any other Saint, and the Sacrifice of the Mass, as they are now used in the Church of Rome, are superstitious and idolatrous. And I do solemnly, in the presence of God, profess, testify and declare, that I do make this declaration and every part thereof in the plain and ordinary sense of the words read unto me, as they are commonly understood by *English Protestants*, without any Evasion, Equivocation, or mental Reservation whatsoever, and without any dispensation already granted me for this purpose by the Pope, or any other person or authority whatsoever, or without hope of any such dispensation from any person or authority whatsoever, or without thinking that I am or can be acquitted before God or man, or absolved of this declaration or any part thereof, although the Pope or any other person or persons or power whatsoever should dispense with or annul the same or declare that it was null and void from the beginning.

At the time of the accession of Edward VII some concern was expressed about language bound to be deeply offensive to the new King's Irish subjects, and a Bill was introduced but not pressed home. Subsequently, however, the new Prince of Wales (later George V) raised the issue with Church and ministers making it clear that he hoped for suitable amendment. The drafting problem was to find a formula which pleased Roman Catholics without displeasing Anglicans and other Protestants. The government's first attempt achieved the former but not the latter. The Archbishop of Canterbury's draft was sent to the Prime Minister on 27 July (the day of the Bill's Second Reading), and incorporated into the Bill which passed through all its stages and received Royal Assent on 3 August 1910.

The question of further amendment is sometimes raised, and there would be opportunity as in 1910 to enact change between accession and coronation. At the same time, as the then Prime Minister pointed out in 1910, it is for consideration whether the Declaration is necessary at all (HC 27 June 1910, col. 2133).

The position of Roman Catholics

If to some extent mitigated by the reformed Accession Declaration, the present law nonetheless maintains disqualifications in respect of Roman Catholicism. This fact has occasionally in recent times led to parliamentary questioning whether they should not be eradicated. In a modern society generally devoted among other things to the extirpation of all forms of discrimination, it is argued that it is anomalous for such features to remain.

A number of attempts have been made to proceed by way of Bills or motions introduced by private Members of both Westminster Houses.[3] There was also a debate in the Scottish Parliament in 1999 which endorsed a resolution in favour of eliminating the discrimination (Pond and Gay 2005: 21). More recently still, Scottish Roman Catholics have drawn attention to the situation. Cardinal O'Brien (the senior Roman Catholic cleric in Scotland) pressed the Scottish First Minister to support repeal of the Act of Settlement: 'It is difficult for a First Minister to tell people you shouldn't discriminate against people on the grounds of their religion when we have an Act of Parliament that does exactly that' (*Scotland on Sunday* 13 February 2005). The Roman Catholic Bishop of Motherwell criticized the Prime Minister for the government's continued inaction on the issue two years later (*The Times* 12 November 2007).

In practice, however, both legislatures have accepted that, because of the complexity of the intertwined legislation involved, there are larger constitutional issues that would have to be weighed before change could be brought about, and that, by the same token, such issues should not be addressed by private members of either House. For example, any change would have to negotiate the requirements of the 1931 Statute of Westminster for the concurrence of the Commonwealth monarchies in any 'alteration in the law touching the succession to the throne or the royal style and titles'.[4] This does not, however, mean that proceeding by a Church of England Measure is necessarily ruled out – a point returned to in Part IV.

The difficulties have so far been presented as difficulties of practice rather than of principle. In his sole formal statement on the position when Prime Minister, Tony Blair responded to a 1999 approach as follows:

> *Ms Roseanna Cunningham*: To ask the Prime Minister if he will make it his policy to seek to amend the law to (a) allow members of the Royal family to marry a Catholic without losing their right to inherit the throne and (b) allow Roman Catholics to inherit the throne; and if he will make a statement.
>
> *The Prime Minister*: The Government have always stood firmly against discrimination in all its forms, including against Roman Catholics, and will continue to do so.
>
> The Government have a heavy legislative programme aimed at delivering key manifesto commitments in areas such as health, education, crime and reform of the welfare system. To bring about change to the law on succession would be a complex undertaking involving amendment or repeal of a number of items of related legislation, as well as requiring the consent of legislatures of member nations of the Commonwealth. It would raise other major constitutional issues. The Government has no plans to legislate in this area. (HC 13 December 1999, col. 57)

A *Guardian* report of 5 June 2001 claimed that the Prime Minister, in an interview with the *Glasgow Herald*, subsequently 'promised to look again at the 300-year-old law banning Roman Catholics from succession to the British throne'. However, the enthusiasm here appears to have been the newspaper's and not the Prime Minister's. When Lord Dubs some years later introduced a Bill on the subject, the Lord Chancellor (Irvine) expressed government sympathy with those who felt strongly on the issues but pointed out the implications for 'major constitutional changes, requiring consultation throughout the Commonwealth', concluding that the Bill was 'not needed at the moment since there is no practical discriminatory effect on the current line of the royal succession' (HL 14 January 2005, col. 512).

The *Guardian* newspaper has continued to campaign on the issue. It has claimed that, while it had been understood that Gordon Brown decided not to seek amendment of the 1701 Act in his original constitutional proposals on taking over as Prime Minister in 2007, he had subsequently decided to pursue change (*Guardian* 25 September 2008). In fact, there appears to be no such commitment. The source, an article by Chris Bryant MP in a collection of Labour essays, specifically stressed the difficulties facing legislation, was not in a position to promise legislation, and gave no such undertakings (Bryant 2008).

Clearly, there are no easy or comfortable answers. For example, permitting the sovereign to be a Roman Catholic would produce difficulties both for the sovereign and the Church of England in a situation where the sovereign's church was not in communion with the Church of England and moreover denied the validity of Protestant orders. There is the important point that the discrimination – if that is the right word – is not uniquely directed against Roman Catholics but affects all non-Christians in addition to certain Christian denominations. The disqualification is not that anyone is prevented from practising any religion they like; rather, it is that the character of the United Kingdom state is predicated on a particular kind of Christian assumption. It is also the case, as the Church of England points out, that it is the requirements of the Roman Catholic Church itself that prevent its members satisfying certain of the statutory stipulations. These considerations by no means exhaust the argument, however, and Chapter 12 returns to the subject in greater detail.

Legislature

The discussion here deals first with legislative procedures, secondly the role of the Second Church Estates Commissioner, and thirdly with episcopal membership of the House of Lords. (The system of episcopal *appointment* is dealt with in the immediately following chapter on the Executive.)

Legislation

Just as the monarchy is a parliamentary monarchy, so for many purposes does the Church of England remain a parliamentary church, though since the Worship and Doctrine Measure of 1974 it has had effective autonomy on those core matters.

A major exception is the status of the canons of the Church of England which, since a King's Bench judgement of 1736, have been directly binding on the clergy alone, though they have some potentially indirect effect against laity in certain limited circumstances. Originally, canons were dealt with exclusively in the Convocations. However, since the Convocations became part of the General Synod on its creation in 1969, canons are now made by the Synod. Canons fall to be approved by the sovereign without any parliamentary procedure. However, on the basis that the sovereign does not act except on the advice of ministers, in practice canons need the approval of ministers, themselves accountable to Parliament.

Under the Church Assembly (Powers) Act 1919 – the Enabling Act – Parliament has given a unique right of legislative initiative to the Church of England Synod. In theory the right of initiative is not exclusive and there is no legal reason why legislation affecting the Church of England cannot be introduced by any member of either House under the normal procedures. In practice, however, Parliament has so far ceded the right of initiative on matters wholly internal to the Church of England. What is in effect a convention has been established that the government will normally expect the Church alone to act in such matters and will not itself exceptionally seek to legislate in such areas without the Church of England's consent.[5]

At the same time, there is nothing to prevent *Parliament* legislating for the Church of England without its consent. However, no Bill introduced by an MP for such purposes has ever made progress. It follows that that was always likely to be the outcome, for example, of the Bishops (Consecration of Women) Bill introduced a few years ago by Andy Reed MP (HC 21 March 2006, cols 170–4). Such initiatives are no doubt taken to make a point rather than in any real expectation of succeeding.

But Parliament does legislate in ways which may affect the Church of England. The extent to which this might be appropriate was, for example, discussed during the passage of the Human Rights Bill in 1998.[6] Similarly, the effect on traditional forms of clerical tenure had to be reviewed by the Church of England as a consequence of the implementation of a European Union Directive on employment rights via the Employment Relations Act 1999. In the same way, there has been recent discussion about how possible changes in charity law should affect the Church of England. But these are issues affecting all churches and not the Church of England alone. As explained in Chapter 7 below, even the Church of Scotland's special status under the Church of Scotland Act 1921 does not free it entirely from taking on board the consequences of action by the civil power not dreamt of in the very different social and political circumstances of 1921. Indeed, as explained in that chapter, legal proceedings

before the House of Lords have recently challenged the scope of the
1921 Act.

Procedure under the 1919 Act is as follows:

The Church of England Synod transmits any Measure (the formal title applied to Church of England legislation under the Act)
it has approved via its Legislative Committee to the Ecclesiastical
Committee of Parliament.

The Ecclesiastical Committee is a statutory joint committee of both
Houses consisting of 15 members from each nominated by the Lord
Chancellor (in future no doubt the Speaker of the Lords) and the
Speaker of the Commons at the beginning – and for the duration –
of each new Parliament. It may continue its business even in a parliamentary recess, and proposed Measures do not therefore fall at the
end of each session if all the necessary procedures remain uncom-
pleted. Although a statutory rather than a parliamentary committee,
the Ecclesiastical Committee has in practice adopted parliamentary
joint committee procedures. The Committee's chair has always been
a peer and, since 1947, a Lord of Appeal – a situation due to
change when the new Supreme Court arrangements get underway.
The Commons' representatives always include the Second Church
Estates Commissioner – see below – who answers for the Church
Commissioners in the Commons.

On receipt of the Measure, the Ecclesiastical Committee has to prepare (after conferring if it wishes with the Legislative Committee) a
report to Parliament. This report has to set out the nature and legal
effect of the Measure and the Ecclesiastical Committee's views 'as to
the expediency thereof, especially with relation to the constitutional
rights of all [Her] Majesty's subjects'. If there has been a conference, the transcript is attached to the report, but the Ecclesiastical
Committee does not otherwise take evidence.

During this process, neither Committee has any power to vary the
text of the Measure. The Legislative Committee may, however, withdraw the Measure – for example, after receipt of the Ecclesiastical
Committee's draft report which the latter is required to show the
former during the considerative process.

A Measure may deal with any Church of England matter, and may
amend or repeal any act of Parliament except those provisions of the
1919 Act itself relating to the composition, powers or duties of the
Ecclesiastical Committee. A Measure may confer powers for Synod to
make subordinate legislation which may, though not automatically,

be brought within the requirements of the Statutory Instruments Act 1946 and become subject to parliamentary scrutiny before entering into full effect. The Synod's own Standing Orders require Measures to provide for subordinate legislation to be laid before Parliament for approval if it affects the legal rights of any person. Following submission of the Ecclesiastical Committee's report to Parliament, a resolution of each House is required to present the Measure for Royal Assent whereupon the Measure attains the force and effect of an Act of Parliament.

Granted that what in an analogous voluntary association would be purely internal adjustments without recourse to a public, let alone statutory, procedure, the Church of England has made regular but not prolific use of the 1919 Act arrangements. In the last two decades, for example, only 1986 has seen as many as four Measures approved; and in some years – 1984, 1985, 1987, 1989, 1996 and 2002 – there have been none.

The scrutiny of the Ecclesiastical Committee is no mere formality or necessarily Parliament's last word. While the rejection of the Prayer Book Measures in 1927 and 1928 are the best-known occasions of parliamentary rejection, there have been others. For example, in 1984 the Commons voted against approving the Appointment of Bishops Measure even though the Ecclesiastical Committee had – as in 1927 – certified the Measure expedient; and in July 1989 it initially declined to approve the Clergy (Ordination) Measure before finally agreeing to do so in February 1990. In a more recent case, the Ecclesiastical Committee's 217th Report dealt with the Church of England (Pensions) Measure which, among other things, sought to continue for a further seven years the ability of the Church Commissioners to expend capital in support of their pension liabilities that had been granted in a Measure of 1997. While the Ecclesiastical Committee had no objection of principle to the proposal, they felt unable in April 2002 to certify as 'expedient' a new proposal that further extensions beyond seven years could be accomplished by subordinate synodical legislation without further reference to Parliament. The upshot was that the Measure in its original form was withdrawn and a fresh Measure submitted in a revised form in November 2002.

Role of the Second Church Estates Commissioner

No government minister is responsible for the Church Commissioners. When the Ecclesiastical Commissioners were created in the 1830s, relations with Parliament were catered for because there were always

Commissioners who were MPs. Increasingly from 1866, however, a convention became established that the government used its powers to appoint the Second (unpaid) Church Estates Commissioner to give that post to a senior government backbencher in the House of Commons, also nowadays appointed to the Ecclesiastical Committee under the Enabling Act 1919. Gradually, and especially after 1926, the Second Church Estates Commissioner came to be regarded as the parliamentary spokesman for the Ecclesiastical/Church Commissioners (Best 1964: 418–19). While it is true that holders of the office are always of the same stripe as the government, they are not strictly *members* of the government.

The present position is that the government business managers arrange that parliamentary time is made available on about eight times a year to the MP to answer Questions concerning the Church Commissioners' activities. The MP is briefed by the Church Commissioners for these purposes. (There is no equivalent arrangement in the House of Lords, because only the Commons may deal with financial matters.) The rationale for an arrangement where the only other non-ministerial MPs who take Questions are the chairs of certain Commons committees is that the Church Commissioners dispose of funds with historic origins partly in parliamentary grants. The arrangement also reflects the established status of the Church of England.

Bishops in the House of Lords

Forty-two diocesan bishops are eligible to sit in the House of Lords as Lords Spiritual by ancient usage. It has been argued that the usage stemmed not from consideration of any spiritual dignity but solely from regard for the lands they held in barony from the sovereign (Pike 1894: 151–68). By the same token, the bishop of Sodor and Man is not included with the English bishops on the grounds that the temporalities of his bishopric were not originally received from the Crown. He is, however, a member of the Manx Parliament.

The number of bishops actually permitted to sit at any one time has, since the Bishop of Manchester Act 1847, been limited to 26 – the number existing at the time of the legislation which that year created additional bishoprics. Of the 42 bishops, the archbishops of Canterbury and York and the bishops of London, Durham and Winchester have seats automatically. The remainder are admitted in order of seniority of consecration when vacancies occur. The episcopal membership constituted 4 per cent of the House at the time of the review by the Wakeham Royal Commission (Wakeham 2000: 150). (In Tudor times before the Reformation, the

Lords Spiritual – who included abbots and priors – actually outnumbered the much smaller lay peerage of the day.)
The United Kingdom Parliament is the only sovereign national legislature in Europe which has explicit religious representation. A majority of the Wakeham Commission recommended that that representation should be widened to include other Christian denominations, and that room be found for such appointments by reducing the Church of England's share from 26 to 16 seats in a reformed upper chamber. Of the 10 seats thus made available, five should go to other denominations in England and five to representatives of Christian denominations in Scotland, Wales and Northern Ireland. Over and above the 26 Christian representatives, the Commission recommended that a further 5 members of the chamber should be 'specifically selected to be broadly representative of the different non-Christian faith communities' (Wakeham 2000: 155–9).[7]

The Church of England was at pains to stress in its own evidence to the Wakeham Commission that it would welcome a wider representation of the nation's spiritual life in the second chamber and 'remains ready and willing to speak in Parliament for its Christian partners and for people of other faiths and none' though without pretending any exclusive claim to do so (Church of England 1999: 9). Archbishop Carey reinforced the point when speaking of a 'hospitable establishment' in the same sense three years later (Carey 2002).

As a Constitution Unit comparative study of second chambers had pointed out, widening religious representation on Wakeham lines is in fact problematic:

> It is widely acknowledged that the representation of only one religious group in a multi-cultural Britain is outdated. However, it is difficult to envisage an agreement being reached on religious representation in a new chamber which fully satisfied all religious groups. Arguments about the relative number of seats to be given to Catholic bishops or Muslim leaders are likely to prove equally difficult as questions about the relative balance of employers and trade unions, or teachers and doctors, in a 'functional' or vocational chamber. (Russell 2000: 330–1)

In its study of House of Lords reform published in 2002, the House of Commons Public Administration Select Committee (PASC) recommended that bishops of the Church of England should no longer sit ex officio from the time of the next general election but one. Observing that the debate had moved on since the Report of the Wakeham Royal

Commission and that removal need not lead to disestablishment, the Select Committee said:

> We entirely accept the case that a healthy variety of opinions, which should include a range of religious, moral and ethical viewpoints, should be represented in the second chamber. However, the political support for a very large second chamber, of the sort that could accommodate the bench of bishops, has diminished, with the Conservative Party for instance now proposing a chamber of 300. The continuing process of reform, with a largely elected second chamber and the active statutory appointments commission we propose, would rapidly make the tradition of ex officio religious membership an anachronism. It is of course the case that distinguished senior figures in the Church of England (and other religious bodies) will be considered for membership of the second chamber through the appointment process (and they should be free to stand for election). This appears to us to represent the fairest approach. (PASC 2002: 35)

This suggestion was not, however, adopted by the government in subsequent White Papers on reform of the Lords. In practice these issues have not been addressed conclusively because, so far, Parliament has not been able to agree how, if at all, the composition (and powers) of the House of Lords should be further reformed. Chapter 13 below considers the future of episcopal membership further.

4
Executive, Judiciary and the Legatine Powers

This chapter explains the extent of the Executive's involvement in Church of England appointments, the position of the Church's own judiciary, and the inherited Legatine powers of the Archbishop of Canterbury.

Current appointments systems are due to change following the Prime Minister's announcement in July 2007 (Government Papers Cm 7170: paras 57–66) that he intended to withdraw from any active involvement in the appointing procedures. Following discussion with and within the Church of England (Church of England 2008), this intention was confirmed in March 2008 (Government Papers Cm 7342, paras 254–6). Because these arrangements are, therefore, in transition, the chapter will first describe the Church appointments arrangements up to the point of change but indicating where change is imminent. It will then discuss some of the background to the proposed changes and offer some preliminary reflections on their significance. How the wider constitutional implications of the changes fall to be regarded will be discussed in Chapter 13.

Executive

The constitutional relationship between the Church of England and the executive stems from the latter's position as advisers, and consequently conduit, to the Crown who, in the person of the Queen, constitutes the Supreme Governor of the Church. Accordingly, all Crown patronage is exercized on the advice of ministers. The Queen, formally advised by the Prime Minister, is at the apex of the system. It is partly in recognition of the Prime Minister's role that the Prime Minister has customarily met with the Archbishop of Canterbury about twice a year.

This relationship does not, of course, exclude contact with other religious leaders. However, that contact is less frequent and of a necessarily different character.

Senior Church of England appointments

This section summarizes the extent of government involvement, current ecclesiastical appointment procedures, and their prospective development.

(a) Extent of Crown patronage

Bishops and suffragan bishops   The Crown appoints 43 diocesan bishops and 68 suffragan bishops. The diocesans include the bishop of Sodor and Man but not the bishop in Europe. Neither of the latter two bishops is eligible to sit in the House of Lords, the first – who *does* sit in the Manx Parliament – because his temporalities were not originally received from the Crown. In addition, both bishops are consecrated to serve in areas which are not part of the United Kingdom.

Cathedral Deans   Under the Cathedrals Measure 1999, all cathedrals now have deans. The Crown appoints 28 of the 44 deans, that is, all except the deans of former 'parish church' cathedrals, and the dean of the cathedral in Gibraltar. There is no dean in the case of the Isle of Man where the bishop is dean of his own cathedral. The Crown also appoints the deans of the Royal Peculiars of Westminster Abbey and St George's, Windsor.

Residentiary canons   There are approximately 160 such canonries. About 30 appointments are in the hands of the Crown shared roughly equally between the Lord Chancellor acting by himself and the Prime Minister advising the sovereign. In practice, the preparatory work for such appointments was undertaken by the Prime Minister's Appointments Secretary (PMAS) who from 1964 had acted additionally as the Lord Chancellor's Ecclesiastical Secretary supported by an Assistant Ecclesiastical Secretary also based at 10 Downing Street.[1] The 30 appointments include those canonries held by the relevant Regius chairs at Oxford, but do not include others at present in abeyance for various reasons. In addition, a small number of the appointments were appointed in turn, shared with the diocesan bishop.

Royal Peculiars   These are churches exempt from the visitation of the customary Ordinary (typically the diocesan bishop) but where the Crown (as supreme Ordinary) has visitatorial jurisdiction. They include Westminster Abbey and St George's Chapel, Windsor, and the Chapels Royal at

St James's Palace, the Tower of London and Hampton Court. As explained above, the deans of Westminster and Windsor are Crown appointments made on the advice of the Prime Minister, as are the appointments of their residentiary canons. Recommendations in respect of the Chapel of the Savoy, a peculiar falling within the Duchy of Lancaster, are made by the Chancellor of the Duchy.

Ministerial advice can reach beyond questions of appointment. Following a difficult episode at Westminster Abbey, a review covering the peculiars at the Abbey, Windsor and the Chapels Royal was set up in 1999 to report to the Queen through the Lord Chancellor on the organization, management and accountability of each. In 2004 the Queen accepted the Lord Chancellor's recommendations based on the report of the review group.[2]

Crown reversion It was the established convention that, where the appointment of a diocesan bishop creates a vacancy even in certain non-episcopal offices, it was the Crown that appointed to the vacancy so created. Thus, the Crown may become involved on those occasions only in appointments to cathedral deaneries, archdeaconries and residentiary canonries not otherwise in its patronage as well as those deaneries and canonries which are.

Benefices The government is also significantly involved in the exercize of patronage for the appointment of clergy to individual benefices, that is, as the incumbents of parishes. A total of 652 benefices is involved: 210 where the Crown appoints on the advice of the Prime Minister, and 442 where the Lord Chancellor is the appointing authority – in 157 as the sole patron, and in 285 cases either alternately or sequentially with other patrons. While all these appointments are exempt from the Patronage (Benefices) Measure 1986, it is the practice of the appointing authorities to observe the spirit of the Measure's requirements.

Since 1964 the preparatory work in all these cases has been undertaken by the Assistant Ecclesiastical Secretary at No 10. He maintains a database of names of clergy actively interested in appointment. The names might reach him from any source, including the Archbishops' Clergy Appointments Adviser, a Church official distinct from the Archbishops' Appointments Secretary (ASA). (The work of the Assistant Ecclesiastical Secretary in respect of the Lord Chancellor's patronage recently received attention from the Select Committee on Constitutional Affairs where the Secretary explained the procedures followed.[3] Essentially the same procedures are followed in the case of the Crown's patronage.)

The Duchy of Lancaster exercizes a much smaller patronage with just over 40 benefices, and operates on the same lines as, if on a different scale from, the Appointments Secretary's office.

Other Crown appointments   These include the six Church Estate Commissioners, the Master of the Temple, six members (including the chairman) of the Churches Conservation Trust, and six members of the Advisory Board for Redundant Churches – the last appointed by the archbishops after consultation with the Prime Minister. (While the Dean of the Arches and Auditor – the most senior ecclesiastical judge – is appointed by the archbishops, the necessary royal consent is forthcoming only on the advice of the Prime Minister.)

(b) Appointment procedures

Archbishops and diocesan bishops   The appointment of archbishops and bishops is determined under the Appointments of Bishops Act 1533, which confers an absolute discretion on the Crown. In its original form, the Act laid down that the sovereign could in effect order cathedral chapters to elect the sovereign's nominee on pain of praemunire. Since the removal of that ancient sanction in 1967 and the substitution of Colleges of Canons for the previous arrangements, the Crown's requirements are nowadays issued to the College.

Appointment: Background   Before 1976, the initiative in those senior Church of England appointments that are made by the sovereign remained entirely in the hands of the Prime Minister who alone advised the sovereign. There were varying degrees of consultation with the archbishops of Canterbury and York, but the whole process was managed in practice by the PMAS, a civil servant with a small staff. (One attempt to improve the arrangements – the Howick Commission – is explained in the Annex to this chapter.)

In due course, the PMAS became counterbalanced by a Church of England official, the ASA. Indeed, from the Church's point of view, the ASA became more important than the PMAS. In internal Church discussions in 1974 about the appointment system, for example, the Archbishop of York thought the ASA's contacts more up to date than the PMAS's; and it was generally accepted that Downing Street was unduly conservative in its outlook and, the ASA claimed, 'seldom produced any surprises' (Notes of meetings 16 and 21 January 1974, GSA/T/CS/1, Church Record Office).

In 1970, the Chadwick Committee proposed changes in the system designed to increase the degree of Church of England influence, and

Synod in 1974 supported that approach in a strongly worded resolution affirming 'the principle that the decisive voice in the appointment of diocesan bishops should be that of the Church'. In the ensuing negotiations, successive Prime Ministers were adamant that they had to have a *real* choice between the names submitted by the Church. Government officials noted that the submission of a single name, as in the case of suffragan bishop appointments, 'could only be regarded as a starter if all concerned were prepared to ignore its major and constitutional disadvantage of treating the Prime Minister as a glorified postman'. Perceiving that the proposed changes would give the initiative in practice to the Church, the PMAS noted that the PMAS

> would cease to be unambiguously the servant of the Prime Minister, and would become a Civil Servant (financed by the taxpayer) carrying out a particular piece of work for the Church. (TNA HO 304/33, letter of 24 July 1975)

A preparatory report by officials approved by Ministers rejected the Church proposal that the Church's nomination should be final:

> The Sovereign would thus be placed in the anomalous position of being able neither to exercize a personal choice nor to have effective recourse to the normal channels of advice – since the Prime Minister could say only that he had no objection but to endorse the Church's decision. Short of altering the present constitution of the House of Lords, the proposal would also mean that nominations for the membership of that House were being made by a body outside the normal political spectrum and not answerable to Parliament. (TNA HO 304/33, memorandum 24 January 1975)

In his statement recording the outcome of the negotiations (about which the leaders of the Opposition parties had been consulted), the Prime Minister, James Callaghan, rejected any notion that it was time to end Prime Ministerial involvement in such appointments:

> There are ... cogent reasons why the State cannot divest itself from a concern with these appointments of the Established Church. The Sovereign must be able to look for advice on a matter of this kind and that must mean, for a constitutional Sovereign, advice from Ministers. The Archbishops and some of the bishops sit by right in the House of Lords, and their nomination must therefore remain a matter for the Prime Minister's concern. (HC 6 June 1976 col. 613)

Since 1976, in a procedure involving the PMAS and the ASA, Crown Nomination Commissions of the Church of England have submitted two names to the Prime Minister for archiepiscopal and diocesan bishop appointments. The Prime Minister was then free to select either of the two names or to reject both and request alternative nominations: he could not substitute a name which had not come from the Church of England in the first place. (The recommendations of the van Straubenzee Working Party in 1992 – see the Annex to this chapter – to cut out the Prime Minister altogether were not acted upon.)

Following the Prime Minister's 1976 statement, the Church's involvement was formalized through its own Crown Nominations Commission, a committee consisting of clerical and lay members, and originally set up as the 'Crown Appointments Commission' in 1977. The operation of the Commission and of diocesan 'Vacancy in See' Committees (which prepare the way in the case of particular vacancies for the work of the Commission) are prescribed in standing orders and regulations respectively of the General Synod.

It is expected that, under the new arrangements, the Crown Nominations Commission will continue – with the exceptions noted below – to function essentially in the same way as before and as follows:

The Archbishop of Canterbury presides when the appointment is in his Province, and the Archbishop of York when the appointment is in his Province, though the presiding Archbishop in either case may invite the other Archbishop to preside instead for all or part of the meeting. In the absence of the appropriate Archbishop the other Archbishop shall preside or, in the absence of both Archbishops, one of the members elected by the Houses of Clergy and Laity shall be nominated to preside by the appropriate Archbishop or in the event of his incapacity by the other Archbishop.

The other members of the Commission are: six members of the General Synod (three clerical and three lay), and six elected by the diocesan Vacancy in See Committee (of whom at least three must be lay). [Both the PMAS and the ASA were formerly ex officio non-voting members of the Commission. It is now expected that the PMAS will be replaced in this role by a senior Cabinet Office official as a Crown appointments adviser.]

In the case of a *Canterbury* vacancy, the Prime Minister nominates the chair. [Whether this will continue has not yet been declared.] In such an instance, there is added to normal membership of the Commission one of the members of the Primates Meeting of the Anglican

Communion elected by the Joint Standing Committee of the Primates Meeting of the Anglican Communion and the Anglican Consultative Council as a voting member. Also invited, but in a non-voting capacity, is the Secretary General of the Anglican Communion. In the case of a *York* vacancy, the Appointments Committee of the Church of England, after consultation with the Archbishop of Canterbury, nominates the chair. (In the instance of the most recent archiepiscopal vacancies, the Canterbury Commission was chaired by a senior Judge and the York Commission by a senior northern figure with wide experience of the Church, both at national and diocesan level.)

The Vacancy in See Committee's function is to prepare a brief description of the diocese with a statement setting out the diocese's needs, and to elect the diocesan representatives to the Crown Nominations Commission. Its ex officio members include all suffragans and stipendiary assistant bishops, the cathedral dean, no more than two archdeacons, any diocesan members of the General Synod, and the chairs of the Houses of Clergy and Laity of the diocesan synod. Elected members are not fewer than two each of clerical and lay members of the diocesan synod. There are also arrangements for the diocesan bishop's council to nominate up to four additional members in order to secure representation of a special interest or to improve the representative character of the Committee as a whole.

Having taken into account the statement of needs provided by the diocese, the national statement of needs provided by the Archbishops and also the memorandum written by the Appointments Secretaries, and after considering eligible candidates, the Crown Nominations Commission submits two names (in order of preference if they so choose) to the Prime Minister for recommendation to the Crown. The Prime Minister may determine which of the names to recommend or invite the Commission to reconsider and submit an alternative name or names. [Henceforward, the Commission will still identify two names but only the first in order of preference will be forwarded to the Prime Minister. The precise function of the civil servant who has replaced the PMAS is unclear.]

Following approval by the Sovereign, cathedral colleges elect the final nominee expressing thereby consent to the outcome of a process in which the diocese's representatives will have played a full part. The election is then confirmed by the relevant Archbishop or by his Vicar General on his behalf. It is at that ceremony that the candidate becomes the diocesan bishop and is given spiritual jurisdiction over the diocese. If not already in episcopal orders, he will be ordained bishop before taking up office. He will also need to make an act of homage to the Sovereign at a ceremony attended by a Cabinet minister. An enthronement service subsequently takes place in the diocese.

The secretary to the Crown Nominations Commission is the Archbishops' Secretary for Appointments (ASA) and she supports the work of the committee. Both she and the PMAS will have attended at least one meeting of the Vacancy in See Committee. In practice the two officials work closely together at all stages, including when they visit dioceses jointly in order to sound out opinion on local needs and preferences. In the new arrangements, it seems likely that the initiative will pass very much to the ASA and the civil servant who replaces the PMAS's former function will have a much more passive role than the PMAS.

Suffragan bishops These bishops are appointed under the Suffragan Bishops Act, 1534. The Act requires the diocesan bishop to submit two names to the Crown for it to choose which of the two is to be appointed.

The initiative for the appointment of suffragan bishops is in the hands of the diocesan bishop in whose diocese the suffragan appointment is to be made. While the Crown Nominations Commission is not involved, there is a formal consideration procedure during which diocesan bishops set up consultative arrangements about the nature of the role and the type of person required, as a minimum involving a small group to advise him and the bishop's council on the vacancy. In addition, the ASA advises as to the field of consideration of candidates, and acts as the vehicle for submitting the diocesan bishop's recommendations through the Archbishop of the relevant Province to the PMAS. While by law two names must be submitted, by convention the first name is recommended by the Prime Minister to the Queen. [Presumably, the PMAS's civil service successor will continue to carry out his predecessor's function.]

Cathedral appointments Where the patronage rests with the Crown, the initiative for appointment of deans and other clergy was taken wholly by the PMAS, and the Church itself had no established selection machinery for relaying its own views. Although the PMAS did not rely on any formal consultative machinery, he generally took careful local soundings, and especially in the appointment of deans took account of the pool of potentially eligible people whose identification might also be assisted by suggestions from the ASA.

Taking on the responsibility for making these appointments was problematic for the Church of England. Not only was there no available machinery for doing so but also there were different views among interested clerical parties about how the respective interests might best be accommodated. Accordingly, a large part of the Archbishops' advice to Synod was taken up in trying to resolve the questions that arose in the new situation (Church of England 2008: paras 26–49).

(c) Reviewing developments in senior ecclesiastical appointments processes

These processes have been the subject of attention *within* the Church on a number of recent occasions. A review in 1992 led to the adoption in 1995 of a code of practice for the appointment of suffragan bishops, deans, archdeacons and residentiary canons applicable to all those appointments not within the patronage of the Crown. Although the code did not bind the Crown, it was understood that the Crown's practices sought to observe the code's spirit.

The Perry Report (Perry 2001) reviewed the operation of the Crown Appointments Commission that had been set up by the Church in 1977 in response to the Prime Minister's statement of the previous year. The Perry Committee was precluded from considering any changes in the law. Further synodical consideration of the report's recommendations resulted in a number of changes in the procedures for nominating diocesan bishops, including renaming the Commission as the 'Crown Nominations Commission'. The purpose of the changes was to increase the transparency of the selection process, to ensure that candidates were considered from as wide a pool as possible, and to improve the candidate information available to the Nominations Commission.

Discussion in Synod in early 2005 resulted in a decision to set up a further review to consider how the current separate processes for making appointments to senior ecclesiastical office (other than diocesan bishops) might be best integrated with one another and made consistent. The terms of reference of the working party extended to reviewing and making recommendations as to the law and practice regarding the appointment of suffragan bishops, deans, archdeacons, and residentiary canons. The Pilling Report (*Talent and Calling*) was published in mid 2007 and recommended, among other things, the abolition of the practice of Crown reversion. In the immediate short term, the report became upstaged days after its publication by the Prime Minister's own July 2007 initiative – *The Governance of Britain* (Government Papers Cm 7170) – which, as already mentioned, proposed that he should withdraw from active personal involvement in senior ecclesiastical appointments. In the longer term, however, it is clear that many of the Pilling Report's detailed recommendations will find a place in the new dispensation.

A new Prime Minister's views made known in July 2007 seemed sensible, though they represented an implicit reversal of a predecessor's reasoning in 1976 that the Prime Minister had to have the last word in the making of appointments. Whether Gordon Brown was made aware of past arguments or not, it is understandable that a modern chief executive might be unwilling to continue to intrude an unrelated political element into what is essentially – in appointment terms alone – an internal Church of England matter. Whereas since 1976 the Church has been able to determine the *field* of choice, the new proposals mean that the Church will actually *make* the choice.

Gordon Brown was right that none of all this betokens disestablishment for the Church of England, even if officials and Ministers thought in 1975 that direct nomination of bishops did. At the same time, the Church of England itself clearly had some anxiety about changes it had not itself proposed. These surfaced in the two papers of model comprehensiveness and lucidity that the archbishops circulated: a consultation paper in Autumn 2007 (Church of England 2007) and final proposals (Church of England 2008) put to the February Synod. The first spoke of the possibility that

> there would be value in an advisory role for someone appointed by the Crown, perhaps after consultation with us, who would have a responsibility for ensuring that the wider 'public voice' was heard in the Church's process for some or all of these Crown appointments. Such a person would also be able to safeguard the interest of the Crown that the arrangements be properly conducted. (Church of England 2007: para. 13)

The paper went on to develop how this might be accomplished working from the PMAS's existing functions.

Following the consultation, the archbishops' recommendations (Church of England 2008: paras 10–17) endorsed the original thinking:

> The clear weight of the representations received is that it would be for the benefit for the Church if someone appointed by the Crown could participate in the selection processes in an advisory capacity. We agree. (Paragraph 10)

That the archbishops entertained some reservation about the sovereign's position may be discerned in this recommendation (agreed by an overwhelming Synod majority) that a residual role should remain for the

PMAS's proposed successor, provisionally called the 'Crown Appointments Adviser'. A number of speakers in the subsequent Synod debate[4] expressed real anxiety about the access to the Prime Minister that this civil servant would have and that he should possess a sufficiently high rank and status, an anxiety apparently shared by the Archbishops. In replying to the debate, the Archbishop of Canterbury defended the proposals on the lines that the expectations and public scrutiny for the appointment of bishops were different from the more purely internal Church appointments, and that one could not ignore the constitutional facts that that represented.

This sounds like accepting change for so long as things remain the same. In fact, the active link with the executive will disappear. The civil servant proposed, who would still have to be a communicant member of the Church of England, was billed as bringing some consciousness of and experience from the world outside the Church of England. But in reality it is difficult to see how such an officer could play anything other than an increasingly redundant walk-on part as a paper shifter for a post-box Prime Minister. The PMAS at least offered some necessary active support in a process where his master, the Prime Minister, retained a real choice and was making a fully responsible decision. The new officer's role will be so different that it may well be asked whether public money should be spent on the post at all. Furthermore, the new system has substantial constitutional implications – both for continued episcopal membership of the House of Lords and for the Crown – which will be discussed in Chapter 13 below.

Judiciary

The jurisdiction of the ecclesiastical courts was much curtailed in the course of the nineteenth century (when, for example, they lost their jurisdiction in cases of defamation, testamentary matters and matrimonial causes). Their jurisdiction, currently regulated largely by the Ecclesiastical Jurisdiction Measure 1963, is now essentially confined to the control of the fabric and contents of churches, churchyards and other consecrated land ('the faculty jurisdiction') and clergy discipline. In the same way that ecclesiastical law forms part of the law of England, however, the courts and judges administering it are courts and judges of the Queen. This is reflected in the appointment of ecclesiastical judges (all of whose appointments involve ministers of the Crown whether royal approval is required or not) and the composition and structure of the ecclesiastical courts.

At the diocesan level, the court is known as the *consistory court*, and is normally presided over by the chancellor of the diocese. The chancellor, who like all other ecclesiastical judges must be a communicant member of the Church of England and has to be legally qualified according to the requirements of s. 71 of the Courts and Legal Services Act 1990, is appointed by the bishop of the diocese in consultation with the Lord Chancellor and the Dean of Arches and Auditor. The last (normally referred to as the Dean of Arches) is the Church's senior judge and is appointed by the archbishops jointly, but with the approval of the Queen on the advice of Ministers.

At the *provincial level* (the Arches Court of Canterbury and the Chancery Court of York) there are five judges presided over by the Dean of Arches. Each of these judges must either have a ten-year qualification under the1990 Act or have held defined high judicial office. They are appointed by the archbishops jointly with the approval of the Queen.

The *Court of Ecclesiastical Causes Reserved* (which deals with offences of doctrine, ritual and ceremonial, as well as hearing appeals in faculty cases involving such matters) has five members all of whom are appointed by the Queen, two of them being persons who hold or have held high judicial office, and three who are, or have been, diocesan bishops.

Furthermore, in relation to faculty cases not involving matters of doctrine, ritual or ceremonial, the final right of appeal lies to a secular court, in the form of the *Judicial Committee of the Privy Council*. (That body also hears appeals against pastoral schemes made by the Church Commissioners.) Similarly, appeals from a commission of Convocation or the Court of Ecclesiastical Causes Reserved relating to offences of doctrine, ritual and ceremonial are heard by a Commission of Review, comprising five persons nominated by the Queen, of whom three must be Lords of Appeal or, from 2008, judges of the Supreme Court.

Like other inferior courts, the ecclesiastical courts are subject to control by the superior courts through the process of judicial review (at least as regards excess of, or failure to exercise, jurisdiction [the position in relation to errors within a court's jurisdiction is less clear]). And, through the doctrine of precedent, the ecclesiastical courts are bound by any applicable decisions of the Judicial Committee of the Privy Council (other than in relation to matters of doctrine, ritual or ceremonial).

Finally, the ecclesiastical courts established under the 1963 Measure have the same powers as the High Court in relation to the attendance and examination of witnesses and the production and inspection of documents; and failure to comply with their orders can be enforced by the contempt process, through the High Court, in the same way as if there had been contempt of the High Court.

Legatine jurisdiction

Before the Reformation, Archbishops of Canterbury commonly exercized Legatine powers delegated to them by the pope. At the Reformation these powers were 'nationalized' by the state and are exercized by the archbishop under legislation originating in the Ecclesiastical Licences Act 1533. The system is administered on behalf of the archbishop by the Faculty Office operating under the supervision of the Master of the Faculties (usually a High Court judge).

The commonly active elements[5] of this jurisdiction include three areas:

- *Special marriage licences* – These may be issued in England and Wales to authorize the solemnization of marriage in circumstances not permitted under normal Church of England *and* Church in Wales requirements, for example, where parties wish to marry outside their parishes of residence.
- *Notaries Public* – These are legal officers of ancient standing. Their functions include the preparation and execution of legal documents for use abroad, attesting the authenticity of deeds and writings, and 'protesting' bills of exchange. Under the Courts and Legal Services Act 1990, the Master of Faculties may make rules for the regulation of the notarial profession.
- *Lambeth Degrees* – The ability of the archbishop to award degrees is also founded on the 1533 Act. The degrees are recognized in law as full degrees. In practice, they are awarded (sometimes after examination) to those – not necessarily Anglicans – who have distinguished themselves in the service of the Christian Church.

ANNEX: Howick and van Straubenzee Committees

Howick Commission

In the 1960s the modalities of appointments came to the fore, at least in part, as a result of the government's refusal in 1961 to appoint the Provost of Guildford, Walter Boulton, to the newly established Deanery of the Cathedral for whose completion he had worked so long and hard (Welsby 1985). In that year a commission was established under the chairmanship of Lord Howick of Glendale to consider Crown appointments: it reported in December 1964, suggesting a modification of the system rather than a radical overhaul. A vacancy-in-see committee of about twenty people under the chairmanship of the senior suffragan bishop or, failing that, the dean or provost would make representations about the needs of the diocese to the Prime Minister and the archbishops but without suggesting names; formal elections by cathedral chapters would be abolished (Howick 1964). The commission also wished to see a wider degree of consultation before the appointment of deans and provosts (Howick 1964: 55). It is difficult to judge the impact of the Howick Commission. Though adopted later, vacancy-in-see committees were not established immediately and, since the process remained strictly confidential, whether there was, in fact, any wider degree of consultation cannot be known.

Van Straubenzee Working Party

The issue was revisited in the late 1980s by a working party chaired by the former MP and Second Church Estates Commissioner, Sir William van Straubenzee, and charged with reviewing the appointment of dignitaries other than diocesan bishops. It reported in 1992 with a series of proposals for the removal of the Prime Minister's part in the appointment of dignitaries. In particular, it recommended that the appointment of deans should be made after an appointing group chaired by the diocesan bishop had considered the matter; the bishop would transmit two names in order of preference to the Archbishop of the Province who, as a Privy Councillor, would submit the preferred name direct to the Sovereign (van Straubenzee 1992: 38–42).

However, the working party was by no means unanimous. Frank Field MP entered a Memorandum of Dissent in which he argued strongly for the Prime Minister's continued involvement in the process, on the grounds that any attempt to diminish the involvement of the Crown in Church appointments would lead to disestablishment by default:

> For what would be left of the Crown's influence if the Government were to accede to the reforms in the [van Straubenzee] report? And if the Crown were to lose its remaining influence in appointments how could the privileges of the Church, particularly its endowments, remain intact?

His preference would be for something like the present system, but

> ... exercized in public. I therefore endorse the ... [van Straubenzee] approach for senior positions. I do, however, believe that the majority of places on any such committee should go to Crown nominees. (van Straubenzee 1992: 115–17)

The recommendations of the working party were not implemented.

5
Financing Establishment in England

This chapter examines the financial relations between the Church of England and the state, putting them into some perspective by comparing them with arrangements in a number of other, mainly EU, countries. It will show in Europe a surprising diversity of systems, and a greater degree of state subvention than might be expected. In Great Britain the largest streams of state money to the churches are indirect: they flow through the tax and education systems, and the chaplaincies in the prisons, the armed forces and the National Health Service (NHS). With the possible exception of statutory requirements for the appointment of Anglican prison chaplains, the Church of England is not privileged since, in principle, the same sources of funding are available to all other religions.

Direct funding

A common fallacy is the belief that 'establishment' means that the state funds the costs of the Church of England. This is not now, and never has been, true. With what veracity the rest of this chapter may assist to judge, the Bishop of London has maintained on the contrary that 'The Church of England is, in financial terms, one of the most disestablished churches in Western Europe' (Church Heritage Forum 2004: 13).

For running costs purposes the Church of England relies on its own resources. Annual expenditure is about £1 billion. The Church Commissioners (the body that united the Ecclesiastical Commissioners and Queen Anne's Bounty in 1948) concentrate on support for dioceses/parishes, bishops, cathedrals and paying clergy pensions. For these purposes, the Church Commissioners manage capital assets amounting in their most recent Annual Report to about £5.7 billion (Church Commissioners 2008). Although the Commissioners have made very respectable returns on their assets, they furnish only about one-sixth of running costs expenses. The dioceses, mainly using funds from parishes, are responsible for paying and housing their clergy, the Church of England's relations with its schools, and support of the parishes. The upkeep of parish churches and cathedrals is in the first instance the responsibility of each individual body.

The last decade has seen important shifts in internal funding responsibilities because of the increased burden of clergy pensions. These now claim one-third of the Commissioners' income within arrangements that permit the Commissioners temporarily to draw on capital for pension payments. The resulting reduction in the amounts formerly given by the Commissioners to dioceses has had to be made up by increased giving from church members, including in respect of pension entitlements arising from service after 1997. At the same time, since 2000, tax changes (the Gift Aid scheme is estimated currently to have helped make covenant giving worth over £200 million) have benefited the Church of England as it has all other charities.

What follows will summarize the range of funding arrangements in some broadly comparable European countries, the historic subventions of the state in England and the current sources of state – concentrating on central government – funding made available to the Church of England.

European funding arrangements

The situation shows great variety, arising from distinctive ecclesiastical histories. In ways which underline the belief that Britain is one of the most secularized European countries, EU practices in general show degrees of state facilitation/subvention far more extensive than in the United Kingdom. For example, even in a famously 'laicized' France the state maintains all church buildings antedating 1905, and the *Loi Debré* of 1969 subsidizes Roman Catholic and other faith schools provided they use no religious admission tests.

In Germany, although the constitution has been secular since 1919, the system of *Kirchensteuer* persists. Religious communities granted the status of a 'corporation under public law' are entitled to levy a church tax (the *Kirchensteuer*) on their members. The state collects this as a proportion of the income tax at rates of from 8 to 9 per cent and for doing so it charges a fee, currently from 3 to 4 per cent of the sum collected (Monsma and Soper 1997). The yield of the *Kirchensteuer* was put at DM16 billion in 2000, and in 2003 the Evangelical and Roman Catholic churches in Germany shared €8.6 billion (£6.8 billion).[1] While the *Kirchensteuer* has been declining since reunification, it still accounts for some 80 per cent of the churches' income (Robbers 2005b: 89). More citizens are opting out (*Kirchenaustritt*, a formal legal process of renunciation), on the one hand, while, on the other, an ageing population and high levels of unemployment have reduced the number of income-tax payers – and only income-tax payers are liable for the *Kirchensteuer*. The result is that only about 35 per cent of the population pays the tax (Barker 2004).

As well as what is raised through the *Kirchensteuer*, the state provides financial support for repairing and restoring some of the religious buildings that existed at the time of the expropriation of church lands in 1803. The *Länder* governments also subsidize certain religious schools and hospitals and, in addition to the church tax, the majority of *Länder* operate a local system of 'church money' (*Kirchgeld*): a low, flat-rate contribution unrelated to income that is devoted entirely to the benefit of the payer's local church community. Because of the decline of the *Kirchensteuer*, the *Kirchgeld* has assumed a growing significance (Barker 2004).

As explained in more detail in Chapter 9, church tax systems persist also in Scandinavia where constitutions guarantee state support for state-recognized churches, and frequently facilitate collection of church-directed funds from worshippers even for other religious groups. In Denmark, the most Erastian establishment system in Europe, support is arranged through a church tax exclusive to the established church and payable only by church members. It provides about three-quarters of the church's income. In addition the government makes grants directly to the church amounting in 2002 to some 12 per cent of its income (Danish Ministry of Ecclesiastical Affairs 2002). In Finland, both established churches (Lutheran and Orthodox) are beneficiaries of church tax collected from their members by the state on reimbursement of the costs of collection. Furthermore, Finnish parishes receive just under a 2 per cent share of corporate tax. In Sweden, despite disestablishment of the Lutheran Church in 2000, the proceeds of church tax collected by the government from their members are available to all registered faith groups. At the same time, in Norway, since 1969 all faith communities have been directly funded partly by the state and partly by municipalities without a hypothecated church tax system. In another variation, Iceland allows no opt-outs from church tax but steers funds to the religious organizations designated by taxpayers, the money of non-believers going to the university. Clergy are paid directly by the government.

While Italy and Spain are in many ways distinct from Northern Europe in the state/church systems (Garcia Oliva 2008), funding systems show some similarities. In Italy, although there is no church tax as such, registered religious organization may request the state to channel to them through the tax system the voluntary contributions of their members. In Spain there are both direct state payments (£18 million in 2003) and voluntary payments of upto 0.5 per cent through the income tax system, which yielded some £90 million in 2003.

As these illustrations show, collection and disbursement by the state of hypothecated revenues has been common in Western Europe and persists. What follows will demonstrate that the history of these matters in England has followed different paths. It seems likely that they have done so because of the considerable degree of continuity between forms of church taxation settled long before the English Reformation occurred in the 1530s and when that Reformation represented initially at least more of a breach with Rome than with domestic, immemorial practices.

The tithe in England originated in Saxon times and was collected under fundamentally local arrangements without the direct intervention of the state though with its support through the civil courts. In many other parts of Europe, the relatively later character of modern state formation and, in some cases, the greater violence of the Reformation experience (including, in France, a later major political and social revolution) meant that the state assumed a larger role than in England. In some European cases, state collection remains open to a privileged few faith organizations, though there appears to have been a tendency to increase access. The degree of direct state subvention varies. It will be interesting to see whether current systems can remain viable in the longer term and, if not, what systems of support will replace them. It is difficult to avoid concluding that the tendency will be to throw more of the responsibility for funding onto the active worshippers, an observable trend in England though its incidence is mitigated by the substantial inheritances from the past available not only to the Church Commissioners but also at diocesan level, and by a limited though vital degree of state support (not wholly confined to the Church of England) for the repair of church buildings.

Historic subventions in England

In the medieval period – when the distinction between the personal rule of the sovereign and the impersonal concept of what is now understood by the 'state' was unknown – the Crown conferred many gifts on the Church *in* England in the days before it became regarded as the Church *of* England. The Chapels Royal, other Royal Peculiars and many cathedral and collegiate buildings continue to testify to this munificence. In contrast, the Reformation both nationalized and alienated much church property. The Crown diverted to itself the taxation revenues formerly received by the pope, and a significant amount of tithe (the local taxation directed to the support of incumbents) fell into lay ownership.

In a measure designed to reduce clerical poverty, in 1704 Queen Anne surrendered the former Papal revenues taken over by the Tudors – the first-fruits and tenths – to the Church of England. These were originally taxes on ecclesiastical dignities and benefices, the first-fruits being the sum paid on entry into possession of any of them and the tenths the smaller recurring charge thereafter (Best 1964: 21). The resulting funding charity – Queen Anne's Bounty – was devoted to raising clerical incomes. Although the state continued to collect the revenues on the Bounty's behalf, they constituted a peculiar kind of gift in the sense that in practice they merely returned to the Church of England its own resources, though in a way which devoted them to particular purposes.

Other subventions were of a different character. In early modern times, there were two church-building initiatives. The first was the early eighteenth century Commission for Building Fifty New Churches which spent nearly £250,000 secured from that part of the coals duty formerly used for the rebuilding of St Paul's and the maintenance of Westminster Abbey. Restrictive conditions and problems, which included negotiating the rights of existing incumbents, meant that only 12 churches were built though 5 were subsidized and 2 others acquired (Port 1986). In the nineteenth century, the two principal Church Building Acts of 1818 and 1825 steered £1.5 million through a Church Building Commission into a process where a significant matching effort from within the Church of England saw a total of 612 churches built by the time the Building Commission was amalgamated with the Ecclesiastical Commissioners in 1856 (Port 1961). These sums were augmented by 'drawback' (exclusive to the Church of England) on building materials, that is, tax refunds similar to current Value Added Tax refunds and estimated to be worth £175,000 over the period (Port 1961: 125). In addition, from 1809, the government made grants of £100,000 a year to the Bounty upto a total of £1,100,000.

All of these were, of course, significant sums. Equally significant was that there were no further parliamentary grants after 1828. Although Parliament continued to legislate for the Church of England, it took no further steps to fund it. The creation of the Ecclesiastical Commissioners in 1835–36 was an occasion for enabling *existing* funding to be managed more equally and efficiently rather than an occasion for additional parliamentary largesse. Peel, the prime mover in 1835, was clear in his ministry of 1841–45 that there could be no question of fresh public funding even when church extension was thought to be an important response to the serious social ills of the day (Gash 1972: 381–4). The only significant government legislation was the Populous Parishes Act 1843 that allowed the Ecclesiastical Commissioners to anticipate upto £600,000 of Queen Anne's Bounty revenue for church-building purposes and for clerical stipends before new churches were completed. In this case no public funds were involved:

> Peel's caution did not result from personal coolness towards the cause of church extension; he personally subscribed £4,000 for church building...Rather, the feebleness of the Act reflected his Government's conviction that there was no longer any consensus for increased State financial support for the established Church. (Brown, S. J. 2001: 341)

In contrast, the Church of England National Society and the largely Nonconformist British and Foreign Society schools continued to benefit from increasing state funding under arrangements initiated in 1833.

At the same time, and to put contemporary funding practices in perspective, it has to be borne in mind that parliamentary grants continued to be made to *other* churches. The *Regium Donum*, payments in support of ministerial salaries begun in 1690, conferred something akin to concurrent establishment on Presbyterian churches, especially in Northern Ireland. It was discontinued only following disestablishment of the Church in Ireland in 1869. Not only were there church-building grants to the Church of Scotland in 1825, but money for the augmentation of stipends from 1812 to 1839 amounted to nearly £370,000. The Church of Ireland received almost as much as the Church of England by way of grants up to 1840 (Established Church Return 1840). Grants were also made for the rebuilding or repair of Roman Catholic chapels destroyed in the 1798 rebellion. From 1795 to 1840, Maynooth, the Roman Catholic seminary, received nearly £400,000 – originally under an Act of the Irish Parliament. The total paid to non-Church of Ireland churches in Ireland from 1690 to 1840 was nearly £1 million (Protestant Dissenting Ministers Return 1840).

In addition, Parliament arranged for the financing of the Church of England abroad. Two Acts in the reign of George IV prescribed both the salaries for Church of England clergy in the West Indies and that, although the payments should issue from the Consolidated Fund in London, the money should come from the colonial revenues (6 Geo IV c 88 and 7 Geo IV c 4). In 1850–51, £31,000 was being paid to support the ecclesiastical establishment in the West Indies, and for clergy in America, New Zealand, Australia, the Gambia, Falkland Islands and

Hong Kong (Religious Institutions Return 1852). Support for Church of England clergy and buildings in India was guaranteed on the Indian revenues, a situation confirmed in the Government of India Act 1915 but repealed in the Government of India Act 1936. In Canadian and Australian territories, proportions of Crown land values had been set aside early on for the purpose of supporting the clergy. In Canada, since 1791 one-seventh of all Crown land sales had been reserved for the support of Protestant clergy, latterly in ratios of two-thirds for the Church of England and one-third for Church of Scotland clergy. Preserving existing entitlements, the system was abolished from 1853 by means of the Canadian Clergy Reserves Act whose scheme of commutation influenced that later adopted for Irish disestablishment (Chadwick 1972 II: 431). In Australia the new responsible legislatures moved to do the same – in Queensland at the first opportunity in 1860 though forms of concurrent endowment (which gave the Anglicans £20,000 a year) survived in Western Australia until 1895 (Selborne 1916: Appx IV 94–191).

Finally, although the state did not supply the funds, it stood behind (that is, collection was enforceable at law) two forms of taxation that benefited the Church of England alone and which were levied on the whole population irrespective of their religious beliefs. Both these forms of funding became increasingly controversial in England and Wales during the nineteenth century and, ultimately, unsustainable. The main one was the tithe. This was originally a tax in kind on the product of the land to support incumbents, made payable first in cash from 1836 and then as a rentcharge from 1891, being finally phased out from 1936. The church tax was raised from all parishioners irrespective of religious denomination for the maintenance of church fabric and worship. After a lengthy campaign, its compulsory character was abolished in 1868 (Ellens 1994). In Ireland the fact that the tithe became for many practical purposes unenforceable was a major consideration leading to disestablishment in 1869 with the concomitant abolition of tithe throughout Ireland.

Current sources of state funding

The legal structure of the Church of England is relevant:

> The Church of England is not a corporation as such, though institutions within it may enjoy the status of corporations sole or aggregate.
> (Doe 1996: 8)

As the present Archbishop of Canterbury has put it: 'I can't speak for the Church of England as a whole (no-one can)' (Williams 2004).

It follows that there is no single conduit for the inward flow of central or local government funds, and identifying their character and extent is not entirely straightforward. The effect of Gift Aid, for example, at different levels of church organization would be very difficult to disentangle. In contrast, with the exception only of assistance to the Church of England's Churches Conservation Trust (the body that cares for redundant church buildings remitted to its care), there is no question but that modern government policy where it does benefit the Church of England does so on criteria equally applicable to all religious organizations.

Church buildings

Apart from Gift Aid and education, most of the state funding available is directed towards buildings. Of the 18,000 listed places of worship, 13,000 are Church of England churches. Put another way, of the total of 16,200 Church of England buildings, over half (approximately 8,400) are listed buildings graded I or II*, amounting to 45 per cent and 20 per cent respectively of all the listed buildings in those categories. This built inheritance constitutes a considerable financial burden for the Church and it has made no fewer than 29 recommendations about how the situation should be addressed (Church Heritage Forum 2004: 4–5). Whereas congregational giving has increased by 8 per cent a year in recent years, local churchgoers and their communities have been able to muster only 70 per cent of what is currently being spent on repairs.

A July 2006 report by the House of Commons Culture, Media and Sport Select Committee – *Protecting and Preserving Our Heritage* – devoted a whole chapter to places of worship and their funding (Culture, Media and Sport 2006). It recommended increasing the reduced and frozen English Heritage (EH) contribution but was not in favour of any general or complete resort to reliance on taxation. The Department of Culture, Media and Sport's (DCMS) response in October (Cm 6947) welcomed the latter recommendation but proposed no increase in funding.

There are five current funding streams (the first three competitive) that benefit Church of England buildings. The principal schemes are operated by English Heritage (EH) and the Heritage Lottery Fund (HLF) under the auspices of the DCMS. The sources are:

1. Places of Worship repair grants (operated jointly by EH and HLF since 1996)
   - For urgent repairs to listed buildings in regular use as public places of worship.

- Worth an average of over £20 million 2000/01–2003/04 (Church Heritage 2004: 11). Money available for offers for 2004/05 and 2005/06 was just under £25 million in each year, and the 2008 Corporate Plan earmarked £20 million for 2008–09. Grants over £100,000 made to identifiable Anglican churches amounted to just under £6 million in 2006–07.

2. Cathedral grants (EH only)
   - For repairs to Church of England and Roman Catholic cathedrals listed grade I or II* and/or are situated within a conservation area.
   - Total grants (including Roman Catholic cathedrals, though chiefly directed to Church of England cathedrals) £2.1 million 2003/04 (English Heritage 2007).
   - For each of the three years 2005/06 until 2007/08 EH proposed to offer £1 million for cathedrals. (It spent £0.9 million in 2006/07.)

3. Heritage grants (HLF only)
   - Grants (or loans) allocated between all applicants on a competitive basis and directed to maintaining or preserving buildings, assets and sites of outstanding heritage significance.
   - Outcome examples: of the 47 projects that qualified in the category for grants of more than £5 million listed by HLF 2006/07 to a total of £510 million, 2 were Church of England projects in line for grants totalling £19 million, or just under 4 per cent of the total. Between them the 2 projects had to raise a further £23 million to cover the total cost (HLF *Annual Report* 2007).
   - Total awarded by Heritage Lottery Fund for projects of all kinds since their establishment in 1994 was £3 billion. They estimate that in the UK as a whole between 1994 and July 2004 they have given a total of nearly £300 million to churches, chapels and cathedrals of all denominations over that time. This includes grants for new facilities, activity and community projects as well as repairs (HLF 2005).

4. Churches Conservation Trust
   - DCMS grant currently pegged at £3.1 million a year. In 2006–07 the Trust added £2.5 million from other sources including £1.29 from the Church Commissioners (Churches Conservation Trust 2007).

5. Refund of Value Added Tax on listed church building repairs
   - Available for reclaiming on cost of listed church repairs carried out since 1 April 2001.
   - Estimated to be worth £6 million a year.
   - As at 30 September 2005, £28 million had been paid out in total since the scheme began to churches in England, an estimated 90 per cent for Anglican churches.

Summarising the 2002 experience on the funding of repair costs (Cooper 2004), the sources were then estimated as follows:

Table 5.1   Major sources of repair funds in 2002

Source	£m
EH/HLF	21.0
Garfield Weston	3.5
Vat reclaimed	6.0
Landfill	2.0
Historic Churches Preservation Trust	1.5
County trusts	1.4
Local church fund raising and other smaller trusts	57.0
Total	**93.0**

On this analysis, EH, HLF and VAT refunds defrayed less than 30 per cent of repair costs. In other words, while the state's contribution is substantial, the larger part of the costs was defrayed from other sources.

Finally, it should be noted that, along with five other religious denominations in England and Wales, the Church of England benefits from the 'ecclesiastical exemption'. This is an arrangement which exempts church buildings from many listed building and conservation area controls. After consultation in 2004, DCMS agreed (DCMS 2005) that the 'exemption' should continue in its existing form for the time being. Access to exemption is in practice conditional on denominations possessing internal control systems comparable with those that would otherwise have applied. While it could be argued that the exemption constitutes an indirect financial benefit to denominations, an alternative view is that it constitutes merely a delegation which spares denominations no labour and subsidizes no expense. Moreover, it could be maintained that the arrangement confers an indirect financial benefit on the state, because the cost implications of replicating the expertise involved in advising on works to churches and cathedrals, much carried out on a voluntary basis by members of advisory committees and central church bodies, would run into millions of pounds.

Indirect funding

The main elements here include the armed forces, prisons, education and health service chaplaincies. It is arguable whether they should be regarded as an activity 'funded' by the state when it is the state which requests or gives room to the services the chaplaincies provide. (Similar considerations may be thought to arise in the case of Church of England schools but the history of their relationship with the state is very different and dealt with separately in Chapter 2.)

Before going on to discuss the services involved, this will be the place to mention the civil service costs arising from the work of the official in the Cabinet Office who now fulfils what remains of the appointment duties formerly undertaken by the PMAS, together with his small staff. While perhaps the real question is whether the costs should be incurred at all, they are at present an unavoidable concomitant of the current form of Church establishment. However, the decision reaffirmed in March 2008 (Government Papers Cm 7342) to remove the Prime Minister from active involvement in the appointment of senior and other Church of England clerics will presumably lead to some scaling down of the role and the costs.

Chaplaincies

In addition to arranging the availability of its ministry through its parochial organization, the Church of England extends that ministry to a range of public and private organizations by the appointment of chaplains. It is not, of course, the only religious denomination that provides such services. Indeed, although the Church of England remains the largest supplier, one of the consequences of increased multiculturalism in the UK is the extent to which not only are other Christian denominations represented through chaplaincies but now also faiths other than Christianity.

Concentrating on public organizations, Table 5.2 summarizes the extent of the Church of England's chaplaincy effort from the latest figures available.

In what follows, estimates will be made of current running-cost expenditure where it is borne by sources other than the Church of

Table 5.2 Church of England chaplaincies 2006

Chaplaincy	Men	Women	Total
Royal Navy	36	0	36
Army	88	1	89
RAF	42	2	44
Prisons	78	38	116
Hospitals/healthcare	194	111	305
Schools	140	16	156
Higher and Further Education	86	23	109
Total	664	191	855

Source: adapted from Church of England Statistics 'Chaplaincy and other ministries 2006' at <www.cofe.anglican.org>, accessed 2 July 2008.

England itself. The baseline will be 2005 costs and therefore the estimates extend to 2005 prices only. Because, with the partial exception of Ministry of Defence data, essential pricing and costs information is not publicly available, some very approximate calculations are involved. Accordingly, the estimates should be treated as representing illustrative orders of magnitude only, a starting point for the more detailed calculations that cannot yet be made. Among the deficiencies of such estimates is that, since they concentrate on running costs, they fail to take account of the costs incurred by the Church of England in preparing individuals to assume chaplaincy roles. Overall, the Church of England estimates that chaplains in public service of one kind or another amount to 5 per cent of licensed ministries as a whole, and 7 per cent of all stipendiary clergy (Church of England 2006).

Armed services

Chaplains are provided as commissioned officers under Queen's Regulations subject to the approval in each case of the appropriate denominational authority. For the Church of England this entails the Archbishop of Canterbury's licence.

In May 2005, the total number of full-time Church of England chaplains in the armed forces was 177, or 58 per cent of the total of 294. (Of the rest, Roman Catholic chaplains constituted 16 per cent, Church of Scotland 12 per cent, Methodists 8 per cent, and the remaining groups 6 per cent.)

Because of the way in which costs are allocated within the defence budget, it is not possible to give an exact figure for total expenditure on Church of England chaplaincy services. Based on capitation rates for the financial year 2004/05 (which include employers' national insurance contributions, education allowances and support etc. costs as well as pay), a reasonable estimate for the current cost of the chaplaincy services would be in the region of the following:

Table 5.3 Estimated Church of England chaplaincy capitation costs 2005

Service	Costs £000s May 2005
RN	4,000
RAF	5,000
Army	9,000
Total	**18,000**

Source: Ministry of Defence

Adding in a conservative estimate of the Church of England share of the additional costs of clerical and other support to the chaplaincies throughout the three services would increase the total to £18.5 million.

Prison Service (England and Wales)

By law (s. 7 of the Prisons Act 1952) every one of the 139 prison establishments in England and Wales must have a chaplain who has to be a clergyman of the Church of England – a requirement which in respect of the establishments in Wales is stipulated (s. 53[3]) to include a clergyman of the Church in Wales.

The prisons chaplaincy is not confined to Church of England clergy or, indeed, Christian denominations. Under the general superintendence of the Prisons Chaplain General, a Church of England priest, the chaplaincy nowadays includes representatives of, for example, the Muslim and Buddhist faiths. This greater diversity reflects significant changes in the character of the prison population where the proportions of the population professing any religious faith were in 2006 as shown in Table 5.4:

Table 5.4 Religions of sentenced prisoners England and Wales September 2006

Religion	%
Anglican	31.0
Free Church	1.6
Roman Catholic	18.0
Other Christian	3.0
Buddhist	2.0
Hindu	0.4
Jewish	0.3
Muslim	10.0
Sikh	0.7
Other	1.0
No religion	32.0
Total	**100.0**

Source: Home Office

There was in 2005–06 a total of 315 chaplains, 184 full time and 131 part time. Of the full time 147 were Church of England. Because of the manner in which expenditure is delegated to individual establishments, cost data are not readily available and, on grounds of disproportionate cost, the government has refused to provide it (HC 26 October 2006, col. 2139). However, on the analogy of Defence costings, it would not be unreasonable to estimate that the annual level of public expenditure in respect of Church of England chaplains ran at about £11 million.[2]

Hospital chaplains

Authorized but not required under the NHS Acts, there are estimated to be something over 400 full-time chaplains of whom slightly more than 300 are Church of England clergy. There were also estimated to be 3,000 part-time chaplains half of whom were from the Church of England (Yearbook 2004). That Church has operated a Hospital Chaplaincies Council, a council of the General Synod, since 1951, which functions at the interface of the Church of England, the Department of Health and the NHS Executive. In addition, the Church of England participates in a Churches' Committee for Hospital Chaplaincies which co-ordinates the relations of all Christian denominations with the Department and the NHS.

Because budgets are delegated to NHS Trust level, it has not been practicable to obtain overall figures constructed on a common basis. Assuming an equivalence with Prison Service chaplains would suggest an annual cost at 2005 prices of over £26 million for full-time chaplains. However, granted that hospital chaplains cost less because there is no housing allowance and probably less in the way of support costs, a more conservative estimate confined to full-time chaplains suggests public expenditure costs for 2005–06 in a range of from £9 million to £10.5 million.[3] There is no statutory requirement that the Health Service should provide chaplains and cost-cutting imperatives have imperilled those services in some cases.[4]

Chaplaincies in Higher Education

There are on one estimate 174 Church of England chaplains in universities, 35 in colleges of further education and 29 in colleges of further education (*Crockfords Clerical Directory* 2004). There is a National Adviser for Higher Education Chaplaincies at Church House generally supporting these chaplaincies.

Estimating costs on the basis of the number of Higher and Further Education chaplains (109) recorded in the Church of England's statistics for 2006 (Church of England 2006) and on the same conservative estimating principles for hospital chaplains, the annual public expenditure costs would fall into the range of from £1 million to £2 million.

Other chaplaincies

These include numbers working in the police service, at airports and in hospices, most of whom work part time, such as the Speaker's Chaplain in the House of Commons who is also Rector of St Margaret's, from their parishes.

Conclusions

There are, of course, those for whom no degree of state subvention to the Church of England will ever be welcome. For them, the fact that the United Kingdom is markedly less financially supportive of religion – let alone church establishment – in comparison with many of its European neighbours is no consolation. At the same time, it would be difficult to maintain in practice that the current, limited flows of public money are excessive. The Churches, after all, manage their running costs from their own resources, and it is not unreasonable to expect the state to pay, for example, for such chaplaincy services as it requests.

However, what looms ahead is whether the present limited arrangements for helping to maintain the listed part of the built inheritance, especially in England, will remain sufficient. The same ageing membership demography that is attenuating the Church of Scotland's finances and causing it to rethink its national mission (see Chapter 6 below) is likely in the longer run to bear down even on the larger resources of the Church of England. How the state should offer support without removing incentives from recipients to continue to raise funds will be a testing policy problem for governments. Moreover, legitimising such aid will have to negotiate a public space characterized by an increasingly pluralized condition of religious belief and a condition of apparently growing unbelief. In the end, the best appeal may be to tradition: even if no longer entirely a Christian country and provided the right terms can be identified, the Christian inheritance should nonetheless be honoured.

6
Establishment in Scotland

The Church of Scotland has from its inception presented an alternative model of church/state relations to that of the Church of England. There, close at home, appeared to be another national church recognized in one of the few parts – the Act of Union – of the UK's constitution that is written down. The result has been that the position of the Church of Scotland has invariably attracted the closest attention of those contemplating the revision of the Church of England's relationship with the state. All four of the twentieth-century Church of England Church and State inquiries considered the Scottish model. More recently, Iain McLean has argued that the Church of England's position should be put on the same footing as the Church of Scotland (McLean and Linsley 2004).

This chapter will attempt to describe the Church of Scotland's status, how it came about, and its relevance to establishment in England. The next chapter will follow up the extent to which the courts appear to be redefining the Church's status.

Background

The pre-Reformation Church in Scotland had no metropolitan until the designation of the Bishop of St Andrews in 1472. In the absence until then of a metropolitan capable of summoning the provincial councils recommended by the Lateran Council of 1215, from 1225 the Church had been enjoined by the pope to hold its own councils. These appear to have occurred irregularly, the membership constituted simply by episcopal summons, and not to have developed any representative form as in the English Convocations. The appointment of the Bishop of Glasgow as a second metropolitan later in the fifteenth century led to metropolitical rivalry, and no council was summoned from then until 1549 (Dowden

1910: 223–41). Authorities differ on whether there was ever a lay presence at the councils. Dowden thought not but the Selborne Committee in 1916 thought there was a lay association and that this was a precedent for the later General Assembly of the reformed church.

The Reformation occurred in Scotland a little later in the sixteenth century than in England and on different lines. While the English Reformation can be described as initially an act of state which sought politically to substitute monarchical for papal governance over an existing church, the changes in Scotland had more popular support and followed Presbyterian lines of Church government to which the state was not finally reconciled until 1690. Indeed, the Stuart kings attempted to enforce episcopacy, and it was not until after their departure in 1688 that the Scottish legislation of 1560 and 1592 establishing Presbyterianism was reaffirmed.

Then as now the Church of Scotland possessed the General Assembly as its supreme decision-making body. Meeting annually, the Assembly is composed of ministers, deacons and elders of the Church, presided over by a Moderator, elected each year. The Assembly has mixed functions: it is a legislature, a court and an executive. (Historically, one of the functions of the General Assembly was to act as the final court of appeal in discipline cases, but since 1988 such appeals have been heard by a Judicial Commission.) The ordinances of the Church are known as Acts of Assembly. Under the Assembly's Barrier Act of 1697, 'overtures' (that is, proposals for Acts) 'which are to be binding Rules and Constitutions to the Church' are referred for a process of approval and ratification to presbyteries. They may be subsequently adopted as Acts of Assembly only when they have received majority approval.

Position of the Crown

Under Article XXV.IV of the Act of Union 1707, and within a formula designed to entrench cited Scottish Acts in respect of Presbyterian Church government, all new sovereigns are bound on accession to swear to uphold the Church of Scotland:

> ... after the Decease of the Present Majesty ... the Sovereign succeeding to her in the Royal Government of the Kingdom of Great Britain shall in all time coming at His or Her Accession to the Crown swear and subscribe that they shall inviolably maintain and preserve the foresaid Settlement of the True Protestant Religion with the Government Worship Discipline Rights and Privileges of this Church as above

established by the Laws of this Kingdom in Prosecution of the Claim of Right.

This oath is customarily sworn at the Accession Privy Council, that is, the first official engagement of the new sovereign immediately after succeeding. It is the only oath required of the sovereign by the Act of Union.

By convention, the sovereign does not normally attend the General Assembly although the right to do so is preserved in a Scottish Act and the present Queen has attended in 1960, 1977 and 2002. Normally, a representative of the sovereign – the Lord High Commissioner (an honorific role given each year normally to a prominent Scottish figure) – attends the annual meeting of the General Assembly but, sitting – like the sovereign – in the balcony as an observer only, in no way participates in its business proceedings. In 2000, the role was undertaken by Prince Charles. In Scotland, it has been argued, the Church and the state are *separate* and *distinct*: in England, even though Parliament has delegated the initiative in legislative functions since 1919 to what is now the General Synod, the Church of England is, save presently for matters of worship and doctrine, *subordinate* to the state.

Secessions and reunions

While other doctrinal and worship matters have occasionally given rise to acute controversy within the Church of Scotland, questions of governance have been the most dramatic and direct cause of secessions of various kinds since the early eighteenth century.[1] The foremost issue has been the extent to which the Church is free to govern its own affairs. In Scotland the theology of the 'two kingdoms' has always possessed particular importance. That is, the state and the Church were conceived as inhabiting simultaneous but separate spheres. Accordingly, it has followed that any intrusion by the state into what have been seen as the Church's affairs have been highly sensitive matters.

One such intrusion was the restoration of lay patronage in an Act of 1712. This was a measure designed to wean landowners from Jacobitism. It was arguably in breach of the Act of Union which included measures to guarantee the then-condition of the Church of Scotland, and differences over governance led to secessions upto and including the 'Disruption' of 1843. The last was precipitated by judicial decisions which challenged the autonomy of the General Assembly in ways hostile to the then-dominant evangelical party. The first decision in 1838

(*Auchterarder*) struck down an Act of Assembly of 1834 (the Veto Act) which had been aimed at mitigating patronage by the addition of elements of popular choice. The second decision (*Stewarton*) in early 1843, by invalidating the Assembly's Chapel Act, effectively eliminated the evangelicals' majority and led to almost a third of the General Assembly leaving to establish their own Free Church. But they did so not because they wished to break the link between Church and state but because they sought a renewed national church in which 'The Crown Rights of the Redeemer' would be fully respected – and which would remain established in accordance with the Treaty of Union. As Thomas Chalmers, the leader of the Disruption, proclaimed in his Moderational address to the first General Assembly of the new church:

> We hold that every part and every function of a commonwealth should be leavened with Christianity, and that every functionary, from the highest to the lowest, should, in their respective spheres, do all that in them lies to countenance and uphold it. That is to say, though we quit a vitiated establishment, we go out on the Establishment principle; we quit a vitiated establishment, but would rejoice in returning to a pure one. To express it otherwise: we are the advocates for a national recognition and national support of religion – *and we are not Voluntaries*. (Free Church of Scotland 1844: 12, emphasis added)

This emphatic act was a defining moment in nineteenth-century Scottish history. Following an enormous effort to raise funds and build new churches, the heirs to the Disruption created a substantial presence outside the Church of Scotland while still sharing adherence to the Westminster Confession.

The Church of Scotland Act 1921

Towards the end of the nineteenth century projects of reunion of various kinds began to be discussed. Characteristic of such events was that there were usually minorities in the uniting forces which stood out obdurately against the proposed settlements. In the case of the union in 1900 between the Free Church of 1843 and the United Presbyterian Church (itself a union of voluntarist secessions of 1733 and 1761), the minority in the Free Church litigated. It claimed that it should be regarded as the continuing, legitimate entity entitled to the whole of the Free Church's property. The House of Lords found (*Overtoun*) for the minority in 1904 on two grounds: that the Free Church was unable to alter the terms of the trust on which it was founded; and that the United Presbyterians (with whom the majority had united) rejected the 'Establishment Principle' on which Chalmers and his colleagues had laid such emphasis. This left the minority in possession of a number of churches, manses and associated property (not all of which had been in issue in, or therefore decided by, the litigation) beyond its capacity to cope, and left the majority contemplating a situation in which it had no physical assets whatsoever. These issues were remitted, effectively for arbitration, to a Royal Commission. Reporting nine months after the Lords' judgement, the Commission opined:

> We are forced to the conclusion that the Free Church, from the paucity of its numbers and the poverty of its resources, is incapable of carrying out the religious work of the Church which it represents, and therefore of putting to their proper purpose the enormous endowments with which it claims to be entrusted. But, on the other hand, it would be unjust that these endowments, or the greater part of them, should be handed over absolutely and without condition to the United Free Church. (Scottish Royal Commission on Churches 1905: 20)

The immediate result was the Churches (Scotland) Act of the same year which implemented the Commission's recommendations for a fair and workable distribution of the assets. Although not involved directly in the events, the Church of Scotland was affected by them in the sense that the Lords decision turned on the view that the Free Church's form of trust did not contain any means of varying it. Opportunity was therefore taken of the legislation to have a clause (s. 5) inserted which put beyond doubt that the Church of Scotland was able to vary its own standing in a way that freed it from the kind of threat, for example in future possible unions, that the litigants had had to confront. Should it wish to vary the basis upon which subscription to the Confession of Faith was required, then the Act laid down that the Church of Scotland could do so by means of an Act of General Assembly following the Barrier Act procedure.

The dramatic character of these events, and the way in which they demonstrated intervention by the state, naturally coloured the character of discussions with a view to union between the Church of Scotland and the United Free Church:

> The Free Church case of 1904 demonstrated, with the utmost clarity, that a Church claiming independence from the State was as exposed to risks in the exercise of its spiritual liberty, as the Church of Scotland had been found to be in the pre-disruption judgements. (Sjölinder 1962: 107)

From the point of view of the United Free Church, union with the Church of Scotland was impossible if it was offered only on a basis which imperilled the principle – avoidance of state control – that had lain at the root of previous secession. In popular language, union could not take place with an 'established' church. Discussions between the two churches from 1909 tried to find a satisfactory solution. (The most up-to-date account of a complicated process may be found in Murray, D. S. 2000). The outcome was the formula of the 'Articles Declaratory of the Constitution of the Church of Scotland in Matters Spiritual' contained as a schedule to the Church of Scotland Act 1921 – 'in effect a treaty between Church and State' (Bogdanor 1995: 237). The Act asserted that the Articles were

... lawful articles, and the constitution of the Church of Scotland in matters spiritual is as therein set forth, and no limitation of the liberty, rights and powers in matters spiritual therein set forth shall be derived from any statute or law affecting the Church of Scotland in matters spiritual at present in force, it being hereby declared that in all questions of construction the Declaratory Articles shall prevail, and that all such statutes and laws shall be construed in conformity therewith and in subordination thereto, and all such statutes and laws in so far as they are inconsistent with the Declaratory Articles are hereby repealed and declared to be of no effect.

The nine Articles themselves (appended to this chapter) state among other things that the Church of Scotland had

the right and power subject to no civil authority to legislate, and to adjudicate finally, in all matters of doctrine, worship, government, and discipline in the Church, including the right to determine all questions concerning membership and office in the Church, the constitution and membership of its Courts, and the mode of election of its office-bearers, and to define the boundaries of the spheres of labour of its ministers and other office-bearers.

As may be seen, in this and other ways the independence of the Church in all matters spiritual is asserted in ringing language. As a modern gloss has put it:

To achieve ... reunion a model had to be found that retained the benefits of the state connection while firmly rejecting the kind of civil control that is a constant worry in any situation of state support of religion. The Church achieved this delicate balance by abandoning the language of establishment and replacing it with the concept of a church that was national and free. (MacLean 2002: 127)

The Bill giving force to the agreement to reunite was a government Bill introduced on Second Reading by the Scottish Secretary, Munro. He made it clear that the Bill was a paving Bill to enable – after a later Bill to deal with property and endowments – union to take place. Strong emotions were expressed. Munro said: 'The nation is weary to death of the wastefulness of the present system, and is deeply conscious of the shame and the peril of ecclesiastical strife' (HC 22 June 1921, col. 1406). The later Church of Scotland (Property and Endowments) Act 1925 then enabled the reunion between the Church of Scotland and the United Free Church eventually to take place in 1929.

Implications for Church and state in England

The special character of the position of the Church of Scotland was a matter of remark for the Church of England even before the 1921 Act. The Selborne Committee on Church and State, which reported in 1916, devoted a whole appendix (Appendix V) to the Church of Scotland and quoted the then-draft *Articles Declaratory* at some length, opining, 'The settlement of the sixteenth century was made not by a government, but by a people: and the constitution after the Revolution was only ratified and confirmed by the State' (Selborne 1916: 35). The committee defended its recommendations for retaining a state veto in what became the Enabling Act of 1919 partly because it distinguished the position of the Church of England from that of the Church of Scotland: 'The Church of England does not represent the mind of the English people as fully as the established Church of Scotland represents the mind of Scotland' (Selborne 1916: 39).

Set up in the wake of Parliament's refusal to accept the Prayer Book Measures in the late 1920s, the Cecil Commission also looked closely at what it called 'The Scottish Solution' after the reunion of 1929. The commission did not, however, recommend following the Scottish model:

We do not think that The Scottish settlement could be an exact model for what should be done in England. The history and conditions of the two countries are not the same. In Scotland there was little or no difference on doctrine or ritual. (Cecil 1935: 5)

The Moberly Commission came to similar conclusions in 1952. Though claiming that the Scottish example showed that establishment was compatible with spiritual freedom, it rejected the model for the Church of England. Its arguments were similar to those used in 1935, namely, the greater co-extensive character of the Church of Scotland and nation, the lack of division over doctrine and worship, the less clear line between clergy and laity, and the longstanding character and prestige of the General Assembly to which the then Church Assembly could not lay claim (Moberly 1952: 27–8). After somewhat briefer consideration than its predecessors, the Chadwick Commission 18 years later came to the same conclusion on the basis that the two churches had very different histories.

The Church of Scotland and 'establishment'

In England there has been a tendency to enlist the Scottish model in aid of whatever argument over establishment is being promoted. Thus, it has for some been a subject of envy and for others – because comparison demonstrates English exceptionalism – not a viable alternative despite apparently attractive features. Because it has been received in England as largely reinforcing pre-existing Scottish tendencies, the Church of Scotland Act 1921 has not by itself much influenced English perceptions, although those coming across it for the first time may be surprised by its content.

In Scotland, there are also different views about the extent to which the 1921 Act disestablished the Church of Scotland. Even during the Second Reading debate on the 1921 Bill, it was pointed out that there was some ambiguity in how the *Articles Declaratory* were seen:

> My friends of the Established Church are told this Bill is to establish the Church of Scotland more strongly than ever ... The people who hold the old United Presbyterian view, or the Free Church view ... are told that this Bill is really equivalent to disestablishing the Church of Scotland ... It is unfortunate that a Bill which is intended to promote union should depend for its support upon exhibitions of casuistry which would have been a credit to the Middle Ages. (HC 22 June 1921, A. Shaw, col. 1451)

As a Scottish lawyer argued over thirty years later

> By this remarkable statute the UK Parliament has admitted the legislative sovereignty which the General Assembly has always claimed

in the ecclesiastical sphere, and, by implication, it seems to have conceded that there is in at least one respect in which the UK Parliament is not sovereign. This power of ecclesiastical legislation is a very real mark of freedom, but not at all a mark of disestablishment. For what established church could ask for a greater measure of state association than to share with the civil authority the legislative power of the state? (Murray, R. K. 1958: 160–1)

At the root of these considerations is just what meaning should be attributed to 'establishment' in the Scottish case. In practice ever an elastic term, its meaning is often stretched to accommodate the rhetorical purpose and policy preferences of particular writers. One commentator has argued that the language of establishment should not be applied to the Scottish situation because it is impossible to do so without giving rise to misunderstanding. Accordingly, the Church of Scotland is neither established nor disestablished but 'a Church both national and free' (Sjölinder 1962: 374). A current member of the Church of Scotland takes the same view: 'The experience of establishment in Scotland is so different from that in England that it is confusing to have the same name applied to both' (MacLean 2002: 126).

Another commentator has reached a slightly different understanding by starting from a not-too-exacting definition of establishment. Whereas the Chadwick Commission had used a definition for the Church of England's established status as stemming from 'the laws which apply to the Church of England and not to others', Colin Munro's starting point was 'A church legally recognized as the official Church of the state or nation and having a special position in law' (Munro 1997: 640). From this standpoint, and asking whether the Church of Scotland could be regarded as an established church at all, he went on to argue that it was:

Generally, it is fair to say that the [1921] Act may be regarded as a *recognition* by Parliament of the Church's constitution, rather than as a *conferment* of a constitution. The underlying notion of co-ordinate jurisdiction of church and state, each supreme within its own sphere, was reinforced by the unusual feature that the Act (by its own terms) could be brought into effect only on condition that the General Assembly adopted the Declaratory Articles. (Munro 1997: 644)

Munro has pointed out that there remain a number of instances where the Church of Scotland is given special recognition. For example, there is the royal oath, a royal appointed High Commissioner, the ability of the Church's ministers to solemnize marriage, and effect (prior to the enactment of the Requirements of Writing [Scotland] Act 1995) the notarial execution of the wills of blind persons. There is also the fact that Church of Scotland as well as Church of England clergy were disqualified from sitting in Parliament under the House of Commons (Clergy Disqualification) Act 1801, now repealed. He concluded in agreement with a previous writer that the Church of Scotland was both established and free (Munro 1997: 645). As against these conclusions, however, has to be weighed the earlier contention of a Scottish witness to the Cecil Commission in 1931: 'The establishment in Scotland has been evacuated of nearly all its connotations' (Simpson 1931: 509).

More recently, it has been suggested that though the Church of Scotland rejects establishment in the narrower sense of a Church 'by law established',

> broader understandings of establishment are more relevant. The Church of Scotland sees itself as more than a sect or a collection of gathered congregations. It has a responsibility to address the whole life of the nation, and to minister to the structures of society . . . It tries to maintain its historic responsibility to be prophetic, to speak truth to power, to be concerned with what used to be called 'the Christian good of Scotland'. And the state, for its part, gives a special degree of recognition to the Church of Scotland, although the 1921 Act makes clear that this does not in any way 'prejudice the recognition of any other Church in Scotland as a Christian Church protected by law in the exercise of its spiritual functions'. (Forrester 1999: 86)

There are, of course, limits to the value of trying to decide where exactly the Church of Scotland should be located on any church/state continuum. Iconoclastically, Callum Brown argues that establishment is a myth (Brown, C. G. 2001). And much of the discussion has a whiff, as the MP observed in 1921, of medieval scholasticism. In the end, more to the immediate point is the need to bear in mind that the 1921 settlement in Scotland was designed for a particular contemporary purpose, and cannot be expected, however it was interpreted in 1921, to be absolutely proof against events and developments, for example EU law and rights approaches, since.[2] The relationship between any Church and the civil authorities is a dynamic process depending on the circumstances of the times and not to be pickled for ever in a single statute or in an 'immutable' formula. One Scottish observer has expressed the position as follows:

> The age of establishment is drawing to a close. Neither the UK nor Scotland can be described, except residually, as Protestant countries.

Since the Reformation, the Kirk has been presented as the authentic expression of national identity. This is no longer tenable and it is time to move forward to a church life that must inevitably be more voluntarist, congregational, countercultural in part, and engaged in new patterns of mission. (Fergusson 2004: 186)

It seems that this change is being reflected in modern judicial thinking. The classical view of the courts of the Church of Scotland has been that they are courts of the realm, exercising a jurisdiction separate from and parallel to those of the Court of Session and the High Court of Judiciary. In *Wight* v. *Presbytery of Dunkeld*, for example, the Court of Session agreed that, though the proceedings in the Presbytery complained of were irregular, contrary to the laws and practice of the Church, and altogether null, they should not be set aside.

However, in a more recent case, Lord President Rodger appeared to take a rather different view of the nature of the courts of the Church of Scotland. The appellant, an associate minister, had her employment terminated in circumstances where, contrary to the Sex Discrimination Act 1975, she claimed a male minister would not have been treated in the same way. In dismissing the appeal on other grounds, the Lord President described the position of the Church courts as follows:

[T]he General Assembly enacts laws which have many of the stylistic and other hallmarks of the kind of legislation which is enacted by Parliament. The procedures of the Church courts are replete with terminology which is familiar to practitioners of Scots law. The language does nothing indeed to conceal the hand which those trained in Scots law have had in guiding such proceedings down the centuries. None the less, despite their outward appearance, the laws of the Church operate only within the Church and her courts adjudicate only on matters spiritual. *In other words, the formality and indeed solemnity of all these transactions and proceedings does not disclose an intention to create relationships under the civil law*; rather, it reflects the serious way in which the Church regulates the matters falling within the spiritual sphere. (Percy 2001, emphasis added)

The course and significance of this case (decided by a majority in the House of Lords for Ms Percy when she appealed the Scottish judgement) is examined in greater depth in the next chapter. Reflecting subsequently on the case, Lord Rodger – in the context of his recent study of the Disruption of 1843 – has remarked that *Percy* marks a significant development in an area of the law which many people hoped had been settled once and for all when Parliament passed the Church of Scotland Act 1921. That Act was intended to put an end to a kind of religious dispute that had been the very stuff of Scottish history. (Rodger 2008: 94)

The general point to make in this part of the narrative is that perhaps no statutory measure, even one as 'strong' as the 1921 Act, can remain perpetually proof against reinterpretations that arise from changed social circumstances and developments in the law unforeseen and unforeseeable at the time. While the Act may, as Vernon Bogdanor has suggested (Bogdanor 1995: 237), be regarded as a treaty between Church and state, it was also a creature of its time – a state endorsed accommodation between two parties that made their union possible. In that sense the treaty was between the parties rather than between them and the state.

Finally, there is the point that the Church's own resources have an important bearing on the extent to which it can live up to its perceived historic position and claims. Whereas Article III of the *Articles Declaratory* speaks of the Church of Scotland's 'distinctive call and duty to bring the ordinances of religion to the people in every parish of Scotland through a territorial ministry', in May 2008 the General Assembly voted to look again at this obligation. Following a recommendation by a Special Commission on Structure and Change – 'We question whether any valuable principle is dependent on retaining the Third Article' (Church of Scotland 2008: 13.4) – a further Commission was set up to report in 2010 on Article III and its relation to parish staffing policy and the financing of the Church's work. Clearly, some sort of modification of or retreat from Article III is envisaged. From this aspect too, therefore, the understanding of the character of the Church of Scotland's 'establishment' seems likely to change.

Articles Declaratory of the Constitution of the Church of Scotland

I. The Church of Scotland is part of the Holy Catholic or Universal Church; worshipping one God, Almighty, all-wise, and all-loving, in the Trinity of the Father, the Son, and the Holy Ghost, the same in substance, equal in power and glory; adoring the Father, infinite in Majesty, of whom are all things; confessing our Lord Jesus Christ, the Eternal Son, made very man for our salvation; glorying in His Cross and Resurrection, and owning obedience to Him as the Head over all things to His Church; trusting in the promised renewal and guidance of the Holy Spirit; proclaiming the forgiveness of sins and acceptance with God through faith in Christ, and the gift of Eternal Life; and labouring for the advancement of the Kingdom of God throughout the world. The Church of Scotland adheres to the Scottish Reformation; receives the Word of God which is contained in the Scriptures of the Old and New Testaments as its supreme rule of faith and life; and avows the fundamental doctrines of the Catholic faith founded thereupon.

II. The principal subordinate standard of the Church of Scotland is the Westminster Confession of Faith approved by the General Assembly of 1647, containing the sum and substance of the Faith of the Reformed Church. Its government is Presbyterian, and is exercized through Kirk Sessions; Presbyteries, [Provincial Synods deleted by Act V, 1992], and General Assemblies. Its system and principles of worship, orders, and discipline are in accordance with 'The Directory for the Public Worship of God,' 'The Form of Presbyterial Church Government' and 'The Form of Process,' as these have been or may hereafter be interpreted or modified by Acts of the General Assembly or by consuetude.

III. This Church is in historical continuity with the Church of Scotland which was reformed in 1560, whose liberties were ratified in 1592, and for whose security provision was made in the Treaty of Union of 1707. The continuity and identity of the Church of Scotland are not prejudiced by the adoption of these Articles. As a national Church representative of the Christian Faith of the Scottish people it acknowledges its distinctive call and duty to bring the ordinances of religion to the people in every parish of Scotland through a territorial ministry.

IV. This Church as part of the Universal Church wherein the Lord Jesus Christ has appointed a government in the hands of Church office-bearers, receives from Him, its Divine King and Head, and from Him alone, the right and power subject to no civil authority to legislate, and to adjudicate finally, in all matters of doctrine, worship, government, and discipline in the Church, including the right to determine all questions concerning membership and office in the Church, the constitution and membership of its Courts, and the mode of election of its office-bearers, and to define the boundaries of the spheres of labour of its ministers and other office-bearers. Recognition by civil authority of the separate and independent government and jurisdiction of this Church in matters spiritual, in whatever manner such recognition be expressed, does not in any way affect the character of this government and jurisdiction as derived from the Divine Head of the Church alone or give to the civil authority any right of interference with the proceedings or judgments of the Church within the sphere of its spiritual government and jurisdiction.

V. This Church has the inherent right, free from interference by civil authority, but under the safeguards for deliberate action and legislation provided by the Church itself, to frame or adopt its subordinate standards, to declare the sense in which it understands its Confession of Faith, to modify the forms of expression therein, or to formulate other doctrinal statements, and to define the relation thereto of its office-bearers and members, but always in agreement with the Word of God and the fundamental doctrines of the Christian Faith contained in the said Confession, of which agreement the Church shall be sole judge, and with due regard to liberty of opinion in points which do not enter into the substance of the Faith.

VI. This Church acknowledges the divine appointment and authority of the civil magistrate within his own sphere, and maintains its historic testimony to the duty of the nation acting in its corporate capacity to render homage to God, to acknowledge the Lord Jesus Christ to be King over the nations, to obey His laws, to reverence His ordinances, to honour His Church, and to promote in all appropriate ways the Kingdom of God. The Church and the State owe mutual duties to each other, and acting within their respective spheres may signally promote each other's welfare. The Church and the State have the right to determine each for itself all questions concerning the extent and the continuance of their mutual relations in the discharge of these duties and the obligations arising therefrom.

VII. The Church of Scotland, believing it to be the will of Christ that His disciples should be all one in the Father and in Him, that the world may believe that the Father has sent Him, recognizes the obligation to seek and promote union with other Churches in which it finds the Word to be purely preached, the sacraments administered according to Christ's ordinance, and discipline rightly exercised; and it has the right to unite with any such Church without loss of its identity on terms which this Church finds to be consistent with these Articles.

VIII. The Church has the right to interpret these Articles, and, subject to the safeguards for deliberate action and legislation provided by the Church itself, to modify or add to them; but always consistently with the provisions of the first Article hereof, adherence to which, as interpreted by the Church, is essential to its continuity and corporate life. Any proposal for a modification of or addition to these Articles which may be approved of by the General Assembly shall, before it can be enacted by the Assembly, be transmitted by way of overture to Presbyteries in at least two immediately successive years. If the overture shall receive the approval, with or without suggested amendment, of two-thirds of the whole of the Presbyteries of the Church, the Assembly may revise the overture in the light of any suggestions by the Presbyteries, and may transmit the overture when so revised to Presbyteries for their consent. If the overture as transmitted in its final form shall receive the consent of not less than two-thirds of the whole of the Presbyteries of the Church, the General Assembly may, if it deems it expedient, modify or add to these Articles in terms of the said overture. But if the overture as transmitted in its final form shall not receive the requisite consent, the same or a similar proposal shall not be again transmitted for the consent of Presbyteries until an interval of five years after the failure to obtain the requisite consent has been reported to the General Assembly.

IX. Subject to the provisions of the foregoing Articles and the powers of amendment therein contained, the Constitution of the Church of Scotland in matters spiritual is hereby anew ratified and confirmed by the Church.

7

Recent Developments in Church/State Relations in Scotland

Marjory MacLean, Frank Cranmer and Scot Peterson[1]

Introduction

As already noted, whenever the Church of England contemplates its connection with the State, the question arises as to whether an interesting, adaptable model might exist just over the Tweed. However, the word 'Establishment' has a different meaning on each side of the border; indeed, its meaning in Scotland is in some ways quite the opposite of any of its definitions down south.

Luther and Calvin each espoused a model of relating to the civil magistrate that differs from the Church of England's pattern. Crudely put, the Lutheran model has more of a separation of powers, with Church and State working separately but (one hopes) in parallel; the secular laws of the civil magistrate pursue common ends with the Church's discipline, but by different means: see generally Cranz (1959). The classical Reformed model gives the civil magistrate a more directly Christian task, which includes the active protection and promotion of the Church and the direct pursuit of the Church's own goals: the Church is in some ways cradled and nurtured by a state charged with guaranteeing a space for the gospel (Höpfl 1982; Hunt 1965).

There are minuses and pluses in the Reformed model today. The obvious drawback is the fact that we rejoice to live in a pluralist and inclusive age, which means that the Reformed model must not give the Church any exclusive right or monopoly. But on the positive side, we live also in an age of rights *in persona*, 'human rights' as we call them; and perhaps the sheltering, cradling, enabling model of the state's protection of a religious body (or a philosophical body, or even an anti-religious one) could be extended indefinitely as a manner of fulfilling one strand of human rights.

Next, a warning: Presbyterianism is not a form of representative democracy, because it is not a system of assessing the will of the people – not even the *prayerful* will of the people. It is a system premised on the placing of spiritual governance in the hands of all the spiritual leaders – ministers, elders and deacons throughout the Church – whose responsibilities may sometimes lead them to do what they believe is right even when it runs counter to the earnest preferences of the majority of the members. One can begin to see the need for an independent spiritual jurisdiction when the Church's jurisprudence is so differently founded compared with secular law and government. One can also see how the temptation arises to seek review of ecclesiastical decisions in the civil courts when those decisions seem utterly wrong and unfair.[2] A theological and prayerful basis for a decision is the core of the Church's polity, but it does not always make the strongest legal defence.

Thirdly, Scottish Establishment ebbed and flowed and changed – with impressive moments and humiliating moments – throughout the period from the 1690s to the 1920s (MacLean 2004, especially Chapter 2). If you imagine the spiritual jurisdiction of the Church of Scotland as some kind of somewhat imprecisely defined 'blob' within the more general jurisdiction of national law, its history has been one that has swung between times when the Church strayed out of its confines – outside the blob – and tried to interfere in the government of the nation, and times when the civil magistrate reached into the area of authority of the Church itself. A vivid and violent example of the first might be the years immediately after the signing of the National Covenant in 1638 and before Cromwell's arrival in Scotland, when the Covenanters practically ruled the country through the Tables in Edinburgh (Stevenson 1974 and 1988): Scotland's own little Terror. An infamous example of the latter would be pre-Disruption cases like *Auchterarder* and *Stewarton* in the 1830s and 1840s, when patrons sought to impose their own choice of minister on unwilling congregations.[3]

Fourthly, the settlement by virtue of the Church of Scotland Act 1921 tried to anchor the relationship at its perfect point of balance. And that brings us to the current ideal, the definition that theoretically pertains.

Article IV of the *Articles Declaratory of the Constitution of the Church of Scotland in Matters Spiritual* (appended to the preceding chapter) declares in emphatic terms the Church's independence in all questions of doctrine, worship, government and discipline. In effect, the Article represents a theological statement of the church/state balance that many others envy. But the sting is in the end of Article VI:

> The Church and the State have the right to determine each for itself all questions concerning the extent and the continuance of their mutual relations in the discharge of these duties and the obligations arising therefrom.

The problem is self-evident: what happens when Church and state determine the same question about the extent of authority and arrive at different answers? Who wins? Deep down, the Church of Scotland has known the answer for 80 years: but it took until October 2005 and the *Percy* case for the blow to fall: *Percy [AP]* v. *Board of National Mission of the Church of Scotland* [2005] UKHL 73; [2006] 2 AC 28; [2006] 2 WLR 353; [2006] 4 All ER 1354 (subsequent references to *Percy* are in parentheses in the text).

The *Percy* case and its aftermath[4]

Helen Percy was ordained in the Church of Scotland in 1991. In June 1994 she was appointed associate minister of a parish in the Presbytery of Angus; her duties included conducting worship on Sundays and acting as part-time chaplain at HMP Noranside. In 1997 it was alleged that she had had an affair with a married elder in the parish; she was suspended and a committee of Presbytery found that there was a case to answer. Preparations began for a trial by libel (a former disciplinary procedure abolished in 2001) but it never took place; instead, at a mediation meeting arranged by the Church she was counselled to resign and demit status as a minister, which she did in December 1997. This step meant that, should she ever in future wish to seek a ministerial appointment, she would have to apply to the Ministries Council of the Church for permission to resume her status as a minister. She later regretted her resignation and demission and in February 1998 initiated proceedings in an employment tribunal, alleging unfair dismissal and unlawful sexual discrimination: in essence, that the Church had not taken similar action against male ministers known to have had extra-marital sexual relationships. The tribunal rejected her application for want of jurisdiction and an employment appeal tribunal dismissed her appeal insofar as it related to sex discrimination (which was all that she had appealed), on the grounds that the disciplining of ministers with regard to their manner of life was a spiritual matter governed by Article IV of the *Articles Declaratory* in the Schedule to the 1921 Act. Her appeal to the Inner House of the Court of Session failed (2001 SC 757) but, undaunted, she took her case to the House of Lords (*Percy [AP][Appellant]* v. *Church of Scotland Board of National Mission [Respondent] [Scotland]* [2005] UKHL 73) who, by a majority of four to one,[5] upheld her appeal and remitted her discrimination claim for determination by an employment tribunal under s. 63(1) of the Sex Discrimination Act 1975.

There were two questions before the Appellate Committee:

- whether Ms Percy's relationship with the Church still constituted 'employment' as defined in s. 82(1) of the Sex Discrimination Act 1975[6] and whether she was therefore protected by section 6 of that Act from unlawful discrimination in the form of a more severe discipline than the Church was accustomed to exercise in the case of a male minister in similar circumstances; and
- whether, if she *had* been discriminated against, her claim nevertheless constituted a 'matter spiritual' within the terms of s. 3 of the 1921 Act[7] and, as such, within the exclusive cognisance of the courts of the Church.

And on those questions there were – and remain – differing views.

The majority decision

Lord Nicholls of Birkenhead noted the line of authorities for the proposition that no contract of service exists between a minister of religion and his or her denomination[8] and pointed out that it is a statutory requirement that in order to prove unfair dismissal one has to be an employee. Moreover,

> an employee is an individual who has entered into or works under a contract of employment, that is, a 'contract of service': see now sections 94 and 230 of the Employment Rights Act 1996 (para. 13).

But that, asserted Lord Nicholls, was not the issue before the Appellate Committee: Ms Percy was claiming sex discrimination, not unfair dismissal. Moreover, he rejected the argument that one was *either* an employee *or* an office-holder. This was a false dichotomy: '[I]f "office" is given a broad meaning, holding an office and being an employee are not inconsistent' (para. 20). He noted that, for example, this approach had been adopted in *Barthorpe* v. *Exeter Diocesan Board of Finance* (1979

ICR 900), in which a stipendiary reader had sued successfully for unfair dismissal. Slynn J had rejected the argument that an office-holder could not be employed under a contract of service and added that

> [I]t may be difficult to establish who is the other contracting party, but we are not satisfied that clergy when working within the framework of the Church cannot be engaged under a contract. It may well be that the contract, if it exists, is for services rather than of service. (*Barthorpe* p. 904)

As to the question of contractual relations, Lord Nicholls conceded that there were certainly instances in Church affairs in which the parties could not be taken to have intended to create a contract (para. 23). But the offer of a post by the General Secretary of the Board of National Mission and its acceptance by Ms Percy seemed to be intended by both parties to create legally binding relations (para. 24), not least because, when Ms Percy attempted to withdraw her resignation, the General Secretary's response referred to 'your letter of resignation from employment by the Department of National Mission' (para. 32).

He then turned to the question of whether the terms of the 1921 Act ousted the jurisdiction of the employment tribunal. A sex discrimination claim could not be regarded as a 'matter spiritual' under Article IV of the *Articles Declaratory* because, by entering into a contract of employment, the parties had 'deliberately left the sphere of matters spiritual ... and ... put themselves within the jurisdiction of the civil courts' (para. 41, quoting Lord President Rodger in the First Division [2001 SC 757, 769, para. 24]). Therefore, because Ms Percy had a contract with the Board, the employment tribunal's jurisdiction was not excluded by the terms of Article IV.

For Lord Hope of Craighead the case was about sexual discrimination, pure and simple: 'it is a fundamental rule of sex discrimination law that it is not possible to contract out of it' (para. 106).[9] He distinguished between 'the contract issue' (whether or not Ms Percy was employed within the terms of the definition in s. 82[1] of the 1975 Act) and 'the jurisdiction issue' (whether or not her complaint was excluded from civil jurisdiction by the terms of Article IV). As to the contract issue, he concluded that there was indeed a contract between Ms Percy and the Board of National Mission and agreed with Lord Nicholls that for the purposes of the 1975 Act (paras 115 and 116) Ms Percy was 'employed'. As to the jurisdiction issue, the exclusion under section 19(1) of 'employment for purposes of an organized religion where the employment is limited to one sex so as to comply with the doctrines of the religion' could hardly apply to the Church of Scotland because there was no doctrinal issue involved: women had been admitted to the ministry since 1968 (para. 119). Unlawful discrimination was a civil matter rather than a spiritual one; and the Church of Scotland had failed to put in place an adequate mechanism of redress for those who felt that they had been discriminated against (para. 132).

Concurring, Baroness Hale of Richmond quoted with approval the dictum of Carswell CJ in *Perceval-Price* v. *Department of Economic Development* (2000 IRLR 380), in which the Northern Ireland Court of Appeal held that full-time chairmen of industrial tribunals and social security appeal tribunals were covered by the Equal Pay Act (Northern Ireland) 1970 and the Sex Discrimination (Northern Ireland) Order 1976 (SI/1042 [NI 15]). Judges, said Lord Carswell,

> ... are all expected to work during defined times and periods, whether they be rigidly laid down or managed by the judges themselves with a greater degree of flexibility. They are not free agents to work as and when they choose, as are self-employed persons. Their office accordingly partakes of some of the characteristics of employment ... (para. 145)

As for judges, so for clergy: Ms Percy's employment 'bore all the hall-marks of a contract' (para. 148). Moreover, Baroness Hale did not believe that Parliament had intended in 1975 that, alone of all organized religions, the Church of Scotland should be immune, not least because at the time that the 1975 Act was passed the Church of Scotland had already decided to admit women to the ministry on the same terms and conditions as men (para. 152).

The argument of the majority seems, in a nutshell, to be this:

- decisions in previous cases have often rested on a false apposition between 'office' and 'employment' whereas, in reality, it is perfectly possible for an office-holder simultaneously to be an employee;
- though not invariably the case, in certain circumstances it is possible for a minister of religion to have a contractual relationship with his or her church as an employee;
- in the absence of express intention (and there was no such intention ever expressed on the part of the Church of Scotland) the provisions of the Sex Discrimination Act 1975 cannot be set aside; and

- by entering into a contract for services the parties bring themselves within the civil law and take the relationship outside the exclusive jurisdiction of the ecclesiastical courts, so that the provisions of Church of Scotland Act 1921 no longer apply.

Part of the problem with the previous case law was that it rested on some rather outmoded assumptions. As Lord Hoffman observed in his dissenting opinion, 'To say, as Lord Templeman did in *Davies* v *Presbyterian Church of Wales* ... that a priest is "the servant of God" is true for a believer but superfluous metaphor for a lawyer' (para. 61). Indeed it is: *any* devout believer might claim to be in some sense a 'servant of God'; but he or she would not expect a stipend and manse in return for that service. And it should also be remembered that the original question raised at the tribunal was not 'is an act of adultery by a minister of the Church of Scotland a disciplinary issue?' but 'has the Church of Scotland treated a female minister differently from a male one in a disciplinary case?'.

Lord Hoffman's view

Dissenting from the majority opinion, Lord Hoffman would have dismissed the appeal; however, his argument is based on narrow civil grounds, not on constitutional ones. Lord Hoffman bases his point on a broad contention:

> The proposition that a minister of a church has no employer but holds an office, subject to rules that impose upon him certain rights and entitle him to a salary, stipend and other benefits, has been stated for so often and for so long that I would not have thought that it was open to question. (para. 56)

Thus, Lord Hoffman determined that Ms Percy was neither employed under a contract of service nor a party to a contract for services. As such, she could not qualify as a 'worker', nor could the circumstances of her demission be termed 'working conditions' under the terms of the Equal Treatment Directive (Council Directive 76/207/EEC) (para. 76). Lord Hoffman would have fallen back on the traditional distinction between ministers as office-holders, who are not employees in any sense of the word, as they have no employer, and those who hold 'employment under a contract of service or of apprenticeship or a contract personally to execute any work or labour', who are protected by the Sex Discrimination Act 1975 s. 82(1).

Equally interesting is Lord Hoffman's rejection of three arguments. First, he discounted certain rhetorical statements about those who are not, technically, employed. Using the language quoted above, concerning a minister's being 'the servant of God', Lord Hoffman labelled the phrase unhelpful and possibly misleading but maintained that ministers, like constables, might hold offices (with attendant rights and duties) without being employees (para. 61). Second, he rejected the Court of Session's imposition of a presumption that the appointment of a minister would not be intended to give rise to obligations enforceable in civil law, since office-holders indeed have such obligations but, nevertheless, are not employees (para. 63). Finally, and most importantly for the Church of Scotland, even Lord Hoffman rejected the potential that the 1921 Act might exempt the Church from the civil jurisdiction of the state:

> if the 1975 [Sex Discrimination] Act ... upon its true construction, applies to ministers of the church, I would think it unlikely that it was not intended to apply to ministers of the Church of Scotland. (para. 77)

Thus, one of the few points of law decided unanimously in *Percy* seems to be that in matters of discrimination law the constitutional status of the Church of Scotland offers it no special protection.

The *Stewart* case

Percy is already beginning to influence the way employment tribunals look at the employment status of clergy, as a recent case has shown.[10]

Mr Stewart was ordained in 1984 into the New Testament Church of God, whose headquarters are in the United States, and ministered at the Harrow church. The Church in the United Kingdom is a company limited by guarantee and a registered charity, with 108 churches and 295 ordained ministers of whom 88 are based in churches. Ministers receive payment for services rendered, sometimes referred to as salary and sometimes as stipend. Pastors' remuneration is paid out of a local tithe paid by church members. In 1999, after an audit suggested to the Church's national office that there were accounting irregularities at the Harrow church, it was agreed that Mr Stewart would in future be paid through the national office. A further audit in January 2005 again revealed financial irregularities and in June 2005 Mr Stewart was found guilty of unbecoming conduct and misappropriating funds and dismissed. He received a P45 that, like his salary slips, indicated that the New Testament Church of God was his employer. He remained an ordained minister but was not appointed to another pastorate nor paid a salary. He therefore took the Church to an employment tribunal. The tribunal found at para. 4.4 of its determination that though there was no formal written contract,

> ... there was ... an agreement, which was not reduced to writing, between the claimant and those representing the respondent that he would perform certain work including administrative tasks and spiritual duties and that he would receive payment for it and be accountable, in part at least, to that National Office ...

and therefore concluded that Mr Stewart's position as pastor at Harrow was governed by a contract of employment and that he was entitled to bring a claim for unfair dismissal. The Church appealed.

In determining whether or not Mr Stewart and the Church had entered into a legally binding contractual relationship, the Chairman of the Appeal Tribunal, Judge Ansell, said that the House of Lords decision in *Percy* had reversed the traditional view of the employment status of ministers of religion:

> Firstly, that they have cast considerable doubt upon, if not reversed, the old presumption, that a minister and a church do not intend to enter into legal relations; and secondly that an individual can be an employee as well as an office holder and thus the task is to determine whether a contract existed at all and if so whether it was a contract of employment, disregarding any presumption against an intention to enter into legal relations. It seems to us that the House of Lords have clearly stated that if the relationship between church and minister has many of the characteristics of a contract of employment in terms of rights and obligations, these cannot be ignored simply because the duties are of a religious or pastoral nature. (para. 27)

The original tribunal had therefore been entitled to conclude that the relationship between Mr Stewart and the Church went beyond the spiritual level and amounted to a legal agreement. The appeal was dismissed.[11]

Whether the conclusion in *Stewart* will have any immediate impact on the employment of clergy in the Church of England and the Church of Scotland is unclear and, in any case, both Churches have been re-examining and updating their employment practices to take account of developments in European law. Its impact on other churches, however, could be quite considerable.

Aston Cantlow and *Percy*: changing status by degrees?

In *Aston Cantlow* v. *Wallbank*[12] a couple owned a farm the ownership of which made them, as lay rectors, liable under the Chancel Repairs Act 1932 for funding repairs to the chancel of the Church of St John the Baptist, Aston Cantlow. They refused to pay, arguing that what was being demanded was, in effect, an arbitrary tax and that, as a public authority, the Aston Cantlow Parochial Church Council (PCC) was acting contrary to the Human Rights Act 1998 and the European Convention – and they took the matter all the way to the House of Lords. One of the principal questions before the Appellate Committee was whether or not a Church of England PCC is, in fact, a public authority for the purposes of the Act and the Convention; and their Lordships concluded that it was not – a conclusion, suggests Augur Pearce, that represents 'a departure from basic assumptions which have characterized England's religious constitution since, if not from before, Tudor times' (Pearce 2003: 167).

Lord Nicholls of Birkenhead put it like this:

> I do not think parochial church councils are 'core' public authorities. Historically the Church of England has discharged an important and influential role in the life of this country. As the established church it still has special links with central government. But the Church of England remains essentially a religious organisation. This is so even though some of the emanations of the Church discharge functions which may qualify as governmental. Church schools and the conduct of marriage services are two instances. The legislative powers of the General Synod of the Church of England are another. This should not be regarded as infecting the Church of England as a whole, or its emanations in general, with the character of a governmental organisation. (*Aston Cantlow*, para. 13).

Perhaps more radically, Lord Hope of Craighead asserted that

> The Church of England as a whole has no legal status or personality. There is no Act of Parliament that purports to establish it as the Church of England ... What establishment in law means is that the state has incorporated its law into the law of the realm as a branch of its general law. (*Aston Cantlow*, para. 61)

Presiding over the first appeal in the *Percy* litigation,[13] Lord President Rodger took a rather similar position, obiter, in respect of the Church of

Scotland. Referring to the exchange of letters between Ms Percy and the Board of Mission, he pointed out that

> [T]he documentation emanated from a board of a church whose constitution is made up of a hierarchy of 'courts' and which asserts the right 'to legislate, and to adjudicate finally, in all matters' of a spiritual nature (Declaratory Article IV). In exercise of that right the General Assembly enacts laws which have many of the stylistic and other hallmarks of the kind of legislation which is enacted by Parliament. The procedures of the Church courts are replete with terminology which is familiar to practitioners of Scots law. The language does nothing, indeed, to conceal the hand which those trained in Scots law have had in guiding such proceedings down the centuries. None the less, despite their outward appearance, the laws of the Church operate only within the Church and her courts adjudicate only on matters spiritual. In other words, the formality and, indeed, solemnity of all these transactions and proceedings does not disclose an intention to create relationships under the civil law; rather, it reflects the serious way in which the Church regulates the matters falling within the spiritual sphere. (2001 SC 757, para. 14)

On close examination, Lord Rodger's conclusions appear less radical than Lord Hope's: as we have already seen, the *Articles Declaratory* themselves refer to the jurisdiction of the Church of Scotland 'in matters spiritual'. Moreover, both *Aston Cantlow* and *Percy* dealt with difficult issues about which there were no simple, cut-and-dried solutions; indeed, so difficult were they that on both occasions the House of Lords reversed the judgement of the lower court. But the remarks both of Lord Nicholls and of Lord Hope prompt a more general speculation: that we may be seeing a gradual change in the way that the judiciary perceives the Church of England and the Church of Scotland.

As to whether or not the Church of Scotland continues to have exclusive jurisdiction in 'matters spiritual', in Lady Hale's opinion in *Percy* the Church of Scotland remains

> ... free to decide what its members should believe, how they should manifest their belief in worship and in teaching, how it should organize its internal government, and the qualifications for membership and office. But the processes whereby they make decisions about membership and office may be subject to the ordinary laws of the land. It will all depend upon what that law says and means. (*Percy*, para. 152)

That said, however, there remains a question mark over an issue that was not raised before their Lordships because it was not relevant to the facts before them. In Scots law there is a long line of decided cases, stretching back to *Auchinloss* v. *Black*,[14] to the effect that the courts of the Church of Scotland have a special status as courts of the Realm and possess a jurisdiction that is separate from and parallel to the jurisdictions of the Court of Session and the High Court of Justiciary. Therefore, though the tribunals of other churches are treated by the secular courts merely as the regulatory bodies of private institutions it is (or, at any rate, was) settled law that actings of the courts of the Church of Scotland are not reviewable.[15] But Ms Percy was not tried by a church court; instead, she resigned and demitted and subsequently sued the Board of National Mission. Had she gone through trial by libel before her Presbytery followed by an unsuccessful appeal to the Judicial Commission of Assembly, would their Lordships have been willing to overturn a determination by the Judicial Commission? The classical response to that question would undoubtedly be 'no': but we cannot know the answer definitively until such a thing happens.

So on the more general question of the constitutional position of the Church of England and the Church of Scotland, both *Aston Cantlow* and *Percy* prompt a series of questions about the way in which relations with the state might develop in the future:

- First, is it the case that the courts are tending to treat churches – whatever their presumed legal status – as private institutions ministering to their members, rather than as public institutions with duties and responsibilities to the world at large?
- Secondly, could it be that the courts are now more interested in principle than precedent and, if so, might the doctrine that the courts of the Church of Scotland exercise a jurisdiction equal and parallel to those of the Court of Session and the High Court of Justiciary one day break down?
- Thirdly, do the courts now take the word 'public' as meaning, in a *general* sense, 'part of government'? And if they do, what does 'part of government' mean? Does it cover, for example, the General Medical Council or the General Teaching Council for Scotland? Or do the courts interpret it in that way only for the purposes of the Human Rights Act?
- Fourthly, what is the meaning of Lord Hope's assertion in *Aston Cantlow* that 'the Church of England as a whole has no legal status or personality'? Does it means merely that there is no overarching body

called 'the Church of England' which one can sue, or does it have any deeper implications for the Church's status in English law *as a church* – and if the latter, does that bring the Church's constitutional status into question more generally?
* Finally, *if* 'the Church of England as a whole has no legal status or personality' does that have any implications for the Church of *Scotland*? Or does the Church of Scotland possess a particular legal status arising from the 1921 Act and the *Articles Declaratory* that the Church of England does not have?

As to this last point, we note Lord Hope's statement in *Percy*, obiter, that

[T]he Church is not a body that has been incorporated by statute. It has, of course, its own distinctive identity and its own Constitution, the lawfulness of which was declared by the 1921 Act. But its status in law is that of a voluntary association, of which its adherents, whether they be elders, communicants or baptized persons, are all members. (para. 117)

This echoes the dictum of Lord President Rodger in the Inner House, quoted above, about the effect of the laws of the Church and the presumed lack of intention to create relationships under them in civil law. Again, does this mean no more than the fact that you cannot sue a body called 'The Church of Scotland' (rather than suing the General Trustees or the Board of National Mission) or does it mean that the courts are tending towards the view that the legal status of the Church of Scotland is no different from that of, say, the Scottish Episcopal Church or the Free Church?

Questions but – inevitably – no answers. However, in broad policy terms, which should at least influence decisions like *Percy*, three perspectives might offer some insight into the potential dissatisfaction that some readers may feel about the House of Lords' conclusion.

First, from an entirely independent perspective, it appears that the decision shows a lack of historical sensitivity – a view supported in Lord Rodgers's Clark Lectures reflecting on the history of the relevant jurisprudence (Rodger 2008). The 1921 Act was explicitly designed to affirm the inherent sovereignty of the Church of Scotland, and it was expected that one consequence would be the prevention of a repeat of the events of 1834–43, when the civil courts interfered in the internal disputes of the Church of Scotland, forcing unwilling congregations in the Church to install ministers against the will of congregations. The arguments that supported the Act at the time may be less coherent now, but there is a certain amount of contemporary evidence that some thought that Parliament was, at least implicitly, recognising that the nineteenth-century judicial decisions had trespassed on what was properly the jurisdiction of the Church. Perhaps the clearest articulation of this position was by Lord Justice Clerk Aitchison in *Ballantyne* v. *Presbytery of Wigtown* 1936 SLT 436, 447:

> [The 1921 Act] is not an Act of Parliament conferring rights upon the Church, but it is a recognition by Parliament of Articles framed by the General Assembly of the Church as its Supreme Court in the exercise of what it claimed to be its own inherent powers ... The Act came into operation by an Order of His Majesty in Council on 28th June 1926, and then only after the Declaratory Articles had been adopted by an Act of the General Assembly of the Church of Scotland with the consent of a majority of the Presbyteries of the Church. This adoption of the Articles by the free will of the Church after the Act was on the statute book, and as a *condition* of the Act becoming operative, was an assertion by the Church of its autonomy in matters affecting its own life and polity.[16]

Although Lord Hope mentions, obiter, that a civil court '*might* not have the power to restore the pursuer to the ministry' (para. 100, emphasis added), powers available to an employment tribunal include recommending that the respondent take action 'appearing to the tribunal to be practicable to obviate or reduce the adverse effect on the complainant of any act of discrimination'.[17] The decision does not entirely foreclose the potential that such a remedy – reinstatement of the minister or payment of a penal sum – might be ordered in another case; though how that might work in practice is not at all clear. In addition, from the same independent perspective it appears that while explicit statutory exceptions protect openly discriminatory churches, such as the Roman Catholics and the Anglicans (s. 19, Sex Discrimination Act 1975), less hierarchical churches that are struggling with issues of gender (for example) at the congregational level are subject to interference by the courts. Thus, a decision like *Percy* can have the unintended, but perverse, effect of making conservative doctrine increasingly attractive to religious organizations that want to stay out of court.

Secondly, from the perspective of the churches, a number of adverse consequences may seem to flow from the decision. Since the court did not establish any clear guidelines about the extent of its jurisdiction with respect to employment and doctrine, any conduct by a church that can be characterized as discriminatory based upon gender (such as, for example, punishment of a female minister's entering into a contract of surrogacy) might give rise to a cause of action. As most litigation lawyers will acknowledge, their professional skills include characterising fact-patterns so that they meet the requirements of a cause of action.

Churches will have to incur some expense in defending against these claims (and settling them, depending on how risk averse the decision-makers might be), whether the claims are well founded or not. Because religious principles may be involved, however, a normal cost-benefit calculus will not always apply. The claimant or pursuer will undoubtedly feel wronged, and if doctrine appears to be affected (or can be understood or characterized as such), the defendant will have a duty to expend resources in order to protect doctrinal integrity (and the specific doctrine to be defended may not even be one that a particular individual holds strongly). Religious believers sign on for packages of beliefs; and, even when some of those beliefs are less firmly held, believers may be willing to defend them, especially from state intrusion, at great expense, as a part of a broader body of doctrine. Religious disputes are a fertile ground for high-level conflict.

Finally, from the point of view of the courts, is it wise to try and adjudicate disputes of this type? Fraught as they are with the risk of treading on doctrinal or other complex principles (including those relating to sexual fidelity and other sexual mores, as was the case in *Percy*), these cases have the potential to consume judicial resources disproportionate to those normally used up in lawsuits that involve financial damages. Moreover, whether or not they discriminate on gender, the primary purpose of the churches is still the advancement of religion and all that flows from that in terms of encouraging care and compassion for others. If the courts cannot articulate a more administrable standard of decision than has been done in *Percy*, can they reasonably expect the churches to expend ostensibly charitable resources paying lawyers to do so? Lord Rodgers's decision, recognising a rebuttable presumption against such judicial involvement,[18] was a tentative step toward trying to avoid that morass.

Conclusion

We have already suggested that the spiritual jurisdiction of the Church of Scotland is an imprecisely defined blob within the more general jurisdiction of national law: both Church and state are trying to decide where the boundary is drawn in terms of Article VI. However, this is not a situation in which the Church's authority could disappear completely.

The spiritual jurisdiction of the Church of Scotland has four elements: church government, discipline in its widest and narrowest senses, worship and doctrine. To varying degrees these are things for which the civil magistrate has no concern. There is nothing in the form of worship that has attracted the attention of the civil law in modern times. There is little in the doctrines of the Church that impinges beyond its own community – though churches take advantage of some legal exemptions, usually in relation to 'sex' in both senses of the word, and that happens for doctrinal reasons. The Church of Scotland has kept at bay civil inspection of its Church government but lives constantly in fear of a litigious party in an internal church case seeking judicial review of a decision of one of its courts or commissions. Most slippery of the four is the concept of the discipline of ministers; and a burgeoning civilian jurisprudence in the area of employment law presses more and more on the Church.

There are, then, parts of the Church's separate jurisdiction that are under no threat: the middle of the blob is perfectly safe. The law's protection of that part of the Church's internal authority is perhaps little more than the safeguarding of confessional freedoms, a human right every belief-system should enjoy in a free country. Then there are things that might once have been left to internal regulation but which the Church is happy to allow the civil law to regulate much better: for example, the law of the Church has quite a lot to say about issues of child protection, but says it entirely to ensure compliance with civil law in that area.

Where the difficulty lies is around the penumbra of the blob, the areas that produce cases like *Percy*. For those there are probably two ways of dividing up the responsibility: the first is to identify the existing provisions of the civil law and then assume that everything else that arises is for the Church to regulate internally, while the second, the converse of the first, is to determine what the Church needs to regulate for the sake of its theological integrity and conscience, then leave everything else to the general law. Both these instincts exist within what is an almost impossibly broad Church.

The Church has lived through the resistance of some ministers to the idea of obeying child protection law because, as they see it, the authority of their Kirk Session over the life of the congregation is perfectly adequate. The Church's response to the Department of Trade and Industry's (DTI's) consultation in 2005 on outlawing discrimination on the basis of sexual orientation in the supply of goods and services[19] has included a request for an acknowledgement that an individual minister must be allowed to exercise his or her conscience in deciding whether to allow the church buildings to be used for, say, a party celebrating a civil partnership. But, on the other hand, most people would prefer Sunday School children to be driven to the picnic by someone with a minibus qualification from the local authority. Once again, the sensible balance has to be found, in a context where people are not agreed where it should lie. Where the Church needs to have her own corpus of law must be *either* where there is serious prospect of such a conflict and difference of principle *or* where the civil law simply does not have an opinion, an interest, a reason to interfere in esoteric matters of doctrine and worship. The rest can well go by default into the general regulation of a safe society.

As mentioned earlier, at the time of writing the British churches are in the middle of a fascinating engagement with the DTI's successor (the BERR) in the area of protection of workers. Thus far, the consultation exercise has resulted in the publication of a *Model Statement of Good Practice* (DTI 2007) covering job-descriptions and terms and conditions of employment, support and training, the establishment of grievance and disciplinary procedures, and consultation and information about significant changes that might affect job-holders.[20] Welcoming the *Model Statement*, parliamentary Under-Secretary of State for Trade and Industry Jim Fitzpatrick said that it represented minimum standards that faith-groups should aim to achieve and that, as a first step, the DTI was asking faith-groups to assess their current positions in relation to the standards in the statement. The DTI (now BERR) would revisit the issue in two years' time and then 'consider if any further action is appropriate, *including legislative action*'.[21]

There are layers of reasons why the churches would not have expected to be subject to those laws in the past: that by nature they are religious and therefore different and 'above that sort of thing'; that by legislation they are exempted, through the 1921 Act in the case of the Church of Scotland or through equivalent provisions enjoyed by other bodies; or that by practice churches have office-holders who are not employees. But no-one is so callous and immoral as to deny the desirability of giving clergy the best possible protection from harassment, discrimination, unfair treatment and constructive dismissal. So the Church of Scotland, setting out from perhaps the clearest starting point of all the British churches, is developing, demonstrating and clarifying an equivalence of protection in all those areas of workers' rights. It is a good and worthwhile exercise for its own sake and for the sake of the clergy. But the technical reason for doing it is to provide BERR with reassurance that the Church of Scotland's self-regulation does give a proper equivalence of protection, in the hope that further encroachment by secular law will prove unnecessary. That is a work in progress; but its outcome will perhaps affect the extent to which the English churches, especially some in the Church of England itself, look to the north for another way of approaching the church/state question.

Part II
Disestablishments

The following two chapters consider how church/state relations have changed in the contrasting environments of the United Kingdom and Scandinavia. Comparing the experiences of changes in church organization emphasizes two things: the vital contribution of local circumstance and the fact that outcomes are dependent on the nature of political interaction over extended timeframes. Ireland stands out as a very special case, a failure of ecclesiastical colonization if you like. But in Wales, where a forced disestablishment was highly hostile, the outcome has been much less of a complete fracture between the disestablished body and the state than originally intended. In Scandinavia, a different concept of the religious community together with stronger Erastian impulses than in the United Kingdom has led to disestablishment – where it has come at all – as a later, whole-state phenomenon without the regional, intra-country forms of the United Kingdom. It is also true that the later a review takes place, the more it is influenced by the degree of religious pluralization then existing. Above all, the experiences show that there is not, and cannot be, any single model for disestablishment. Rather, whether or not the language of 'establishment' is used, there are simply different ways of structuring church/state relations over time in response to changed circumstances.

8
Disestablishment in Ireland and Wales

John Lucas (with Bob Morris)

Introduction

There are two established churches in the British Isles – the Anglican Church of England and the Presbyterian Church of Scotland. Until the middle of the nineteenth century the Anglican Church was also established in Ireland and Wales. These churches were disestablished, however, in 1871 and 1920 respectively as the result of long campaigns culminating in Acts of Parliament.

What establishment meant in Ireland and Wales

The Church of Ireland and the Church in Wales were reformed by the English Crown with the Church of England during the mid-sixteenth century. Until its disestablishment, the Welsh Church consisted of the four sees of the province of Canterbury that roughly corresponded to the geographic area of Wales, but had no separate status within what was a unitary church organization for England and Wales together. Though Anglican in form, the Church of Ireland was an independent church until the Act of Union of Great Britain with Ireland in 1800 explicitly united the Church of Ireland and that of England and Wales.

Establishment contained the following principal features:

- It provided identical financial benefits. The established churches controlled the traditional lands and revenues of the pre-Reformation churches, including rights to tithe and church tax (known in Ireland as church cess) regardless of parishioners' confessions.
- Establishment also conferred membership of the relevant legislature and therefore a degree of political power. The bishops of the Irish

Church sat in the Irish House of Lords in Dublin until the Act of Union, after which a rota was created giving four Irish bishops the right to sit alongside their English and Welsh counterparts at Westminster. In all cases, other clergy were forbidden to sit in the House of Commons. Political influence was also given to the Church of Ireland through places for two archbishops on the Irish Privy Council.

- Establishment meant that ecclesiastical law was enforceable under the authority of the Crown, and, following the Court of Delegates Act 1833, all matters that involved questions of doctrine, ceremony and ritual were decided ultimately by the Judicial Committee of the Privy Council.

- Until the 1828 repeal of the Test and Corporation Acts and the grant of Catholic Emancipation in 1829, establishment entrenched a privileged position for the laity of the established Church, while suppressing non-members. Additional penal laws had been directed in Ireland against the majority Roman Catholic population, although most of the laws were repealed by the Irish Parliament at the end of the eighteenth century. In Wales, the growth of Protestant dissent embarrassed a Church increasingly associated with an Anglican and anglicized ruling class. Establishment was consequently a symbol of repression and inequality to the non-Anglican populations of both Ireland and Wales, especially during periods when franchise limitations denied participation in the legislatures to large numbers of people.

Ireland

Prior to 1870, the Irish Church was viewed by many as 'a badge of conquest' (Marx and Engels 1869: 421). The members of the Church of Ireland were vested with political and economic power, and owned the majority of the land. They were the descendants of predominantly English settlers from the sixteenth to early eighteenth centuries. This 'Protestant Ascendancy' over Catholics in Ireland was supported in Ulster by Presbyterian Scots, who had settled in Ireland during the early seventeenth century. In return for their loyalty to William III during James II's attempts to win back the British crowns, the Presbyterians were awarded a grant called the *Regium Donum* to support their clergy.

Despite English pressure, the majority of the Irish population, who were descended from the native Gael population, and the 'Old English' families from the thirteenth century, remained Roman Catholic. The census of 1861 in Ireland contained a question on religion. The results illustrated the absurd position of the Established Church, which made up only 11.9 per cent of the population, while Roman Catholics constituted 77.6 per cent, and Presbyterians 9 per cent (Bell 1969: 41).

Political background

Before the Act of Union, the Irish Parliament had achieved a degree of independent action from 1782, and had relaxed some of the Penal Laws which had heavily discriminated against Catholics in civic and economic life. Catholics were allowed to vote in elections from 1793 (although the high franchise excluded the majority of Catholics), and a Catholic seminary at Maynooth was founded in 1795 with state support. The Union was meant to be accompanied by emancipation legislation, although George III refused to sanction this as he considered it to be in violation of his coronation oaths.

Emancipation in 1829 was followed in 1833 by the Irish Church (Temporalities) Act which, as already noted, abolished church cess, reduced the number of archbishops from 4 to 2, and the number of bishops from 18 to 10, and established a commission to administer the funds released by the changes. Although the Act, an unprecedented and swingeing intervention by the executive, sought to strengthen the Church through reform, it also signalled that ecclesiastical change was possible throughout Britain – a point not lost on churchmen and non-churchmen alike in England and Wales as well as in Ireland. To reduce resistance to tithe (which had become acute in the 1830s) an act of 1838 converted it into a rentcharge. De facto limited concurrent endowment in the Maynooth grant and *Regium Donum* was continued. Indeed, Robert Peel's Tory government increased Maynooth's endowment in 1845. It was over that issue that William Gladstone left the government, though he later became the champion of disestablishment under the Liberal Party banner.

Irish political action

Establishment and the Protestant Ascendancy were meant to increase British security. However, it became clear in the nineteenth century that Catholicism was no longer a threat to British security though political instability *within* Ireland was. This threat was exemplified by the birth of unified Catholic political action in Daniel O'Connell's Catholic Association. It was the election of O'Connell as the MP for Clare in 1828 that forced the hand of Wellington's Tory government over emancipation. Irish political grievances were later internationalized by the formation in the United States in 1858 of the Irish terrorist group called the Fenian Brotherhood, and the threats it posed to Canada.

A national issue

Political articulation was also given to the Irish question in England itself with the formation of the Liberation Society by Edward Miall in its original form in 1844. Although seeking to disestablish and disendow churches throughout the United Kingdom so that all Christian churches would have equal status, the Society quickly picked out Ireland as the weakest point in the armour of established religion. As Ireland's political problems became more pronounced, Westminster politicians were forced to pay them more attention. By the late 1860s both Tory and Liberal politicians had begun to accept the necessity of resolving the Irish problem. Prime Minister Benjamin Disraeli stated that the Church of Ireland was 'an alien church' and a central part of the 'extreme distress' of Ireland.

The Tories, however, favoured the concept of concurrent endowment rather than disestablishment and disendowment. The Earl of Mayo, Disraeli's Chief Secretary for Ireland, maintained 'that Justice and Policy may demand a greater equalization of ecclesiastical arrangements than now exists ... If it is desired to make our churches more equal in position than they now are, this should be secured by elevation and restoration, and not by confiscation and degradation' (Moneypenny and Buckle 1929: 589–90).

Despite Tory views on the matter, the mantle was stolen by William Gladstone who, in the course of the mid 1860s, sought to unite all Nonconformist and Catholic opinion with Whigs and Radicals under a Liberal Party banner throughout the British Isles, capitalising on the expanded franchise of the Reform Act of 1867 – which also delivered a phalanx of Irish nationalist MPs into the Commons. Despite being a high-churchman, Gladstone decided that, as part of his programme for reform in Ireland, the interests of the British State would be better served by the disestablishment and disendowment of the Anglican Church in Ireland. Accordingly, the Liberals went on the parliamentary offensive and in March 1868 Gladstone carried a motion against the government in favour of Irish disestablishment.

Later that year, the country went to the polls in a campaign largely fought on the issue of Irish disestablishment and disendowment. Liberals supported the issue using the arguments of justice in terms of population and the disproportionate wealth of the Church compared to its membership, alongside the need to resolve the Irish political situation. The election proved a success for Gladstone and his coalition of Radicals, Whigs, Catholics and dissenters under the wing of the Liberal Party, winning 387 seats to the Conservatives 271. As a result, Gladstone had a mandate to move ahead with a bill to disestablish and disendow the Irish Church.

Finally introduced on 1 March 1869, the Bill was vigorously attacked by Disraeli's Tories in committee stage, but all amendments were voted down. When it reached the Lords in June, the Bill was heavily amended to reduce its financial effects and there was some toying with possibilities of concurrent endowment. The Commons rejected the Lords amendments and it was only after high-level mediation involving the Queen and some mitigation of compensation terms that a major constitutional crisis was avoided and the Bill finally passed, receiving royal assent on 28 July 1869.

An Act to put an end to the Establishment of the Church of Ireland, and to make provision of the Temporalities thereof (32 & 33 Vict c 42)

The date of Irish disestablishment was set for 1 January 1871, at which time the union of the Churches of England and Ireland, Crown patronage, appointments and lay patronage ceased. The Irish bishops also lost their places in the House of Lords, and the archbishops their ex-officio places on the Irish Privy Council (though the then-archbishops continued while remaining in office). The other main provisions were as follows:

- Ecclesiastical law ceased to have effect other than by the operation of the normal civil law of contract.
- Ecclesiastical corporations were dissolved and their property handed over to the new commissioners appointed to receive the property of the Church, including that formerly administered by the Irish ecclesiastical commissioners.
- The Crown was empowered to grant a charter to a new representative body of the Church to enable it to receive property, which included church buildings and movable goods for the use of worship. The Church was also given the opportunity to buy its glebe-houses at favourable rates.
- The Church kept endowments that it had obtained after 1660 when the Church assumed its post-Restoration form. Endowments before that time were put towards the good of the greater Irish community, but only after vested interests had been compensated.
- Clergy who held the freehold to their benefice or were permanent curates received a net income for life on the condition that they

continued to perform their duties, and with a right to voluntary commutation. Non-permanent curates received compensation of between £200 and £600. Lay patrons were also compensated, as were others who worked within the Church.

- Tenants were given first refusal where the new commission sold land. Likewise, the tithe was put up for sale on the same terms, but few if any took up the offer, and the tithe effectively died.
- The Maynooth Grant and the *Regium Donum* ceased, but were compensated both by preserving existing life interests and the payment of final capital sums.
- The new Church of Ireland was allowed to hold a synod, which was to form the backbone of future church governance alongside the representative body.

Church of Ireland organization

Between 1869 and 1871 the Church designed its new General Synod, which was to meet annually. It consisted of the House of Bishops and House of Representatives, made up of clerical and lay orders. Legislation could only pass if approved by a majority of each order. Thus, each house could operate a veto, although the bishops' veto was limited.

A Representative Church Body was formed to hold the property that remained with the Church. It consisted of the episcopate, 1 clergyman and 2 laymen from each diocese, and 12 laymen. Meeting regularly, it was the civil service of the Church, and responsible to the General Synod.

Bishops and the Archbishop of Dublin were elected by the synods of their dioceses, while the Archbishop of Armagh, elected in the same way, was approved by the House of Bishops. Clergy were appointed by vestry councils operating with diocesan appointment boards.

Post-disestablishment

The Church of Ireland declined into the twentieth century, especially in southern Ireland, although it remained unified after the creation of the Irish Republic in 1922. The new constitutional arrangements functioned successfully and the Church managed to agree on a new prayer book.

Gladstone's Church of Ireland Act was, of course, only the first in a series of measures that were designed to resolve the Irish issue. Gladstone's Liberal Party held together its coalition of Whigs, Protestant dissenters, Catholics and radicals until the issue of home rule split the party in 1886. Whereas the Act succeeded in removing the religious issue, it could not by itself redress all Irish grievances whose residue remained an intractable puzzle for both the Irish and British governments.

Wales

A situation where the Welsh Church was the Church of England in Wales was not seriously challenged until the growth of nonconformity became increasingly apparent in Wales from the mid-eighteenth century, a growth which was itself a symptom of the neglect that had characterized ecclesiastical affairs in the country where the Church became increasingly distant from the people.

No Welsh-speaking bishop was consecrated after Anne's reign (1702–14) until Gladstone appointed Joshua Hughes to St Asaph in 1870. The Church was inflexible and monolithic and unable to respond to the needs of the growing Welsh population, especially in quickly industrialising South Wales. New parishes could not even be created without legislation. It was much more thinly endowed than in England, with a higher proportion of its anyway less valuable tithes in the hands of lay impropriators. Nonconformity, in contrast, was flexible and responsive to local needs. Moreover, it catered much more assiduously for a monoglot Welsh-speaking as well as bilingual Welsh population. However, although there were certainly special cultural and linguistic features unique to Wales, their exact contribution to the decline of Anglicanism in Wales might be in danger of being exaggerated when it is remembered that Anglicanism also lost support in England at the same time.

Political background

In 1851 Henry Mann conducted the first census of religion. It revealed the strength of Nonconformity in the four Welsh dioceses. Of the 52 per cent of the Welsh population who attended services on 30 March 1851, 78 per cent were dissenters, while only 21 per cent went to services within the Church (Morgan 1980:10). The results provided a clear insight into the conditions of religious activity in Wales and demonstrated that the Church constituted much the smallest part of active Christianity.

Although the Church did go through a mid-century revival and became more responsive to the needs of the population that it served, the strength of the combined Nonconformist groups continued in the period before disestablishment. By 1906, when the Royal Commission was appointed to investigate the state of the Church in Wales, 27 per cent of active Christians were from the Church, while 73 per cent practised in dissenting chapels (Bell 1969: 274), although the 'national' Church laid claim to the 50 per cent of the population that did not practise any faith at all.

Although the grievance of church tax was removed for Wales as for England in 1868, the Church's unpopularity was aggravated by the existence of tithes as a major part of the Church's endowment, regardless of the confession of those who had to pay it. Anger boiled over in the 1880s with forced sales during the collapse of the agricultural market, and legislation was passed in 1891 to hand the responsibility of paying tithe to the landlords rather than tenants.

Disestablishment and Liberal Radicalism

The progress of disestablishment in Wales was not simply a struggle of religious affiliation; it was intrinsically tied to the growing awareness of Wales as a political body, especially as political enfranchisement increased at both the local and national levels.

The Liberation Society quickly took root in Wales and encouraged those favouring radical political change to support disestablishment as the vanguard and symbol of that change. In the election campaign of 1861, the Society placed pressure on Liberal candidates in Wales to come out in support of disestablishment and disendowment (Bell 1969: 18). Disestablishment quickly became the centre of Welsh political consciousness. The campaign for religious equality came to represent the rejection of the political subjugation of Wales as a whole.

The process was advanced by two events in the latter half of the 1860s. The first was the election of 1868, which was fought with a widened franchise after the Reform Act of 1867. This act gave the vote to thousands of Welsh nonconformists for whom disestablishment was a key issue. Liberal candidates campaigned on the slogan 'the nonconformists of Wales are the people of Wales' (Morgan 1980: 28). The second event was Irish disestablishment which provided a blueprint for nonconformists and radicals to consider the possibilities for their own nation.

Wales as a separate political identity

The political identity of Wales became further pronounced during the 1870s. Politicians began to understand and exploit the potential of the Welsh bloc in the Commons. Gladstone's attendance at the 1873 Mold Eisteddfod, at which he defended Welsh nationalism and language, was a key example of this recognition.

Stuart Rendel, an English Anglican, saw the possibilities of Welsh action. Standing in Montgomeryshire on a disestablishment ticket and claiming that the Church was anti-Welsh, he ousted the sitting Tory MP,

Sir Watkin Williams Wynn, whose family had held the county seat since 1799 (Morgan 1980: 40). Observing that the Liberal voting block in the Commons consistently won from 27 to 30 out of 34 possible seats, Rendel sought to organize the Welsh block to further Welsh interests, placing disestablishment at its fore.

This goal was also taken up by the radical Liberals of the main party. In 1882, Joseph Chamberlain visited Wales, spoke about disestablishment and added the issue to the radical Liberal 'Unauthorized Programme'.

One of the clearest signs of the Welsh political voice's growing power was the first ever separate legislation for Wales in 1881. The Nonconformists' opposition to intoxicating liquor gave rise to an influential temperance movement which bore fruit in the form of the Welsh Sunday Closing Act 1881. This was a major political landmark for Wales as, together with the Welsh Intermediate Education Act 1889, it set the precedent that Wales could be legislated for separately from England.

Dependence on national events

Despite these developments, the issue of Welsh disestablishment remained on the agenda with little effect for fifty years, although various motions and bills about it were presented to Parliament. The issue did, however, rise on the *Liberal* agenda. After the Liberal Party split over the issue of home rule for Ireland in 1886, Gladstone had to rely on the Welsh Liberal voting bloc. Gladstone himself said, 'the Welsh vote is a strong vote, and they are right to try what they can do with it' (Bell 1969: 230–1).

The Liberal Party was out of office between 1886 and 1892, which effectively destroyed the chances of disestablishment even if the certainty of a Lords' veto was discounted. Further resolutions of the Commons in 1889, 1891 and 1892 failed, although the Welsh bloc remained solid. The importance of the bloc to the Liberal Party was highlighted in 1891 when the issue was placed second only to Irish home rule on the Newcastle Programme of Liberal Party objectives.

In a nod to Welsh members after Gladstone won the 1892 election, Asquith, the Home Secretary, introduced the Welsh Church Suspensory Bill in February 1893 in preparation for disestablishment. However, it made no progress because of the preference given to the Irish Home Rule Bill.

In 1894, Rosebury, Gladstone's successor, failed to introduce a Bill despite his stated commitment to Welsh disestablishment (Morgan 1980: 143). Three Welsh Liberal members, including Lloyd George, declared themselves independent of the whip in protest. The worried government then introduced the first Welsh Disestablishment Bill, but the Liberals lost the 1895 election and the Bill failed. The issue remained a low priority until the next Liberal government, which appointed a Royal Commission in 1906 to examine Church affairs in Wales. This was a sign that the government intended to press ahead with disestablishment legislation but was in no immediate hurry to do so.

Despite disestablishment being a major issue for the party, Irish home rule dominated the last decades of the nineteenth century. Home rule caused Liberal governments to fall, or meant that not enough parliamentary time could be found to take the Welsh bills past their second readings. Likewise, the 1909 Bill failed to progress because the Government was consumed by the budget crisis. But at all times it has to be recalled that the handling of such legislation by the government's business managers was dominated by the fact that Bills had to pass both the Commons *and* the Lords. For so long as the Lords veto remained, disestablishment in Wales was simply not on the cards. Accordingly, the Bills that were introduced by Liberal governments could function only as a sop to the Welsh lobby in the knowledge that they would not be approved by the upper house. (Wittingly introducing Bills that could in fact never become law was a standard Liberal government technique for managing their radical supporters.) It followed that there was no incentive to give such Bills parliamentary time. It was only after the Parliament Act of 1911 removed the Lords' veto that a Bill for Welsh disestablishment became a practical proposition.

Disestablishment and beyond

By the time Home Secretary Reginald McKenna introduced the final Bill, much of what disestablishment represented to the people of Wales, especially the fusing of religious with political equality, had already been achieved. Two-in-three men had the vote; Wales was recognized as an area with a separate custom; Welsh culture and language had been recognized by the foundation of a university and national library (Morgan 1980: 274); the Local Government Act 1888 had removed Anglican oligarchic county rule; and a Welshman was Chancellor of the Exchequer. The fire that had raged over the cause of disestablishment in Wales was burning itself out: the Bishop of St Davids commented to the Bishop of London that the disestablishment movement was dying at its roots from old age.

The Lords failed to pass the 1912 Bill twice, but the terms of the Parliament Act were invoked on its third introduction in April 1914. While in the Lords committee stage war broke out. Although the government toyed with the idea of suspending the Act altogether, the Welsh Church Act and supporting suspensory legislation received royal assent on 18 September 1914 and merely postponed the principal Act's coming into force until after the conclusion of hostilities and therefore cleared the way for preparatory steps to be taken.

An Act to terminate the establishment of the Church of England in Wales and Monmouthshire, and to make provision in respect of the Temporalities thereof (4 & 5 Geo V c 91)

The Act dissolved ecclesiastical corporations, abolished patronage, removed the Welsh bishops from the House of Lords and allowed Welsh clergy to sit in the Commons. The ecclesiastical courts ceased to have jurisdiction, and ecclesiastical law no longer had force except as contract under the normal civil law. The Welsh bishops and clergy were removed from the Convocation of Canterbury.

The Act also made provision for the temporalities of the Church by supplying a measure of disendowment. A body of commissioners – the Commissioners of Church Temporalities in Wales (CCTW) – was established to receive the Church's property. Where income-generating property had been acquired before 1662 (about five-eighths of the total) it was to be passed to the Welsh county and borough councils and the University of Wales. All real and personal property, and anything acquired post-1662, was to go to the representative body of the disestablished Church. The date of 1662 was chosen to mark the point when it was argued that the Church ceased to minister to the nation as a whole. On that basis, disendowment could be justified as returning to the nation what could not legitimately be claimed by the Church.

Roughly one-quarter of income-producing property was derived from English sources, namely, the Ecclesiastical Commissioners' common fund and Queen Anne's Bounty. The Act made provision for these sources to be transferred to the Representative Body. The final eighth fell under the description of 'modern endowments', or those which had been given to the Church after 1662. Life interests in 'freehold' livings were preserved. Likewise, lay patrons of the Church, whose rights over livings were ended by the Act, received compensation of not more that one year's revenue from the benefice in question. Curates, however, were not compensated.

The suspension of the Act's entering into force gave more time to prepare for what not all regarded or hoped as necessarily inevitable. For example, some churchmen felt that a post-war Conservative government might look more favourably upon the Church, or repeal the Act.

But as the war progressed, the Church, led by Alfred George Edwards, Bishop of St Asaph, sought to organize its affairs in order to prepare for disestablishment.

Although a Conservative government did not emerge after the armistice, the political situation did change favourably. This was because the majority of the membership of the post-war coalition led by Lloyd George was Unionist and therefore, even if there was to be no going back on disestablishment, at least sympathetic to the Church's financial position. Equally, the Welsh MPs most interested in sustaining the force of the original disendowment provisions, as well as being bamboozled by Lloyd George keen to preserve his coalition with Unionists, were politically too weak to insist on having their way, and they were without the support of the bloc of Irish MPs then no longer in the Commons. In practice, and by routes by no means patent at the time to all except the very closest observers, the way in which the government responded to wartime movements in tithe values and sought to give both overt and covert compensation to the Church vitiated the ability of the Commissioners to deliver the degree of disendowment originally intended and the Church suffered less severely as a result. While the Commissioners eventually transmitted £3,455,813 10s 8d to the beneficiaries during 1942–47 (Bell 1969: 312), it has been pointed out that this sum was very substantially less than the total of £13,486,113 that might have been expected from the calculus of the 1914 Act (Peterson and McLean 2007: 153).

Legislatively, the outcome was the combined effect of the Tithe Act 1918 and the Church in Wales (Temporalities) Act of August 1919. The latter set the date of disestablishment at 31 March 1920, and provided £1,000,000 from the taxpayer towards the CCTW's responsibilities for commutation. Moreover, the 1919 Act returned to the Church one important element that the 1914 Act had sought to take away. Whereas the 1914 Act had removed the Church's ability to continue to solemnize marriage without the presence of a civil registrar and thus put the Church on the same footing as nonconformist chapels, the 1919 Act returned to the original position. Accordingly, in this respect the disestablished Church in Wales remained after all in the same position as the established Church of England.

Thus, on more favourable terms than the original 1914 Act, the Church in Wales became in 1920 an independent province within the Anglican Communion. The Archbishop of Canterbury released the four Welsh bishops from their oaths of obedience, and they duly elected Bishop Edwards as their metropolitan.

Effects of disestablishment

Financially, in addition to the taxpayers' subvention, Queen Anne's Bounty and the Ecclesiastical Commissioners behaved generously to the Welsh Church. More dependent on securing its own resources, the Church had by 1935 raised over £700,000 in new endowment by voluntary subscription and a further £45,000 from a Provincial levy. After World War II, the Church made a fresh appeal for £500,000 and succeeded in raising £600,000. In 1955 the Governing Body relaxed its investment rules so that investments no longer had to satisfy Trustee criteria. Having as a result bought Bush House in London, the Church sold it for a greatly enhanced price of £20 million in 1972 (Walker 1976).

Tithe was not abolished but the ownership of the rentcharge passed to county councils before abolition as in England, from 1936. Noting with relief in 1935 that the Church in Wales no longer had the responsibility of tithe, Archbishop Green thought that one net effect of the overall financial provisions had been actually to see an improvement in net clerical incomes (Green, C. A. H. 1937: 9). In addition, the length of time it took to implement disendowment made it more difficult to judge final outcomes. This was not unwelcome to the Church in Wales since it probably did not want to draw undue attention to how far disendowment had not been anything like as ungenerous as the 1914 Act had intended. As Bishop Owen of St Davids remarked of the 1919 Bill:

> [T]he Bill is a huge hanky-panky job after [Lloyd] George's best style and much, much better than it looks. Lord Robert [*Cecil* – and Anglican leader in the Commons] thinks we bishops have been gulled, which is, to me, a very good joke, but we shall have to play the part of silly lambs for a bit. (Quoted Peterson and McLean 2007: 164)

Organizationally, two new dioceses were later founded the better to serve Wales: the see of Swansea and Brecon was carved out of St Davids in 1921, and the see of Monmouth was created out of Llandaff in 1923. The sole substantial untidiness left from the legislation related to the upkeep of usable pre-1662 churchyards. The legislation made these available to county councils should they want them. By 1935 out of 819 the Church still had 670 on its hands, and legislation was later necessary in 1945 – the Welsh Church (Burial Grounds) Act – to deal with the situation and in effect reverse the 1914 Act's provision by vesting burial grounds in the Representative Body. Meanwhile, the Prison Rules for England and Wales remain adjusted following disestablishment to put the statutory duty for providing prison chaplains in penal establishments in Wales upon the Church in Wales.

There is, finally, the question just what kind of disestablishment actually occurred in Wales? The position over marriage and burial – and, to a lesser but still notable extent, in the case of prison chaplains – suggests that it was not complete. Although the Archbishop of Wales and the Bishop of Monmouth decided in 1922 not to attend a levee because the Lord Chamberlain had declined to issue invitations adequately reflecting what they thought was their proper precedence (TNA HO 144/6935 Boyd to Stamfordham, 8 July 1926), this did not result in ostracism. Indeed, royal visitations requiring religious observance see them carried out in cathedrals. The 1982 distribution of Maundy money took place at St David's Cathedral. More

In a way that would have scandalized many Welsh politicians at the time of disestablishment, the National Assembly for Wales was inaugurated in the presence of the Queen at Llandaff Cathedral ... It was an ecumenical service, sensitive to the religious beliefs of all the people of Wales, but it took place in an Anglican cathedral. (Taylor 2003: 236)

Ecclesiastical lawyers have also pointed to aspects of the legal status of the Church which indicate that disestablishment was less climactic than supposed. Reflecting that it was not the Church in Wales that was disestablished in 1920 but the Church of England,

there is modest judicial support for the view that the Church in Wales is a re-established church. Indeed, two notable vestiges of establishment remain today in the duty of the clergy ... to solemnize the marriages of parishioners and the right of parishioners to burial in the churchyard. These and other instances of establishment may suggest the view that the Church in Wales is a quasi-established church, being for these purposes as if it were established. (Doe 2002: 11)

Another observer has argued even that the royal supremacy was untouched by the 1914 and 1919 Acts (Jones, P. 2000: 68). Focusing on the way in which disestablishment left the Church in Wales to make its own law, an ecclesiastical lawyer has maintained that it was thereby freed from the control of governors who were no longer representative of the Church: 'In a sense, the Welsh dioceses were returned to the position which had obtained centuries earlier when the members of the Church governed themselves' (Watkin 1992: 31). Granted that the Church of England for all its greater autonomy under the Enabling Act 1919 is still tied to Parliament, that observation has force. Among other things, it means that the Church in Wales was spared the English crises of 1927 and 1928, as well as the anxieties of the Archbishops' Commissions that followed. Lastly, quoting Bishop Morris of Monmouth's 1946 charge to his clergy that they should minister to *all* the souls in their parishes, a historian of disestablishment has observed that disestablishment clearly did not prevent the bishop giving such an injunction:

> Yet the importance of establishment as conferring a duty and opportunity to minister to all people in a country was an argument prominent in the campaign against establishment in Wales. It is still used on occasion about the position in England. (Bell 1969: 328)

The two disestablishments in perspective

Just as the mid-nineteenth-century debates about the degree of autonomy to be conceded to Canada and Australia in church matters recognized in the end local political realities, so may the two disestablishments be seen as part of a process – with ultimately rather different constitutional outcomes – of conceding the status of political personality to Irish and Welsh people. Ultimately, Church establishment in Canada and Australia could not be sustained if it was not wanted. Essentially, that principle had been conceded in the Clergy Reserves (Canada) Act 1853 which allowed the local legislature to dispose of the reserves introduced in 1791. Similarly, after a decade-long discussion about the right modalities, the Privy Council in 1856 accepted a Victoria (Australia) Bill that set up the Church of England there as a voluntary, self-governing denomination (Daw 1977). However, what could be tolerated in far-off countries was one thing: nearer home questions of long-vested property rights, tradition and – in Ireland at any rate – security were at stake. If the political logic was in the end the same as for the colonies, domestic anxieties greatly prolonged resolution. Alien establishment/concurrent endowment could survive only where there was oligarchic or wholly undemocratic control: significantly, it was the Government of India Act 1935 and its concern with conceding greater local political autonomy in the sub-continent that abolished its main manifestations in India.

Both disestablishments assumed that they would be accompanied with measures of disendowment. On the whole, it could be maintained that the disendowment in Ireland was in principle at least less punitive than that in Wales, though there it is also true that each successive Welsh Bill was less severe than the last. Finally, neither disestablishment could necessarily function as a model for disestablishment in England. Apart from the fact that attitudes and circumstances have moved on greatly from the ancient controversies, dealing with peripheries is quite distinct from tackling the core. In that case, forms of disestablishment which severed links with the Crown would require revisiting not only state formularies but also the whole constitutional settlement of the late seventeenth and early eighteenth centuries.

'Forms of disestablishment' is used advisedly. It is clear that the Welsh disestablishment did not obliterate all that went before. Significant 'civic' functions were retained, some by law and some by perpetuated custom. Even in Ireland where the Anglican Church of Ireland has only a small presence, the Queen in 2008 nonetheless went to distribute Maundy money, and she did it – however symbolically ecumenical the service – in the Anglican cathedral at Armagh. Like the politics in Lampedusa's *The Leopard*, things sometimes have to change so that they can stay the same.

9
Church/State Relations in Scandinavia

Frank Cranmer

Lutheranism and the 'folk-church'

At the Reformation, the Scandinavian churches were restructured in accordance with Lutheran principles; however, though they all subscribed to Luther's theology the resulting institutions were by no means identical. Sweden, for example, made a point of preserving the historic 'apostolic succession' of bishops while Denmark decisively rejected it. Almost inevitably, the paths of the Nordic churches have diverged since then to some degree; but what they have in common apart from Lutheran theology is that all began as state churches established by law and all identify strongly with the people of the country that they serve: the 'folk-church' concept.

For Luther, the conduct of secular affairs was to be reserved to the civil power while the government of the Church was to be conducted by the superintendents and clergy (Höpfl 1991: 28).[1] However, Luther had no strong desire to supplant the traditional ecclesiastical hierarchy with the kind of conciliar system of governance espoused by the followers of Calvin. Similarly, though no great admirer of the nobility, he was prepared to concede a place in the system for the Christian prince, always provided that the prince did not act capriciously. Superintendents were to rule the Church unfettered but they, in their turn, were to be subjects of the secular authority (Höpfl 1991: 32).

Bernt Ofestad has suggested that, given the troubled times he lived in, Luther regarded the role of the secular arm in relation to the Church as no more than a temporary expedient (Ofestad 1996: 23, though see also Fergusson 2004: 37–9). But once one has conceded that the Church, though independent in spiritual matters, is subordinate to the secular authorities in temporal ones, it is a fairly short step to conceding the interest of those secular authorities in such matters as senior Church appointments, or even acknowledging that, as protector of the Church's independence, they should have some say in the polity of the Church whose independence they are to guarantee. Therefore, though Lutheran ecclesiology provided a degree of theological justification for the particular form of the Scandinavian Reformation, it also rested to a considerable degree on *Realpolitik*.

In Denmark–Norway–Iceland, the Reformation began with a decree by Christian III on his accession to the Danish throne in 1538; and the process of reformation in Iceland was not completed until the execution of the last Roman Catholic bishop, Jón Arason of Hólar, and his sons in 1550 (Fell 1999: 90, 97). Similarly, though the Swedish Reformation had been begun by Gustavus Vasa, a Roman Catholic restoration was only narrowly averted on the death in 1592 of Johan III, who had allowed his son Sigismund to be brought up as a Roman Catholic and who in 1577 had offended many clergy by introducing a new liturgy – *Liturgia Svecanae Ecclesiae Catholicae et Orthodoxae Conformis*, commonly called the *Red Book* – which many thought romanising. Sigismund's uncle, Duke Karl Gustafsson Vasa, summoned a synod at Uppsala in 1593 which condemned the new liturgy, elected as archbishop a militant Lutheran, and adopted the *Augsburg Confession*. Karl became Regent in 1599 and succeeded Sigismund as Karl IX in 1604. Under the Act of Succession 1604 the Crown was secured to the heirs of Karl IX and the Reformation settlement firmly established (Derry 1979: 99–101).

The idea of ministering to the people at large, rather than to a series of gathered congregations, is by no means unique to Scandinavia. The Church of England, the Church of Scotland and the Church in Wales all see their mission in that way and, in the case of the Church of Scotland, Article III of the *Articles Declaratory* annexed to the Church of Scotland Act 1921 speaks of the 'distinctive call and duty to bring the ordinances of religion to the people in every parish of Scotland through a territorial ministry'. But the theology of the folk-church is probably more developed in Scandinavia than in Britain, given that the vast majority of Scandinavians still regard themselves as members of their national churches even if they hardly ever attend a service. The 'folk-church' concept has been described as 'the Scandinavian speciality in the field of church characteristics' (Myrhe-Nielsen 1990: 85: see also Aurelius 1998) and it is basic to the Nordic churches' self-image.

In Denmark, for example, the Church is often referred to as *Den Danske Folkekirke*: two possible translations might be 'The Church of the Danish People' or 'The Danish National Church', while the Church of Sweden even goes so far as to declare that its members 'are under no obligation to attend church on a regular basis or to be of a strong faith. Membership is an expression of a desire for fellowship with the Church' (Church of Sweden 2007).

So when, for example, in the early part of the twentieth century the inclusivist approach of the leaders of the Church of Sweden was attacked by its evangelical wing, who wanted gathered congregations united by personal conversion instead of territorial, inclusive parishes (Hope 1995: 584), territoriality was stoutly defended by the bishops. Perhaps the most telling response was by Bishop Einar Billing of Västerås, who argued that territorial ministry demonstrated in a practical way that the services of the Church were available to everyone and bore witness to the fact that every person lives within the borders of the grace of God (Billing 1930, quoted in Wingren 1969: 85; see also Gustafsson 1990: 7 and Toy 1998: 19). It was because of this desire to include everyone that for almost fifty years the Church of Sweden's test of membership was *citizenship and inheritance* rather than baptism; if either of its parents was a member of the Church then a child automatically became a member in its turn, whether baptized or not (Ahrén 1960: 32).

The folk-church concept remains very strong in all the Scandinavian countries, irrespective of the legal status of the Church in question. In 2001 a black Muslim teenager, Benjamin Hermansen, was stabbed to death in an Oslo suburb in what was thought to be the first racially motivated murder in Norway. Because the local mosque was not big enough to accommodate everyone expected to attend his funeral, it was decided to hold it in the parish church – and it was then decided that the service should be conducted by the Bishop of Oslo rather than by the local imam. Jan-Olav Henriksen, of the Oslo Free Theological Faculty, explained that the decision was in accordance with the self-understanding of the Church of Norway as

> a church that is there for all people living in Norway. Given that this is the organizing point of view, the cultural function of the church cannot be restricted to that of an organization only for those who happen to believe in God the Christian way. The bishop is the bishop for all, and the church is the place for everyone. (Henriksen 2001, quoted in Cranmer 2002: 174)

Similarly, when in 1994 the Baltic ferry *Estonia* sank with the loss of some 900 lives, the Swedish people went to their churches to light candles and to mourn privately in the anticipation that the Church of Sweden would articulate – vicariously – the meaning of the tragedy on their behalf. The only obvious English parallel to this is the series of events that unfolded after the death of Princess Diana (Davie, G. 2002a). Canon John Toy, a long-standing Anglican observer of the Scandinavian scene, concludes that the Church of England has never held the dominant position in England that the Scandinavian churches retain even in today's heavily secularized society, so that 'the connection between people and church has never had here the ideological basis which makes it so strong over there' (Toy 1998: 21–2). That seems to be fair comment. It may be that one of the reasons for this is historical: though the Scandinavian state churches and the Church of England operated within fairly similar legal and constitutional frameworks after the Reformation, toleration both of Dissent and of Roman Catholicism came much earlier to England than to Scandinavia and it was toleration that tended to relieve pressure on the Church of England to be inclusive. But the inclusiveness of the Scandinavian churches may also be, at least in part, the result of a conscious desire on their part to emphasize community rather than theological conformity. To take Norway as an example, Henriksen suggests that the Church is anxious to minimize conflicts within society and be seen as 'the common voice' and, in consequence, upholds 'a rather privatized mode of ... religiosity' (Henriksen 2001: 8). He concludes that the Scandinavian churches as a whole have been able to survive in a post-modern, largely secularized society because they continue to provide 'resources of morality, history and cultural identity etc. that is recognized by most members of society as relevant for their own shaping of identity, *irrespective of their personal faith*' (Henriksen 2001: 18 – emphasis added).

The individual churches

Because of their common Lutheran heritage, the national churches of Scandinavia still have a strong family resemblance. But in spite of the unifying factors of the Lutheran tradition and the folk-church concept, the church/state relationship in Scandinavia has developed differently in each country, with the result that no two churches are exactly alike, while the outliers – Denmark and Sweden – are no longer very similar at all, either in terms of governance or in their theological emphases. The Church of Sweden (or at least a significant part of it) has tended towards the Catholic, sacramental wing of Lutheranism, while the Church of Denmark (the only Scandinavian Church that decided not to sign up to the Porvoo Agreement with the Anglican churches of Europe) has been inclined to a more overtly Evangelical stance.

Denmark

The Reformation in Denmark was probably the most radical in Scandinavia: the bishops were deposed and the link with the historic episcopate was intentionally and decisively broken. In 1537 King Christian III secured the services of Luther's colleague Johann Bugenhagen to help in the continued reform of the Church; and though, traditionally, coronations had been performed by the Archbishop of Lund (Skåne then being part of Denmark rather than a province of Sweden), Bugenhagen crowned the king and queen and later ordained seven clergy as superintendents to replace the deposed bishops.

The English version of the Danish Constitution published by the Danish Parliament (*Folketinget*) defines the position of the Church as follows: '[T]he Evangelical Lutheran Church shall be the Established Church of Denmark, and, as such, it shall be supported by the State' (Part I s. 4). In addition, Part VII s. 66 declares that '[t]he constitution of the Established Church shall be laid down by Statute'. Part VII also provides for public regulation of other religious organizations: 'Rules for religious bodies dissenting from the Established Church shall be laid down by Statute' (Part VII s. 69).[2]

Paradoxically, some argue that with the abolition of absolutism in 1848 the Church of Denmark *ceased* to be 'established':

> In a legal sense, the state has no religion; hence it is not stipulated that either the minister for the church, the members of Parliament or any other citizen *must* be members of the people's church. State and church have been separated; civil and political rights apply regardless of whether one belongs to the people's church, some other community of faith, or prefers to live with no association with any faith whatsoever. (Lausten 2002: 229–30)

Moreover, the official English text of the Constitution Act is itself slightly misleading, since it renders *Den Danske Folkekirke* as 'the Established Church of Denmark'.

It is undoubtedly true that the modern Church of Denmark has no privileged position in terms of particular religious freedoms and civil rights; but in terms of its own governance it is possibly the last quasi-Erastian church in Western Europe. In spite of the declaration in section

66 of the Constitution, the Church still has no national system of synodical government, the Minister for Ecclesiastical Affairs is its supreme
administrative authority, its canons are promulgated by the *Folketing* and
its regulations are part of public law (Dübeck 2005: 60) – though there
is a very strong convention that church legislation will only be enacted
if there is broad cross-party agreement about its content (Lausten 2002:
282). The responsible minister in 2008, Birthe Rønn Hornbech, held
the Ecclesiastical Affairs portfolio with that of Refugee, Immigration and
Integration Affairs.

The Church's most important source of income is the church tax,
payable *only* by members of the National Church and accounting for
about three-quarters of the Church's budget (Church of Denmark 2008) –
though members of other churches can claim an income-tax rebate on
their contributions to their own denominations (Danish Ministry of
Ecclesiastical Affairs 2006). In addition, the government makes grants
directly to the Church, which in 1997 accounted for some 12 per cent
of the Church's total operating costs (Sørenson 1997). Possibly because
there was no ecclesiastical counterweight to balance the views of secular
politicians, legislation to permit the ordination of women in the National
Church was enacted in 1947 and the first ordinations took place in the
following year – though the legislation did provide a 'conscience clause'
for those bishops who were opposed to the ordination of women. In comparison to the rest of Scandinavia this was very early; the first women
were ordained in Sweden in 1960 and in Finland in 1988.[3] Similarly, the
Danish service book of 1995, *Den danske Salmebog*, was *autoriset ved kgl.
resolution af 12 juni 1992*: 'authorized by Royal decree'; in contrast, the
Church of Sweden was given autonomy over matters of doctrine and
worship in 1983 and its *Psalmboken* 1986 bore the colophon *antagen ...
års kyrkomöte*: 'approved ... by a Church Assembly'.

Even though there is no national synod, since 1903 each parish has
had an elected council which has considerable influence in the choice
of a new incumbent. The final appointment is made by the Crown on
the recommendation of the minister, but where the nomination of the
parish council is unanimous, the candidate *must* be appointed. If, however, the nomination is not unanimous, the minister is free to present
any of the candidates for appointment. That was the system described by
W. Westergard Madsen over forty years ago (Madsen 1964: 92) and
nothing appears to have changed since then.

Bishops and deans are appointed by the Crown in accordance with the
recommendation of the minister; but a new bishop is appointed only
after an election in which all clergy and parish council members of the

diocese can nominate candidates and vote – and a candidate receiving more than 50 per cent of the votes will be appointed automatically. The Ministry of Ecclesiastical Affairs also approves the construction of churches and functions as a court of appeal from decisions of diocesan or other authorities (Danish Ministry of Foreign Affairs 2008). As well as their purely ecclesiastical functions, the Church of Denmark's parish clergy also act as civil registrars. To gain official recognition to maintain legal registers and issue legally valid certificates of marriage and baptism for their own communities, other religious groups must either be 'recognized' by Royal Decree or 'approved' under the Marriage Act 1969. The Ministry of Ecclesiastical Affairs is the competent authority for approval; and it must also approve the laying out of cemeteries for members of faith-communities other than the Church of Denmark.

Before 1969 only a limited number of other faith-communities had been given official recognition; and even after the passing of the Marriage Act the minister would refer any application for approval to the Bishop of Copenhagen for an opinion as to whether or not the group applying for recognition was 'genuine' (Lodberg 2000: 49). That practice was discontinued in 1998 and there are currently over a hundred religious organizations that have either been recognized by Royal Decree or 'approved'. By 'approving' religions under the Marriage Act, the government allows individually named clerics to conduct officially recognized marriage ceremonies and thereby legally 'approves' the religion. In addition, where a church is recognized by Royal Decree, its clergy may name and baptize children with legal effect, keep church registers, and transcribe certificates on the basis of such registers (United States Department of State 2007).

The Faroes and Greenland

Until recently, the Church of Denmark had 12 dioceses: 10 in Denmark itself and 1 each for the Faroes (established in 1990) and for Greenland (established in 1993). Neither of the extra-territorial dioceses was subject to domestic regulation.

From the re-establishment of the Faroese Parliament (*Løgtinget*) in 1848 until its reorganization in 1923 the dean (who was then the highest ecclesiastical authority in the islands, there being no separate diocese) was a member ex officio. *Løgtinget* still begins its annual session on 29 July, St Olaf's Day (*Ólavsøka*), with a service in Tórshavn Cathedral followed by a procession to the Parliament House for the St Olaf's Address given by the Prime Minister – the Faroese equivalent of the Queen's Speech.

When the Diocese of the Faroes was established in 1990, legislative authority for church affairs was devolved to *Løgtinget* and administrative responsibility to the Faroese Minister of Education and Culture. However, ultimate responsibility for the diocese was finally handed over to the Faroese Government under the terms of the 'Takeover Act' of 2005 – the schedule to which provides for the negotiated transfer of responsibility for a range of domestic matters including the church affairs – and the diocese became completely independent of the Church of Denmark on St Olaf's Day 2007.

Greenland was granted home rule on 1 May 1979. The legislative authority for the Diocese of Greenland is the Greenlandic Parliament (*Landstinget*) which in October 1993 introduced considerable changes in the Church's organizational structure. The ecclesiastical functions remain with the Bishop, who is responsible for the overall supervision of the three regional deans, the parish clergy and catechists, while the administration of ecclesiastical affairs has been integrated into the Greenlandic Government's Directorate of Culture, Education and the Church, which also provides financial support for the diocese.

The governance of the Church

Perhaps surprisingly, the current status of the Church of Denmark does not appear to be a matter of great concern to many of its members. It had always been the intention of those who framed the Danish Constitution that a legal framework should be established for the Church that would free it from the state. However, it has never proved possible to reach agreement about a mechanism under which the Church could be given autonomy; and even though the Social Democrats have for many years wished, at least in principle, to see separation between Church and state, there seems to be no great political enthusiasm for a change.

The result of this, suggests Martin Schwarz Lausten, is something of a vacuum; quite apart from the question of church legislation, even on ethical issues there is no single individual, organization or movement that is able to speak on behalf of the Church as a whole (Lausten 2002: 283). Peter Lodberg notes that Danish society is becoming more pluralistic and bemoans the fact that this has not been reflected in any loosening of the ties between Church and state:

> The Established Church is still dependent on the State and the Minister for Ecclesiastical Affairs. All important decisions on the structures and finances of the Established Church are taken by the Minister for

Ecclesiastical Affairs and the relevant departmental civil servants in Copenhagen. (Lodberg 2000)

The constitutional status of the Church continues to be a matter of debate. The previous Minister of Ecclesiastical Affairs, Bertel Haarder, defended the status quo on the grounds that, in effect, it guarantees theological pluralism:

> the church is a free battlefield on which you cannot use anything else than spiritual weapons against your opponents. It is just because the politicians have retained the power that the parties to the dispute have not driven each other out of the Church. (*Church News from Denmark* February 2006: 1/6)

At the same time, there evidently remains some concern about the degree to which politicians can interfere in matters that have important theological and ecclesiological consequences. In 2007 Haarder sparked a major row with his proposal for new regulations on baptism, the original version of which declared that every child and adult had the right to baptism and the resident parish minister had a 'duty' to baptize. This provoked widespread protest; and a large majority of the 2000 clergy in the Pastors' Union sent a strongly worded response to the Minister in which they stated that an absolute duty to baptize without regard to any education in the Christian faith threatened the character of the Church as a faith-community (*Church News from Denmark* April 2007: 2/6). After further consideration, Haarder withdrew the word 'duty' and issued a revised version in which it is 'incumbent upon' pastors to baptize on request (*Church News from Denmark* June 2007: 3/6).

The status quo still has powerful support from no less a person than Queen Margrethe herself. It is reported that she told her biographer that she was afraid that disestablishment would only serve to marginalize religious belief:

> I am not fond of the free congregations that are so fine and feel they are the genuine Christians ... What about all of us? Where do we belong? There is one entrance, baptism, and that is enough. I am afraid that if you separate church and state then we will for real get a de-Christianization of the country. (*Church News from Denmark* June 2005: 3/6)

The qualms of academic commentators apart, there seem to be few signs of any mass movement for democratization. After the general election in November 2007 the Centre-Right Government put forward proposals to limit the tenure of bishops and to replace the direct public subvention to pastors' salaries with a block grant to the Church as a whole – which would then be able to spend the money as it wished but which would also have to live within its means (*Church News from Denmark* December 2007: 6/6). The proposal of limited tenure for bishops sparked off an argument that is as yet unresolved – but no-one seems to be suggesting that the Church should take control of its own affairs.

Finland

Section 76 (The Church Act) of the Constitution that came into force on 1 March 2000 reads as follows:

(1) Provisions on the organization and administration of the Evangelical Lutheran Church are laid down in the Church Act.

(2) The legislative procedure for enactment of the Church Act and the right to submit legislative proposals relating to the Church Act are governed by the specific provisions in that Code.

Finland has *two* Established Churches. As well as the Evangelical-Lutheran Church, there is also an autonomous Orthodox Church of about 60,000 members under the ultimate jurisdiction of the Oecumenical Patriarch. When Finland became independent after the Russian Revolution, administrative ties with the Patriarchate of Moscow were severed and the Orthodox Church of Finland had to be reorganized. Though small, it was formally recognized by the Decree on the Orthodox Church of Finland in 1918 and is currently regulated by the Act on the Orthodox Church of Finland 1969. The Church is governed by a General Assembly of bishops, priests and laity; but the Assembly's decisions (like those of the Synod of the Church of Finland) have legal effect only if approved by the state – possibly because the Orthodox Church is a beneficiary of the church tax. Until 2000, the Orthodox bishops, like the bishops of the Church of Finland, were appointed by the President; the right of appointment was surrendered under Ordinance 880 of 2000, amending s. 153 of the Ordinance on the Orthodox Church (Heikkilä, Knuutil and Scheinin 2005: 530).

As to the Evangelical-Lutheran Church, in 1972 a parliamentary committee was established to re-examine the relationship between Church and state. Its report in 1977 recommended an increase in the Church's internal autonomy and a broadening of the areas of separate responsibility. The tempo of reform slowed during the 1980s, during which both the Ministry of Education and the Church considered the parliamentary committee's findings. This eventually led in 1994 to the division of the material covered by the Church Act 1869 into three sections: the new Church Law, the Church Order and the Church Election Order (Heino, Salonen and Rusame 1997). The result was that the majority of matters covered by the old Church Law became entirely the Church's internal business, so that regulations concerning the Church's operations and internal affairs would henceforth be determined directly by the Synod (Seppo 2002: 155). Crucially, the provision of the Church Act 1869 that 'final authority over the Church throughout the country is to rest with the national Government' was repealed.

The supreme legislative authority for the Church of Finland remains the Finnish Parliament (*Eduskunta*) but it exercises its authority in a rather unusual form. Unlike the Westminster Parliament, the *Eduskunta* has no right to initiate church legislation: under the Church Act 1869, that power rests exclusively with the Synod. Although Parliament must ultimately ratify church laws, it has no right to amend the proposals it receives from the Synod; they must either be accepted in their original form or rejected altogether. However, since changes to church law must be presented to Parliament by the government, it is always possible for ministers to prevent a proposal of synod from coming before Parliament in the first place. This has happened, though extremely rarely; but Parliament has never rejected a change in church law proposed by the Synod (Seppo 2002).[4] An example of the kind of legislation approved by the *Eduskunta* is the Act on Amending the Church Act 2001: Chapter 6.1 provides that offices within the Church may only be held by Evangelical-Lutherans, while Chapter 6.2 provides for dispensation in the case of clergy of churches with which the Church Assembly has approved reciprocal arrangements for recognition of ministry (Seppo 2002: 155).

There are nine dioceses; eight are territorial, while the ninth – Porvoo (Borgå in Swedish) – is the extra-territorial diocese for the Swedish-speaking parishes, most of which are situated around the coastline and in the Åland Islands. Prior to 1994, bishops were appointed by the President of the Republic from among the top three candidates in a diocesan election. The Church then moved to a system where the result of the election was conclusive and could, if necessary, go to a second round (Mäkeläinen 2001). In 1999, the Synod decided on further reforms to the procedure. Candidates are now nominated by electors' associations which can be set up by a minimum of ten electors. The President of the

Republic no longer appoints the bishop: under the new procedure a letter of appointment is presented by the diocesan chapter to the candidate who has obtained more than half the votes in the election (Salonen, Kääriänen and Niemelä 2001: 25).

For historical reasons, the diocesan chapters (each of which consist of the bishop, the cathedral dean, two clergy assessors and a legally-trained assessor) were state-funded offices for 450 years. The maintenance of the chapters was transferred entirely to the Church at the beginning of 1997 and their employees ceased to be state officials (Salonen, Kääriänen and Niemelä 2001: 25).

Under the 1994 settlement the church tax remains. All citizens belonging to either of the two State Churches pay it as part of their income tax and the Churches reimburse the state for the cost of collection. Those who do not want to pay the tax must resign from the relevant church. In addition, the Church of Finland receives part of the corporate tax that is levied on private companies and public communities: in 2005 the parishes' share of the corporate tax was 1.94 per cent (Hietakangas: 2005) Because church finances continue to be the subject of parliamentary legislation rather than of church regulation, in the case of the Evangelical-Lutheran Church it is the *Eduskunta*, rather than the synod, that has the decisive voice (Salonen, Kääriänen and Niemelä 2001: 25).

The legal framework for faith-communities other than the Church of Finland and the Orthodox Church is now the Freedom of Religion Act 2003. Chapter 1 §2 of the Act states that ' "religious community" refers to the Evangelical Lutheran and Orthodox Churches and to a religious community registered in the manner laid down in chapter 2', while chapter 2 §7 defines the purpose of a religious community as 'to organize and support the individual, community and public activity relating to the professing and practising of religion which is based on confession of faith, scriptures regarded as holy, or other specified, established grounds of activity regarded as sacred'. Under Chapter 2 §8 of the Act, any group of 20 persons or more aged 18 or over may acquire legal personality by registering as a religious community with the National Board of Patents and Registration, while 2 §9 sets out a series of obligatory heads for the by-laws of any group applying for registration. At the same time, the centuries-old custom whereby the national government used to decree public days of prayer was discontinued.

The 2003 Act was followed by the Burial Act 2004, which obliges the parishes of the Church of Finland to maintain public cemeteries and to establish non-denominational burial grounds if needed. Burial charges are to be equal for everyone, whether a member of the Church or not. The

Burial Act has subsequently been the subject of a degree of controversy. Supporters of the Act contend that the obligations laid on the Church are reasonable, since the Act also requires the government to contribute to the costs of cemetery maintenance; opponents, however, argue that members of the Church pay twice over: once through general taxation and again through the church tax (Seppo 2002).

Commenting on the recent changes, Markku Heikkilä and Jyri Knuutil feel that the Freedom of Religion Act is likely to have considerable influence on future developments in church/state relations:

> It seems inevitable that the bond between state and church will become progressively looser. This development will not necessarily be obvious. Old traditions will probably remain. Thus, the President of Finland and other representatives of government will continue to take part in the hour of devotion on Finnish Independence Day ... However, the guidelines ... will not any more [be set] by the state but [by] the Finnish Ecumenical Council. (Heikkilä, Knuutil and Scheinin 2005: 535–6)

Iceland

Chapter VI of the Icelandic Constitution begins as follows:

> The Evangelical Lutheran Church shall be the State Church in Iceland and, as such, it shall be supported and protected by the State. (Article 62)

> All persons have the right to form religious associations and to practice their religion in conformity with their individual convictions. Nothing may however be preached or practised which is prejudicial to good morals or public order. (Article 63)

Article 64 guarantees the freedom to exercise a religion or not, but includes an interesting provision about financial support for religious organizations. Individuals are free to direct their church tax payments to any of the religious groups officially registered and recognized by the state, but '[a] person who is not a member of any religious association shall pay to the University of Iceland the dues that he would have had to pay to such an association if he had been a member'.

So the combined church and cemetery tax (in 2003 just over 10,000 kronor or about £80) is payable in one form or another by all taxpayers: not even atheists escape.

Though the Church holds an election when there is an episcopal vacancy, it is the President of Iceland who signs the successful candidate into office.[5] In addition, the clergy are paid directly by the Government and are regarded as public servants under the aegis of the Ministry of Justice and Ecclesiastical Affairs; however, in March 2007 the Parliament (*Alþingi*) amended the law to transfer their appointment from the minister to the bishop and, at the same time, to hand over ownership of parsonage-houses and associated lands to the Church.

Synodical government, of a kind, began in Iceland in 1639 with the establishment of a diocesan synod for the Diocese of Skálholt, to be held annually at Thingvellir in conjunction with the open-air meeting of the mediaeval Parliament (Fell 1999: 323). When the Diocese of Skálholt was merged with the Diocese of Hólar to form the present single See of Iceland the Synod became an annual gathering of all the Church's clergy.[6]

The first modern synod was the Church Council established by Parliament in 1931; it consisted of the bishop, two theologians and two representatives chosen by district meetings. Its remit was to make recommendations to the Bishop of Iceland on the internal affairs of the Church which became binding if approved by the bishop. It continued in existence until 1957, when it was superseded by the Church Assembly (*kirkjuþing*), which meets annually and currently consists of 29 elected delegates: 12 clergy and 17 laypeople, with a lay president (Fell 1999: 323).

Under new legislation that came into force on 1 January 1998, the Church's relationship with the government was modified so that most of the legislation that would previously have been enacted by Parliament is now the province of the annual Church Assembly. The highest executive authority is the Church Council (*kirkjurád*) of two clergy and two laymen elected by the Church Assembly, together with the Bishop of Iceland as chairman (Sigurbjörnsson 2000). The council is responsible for day-to-day decision-making over a wide range of matters referred to it by the Church Assembly, the bishop himself, Parliament and the government. Together with the bishop it prepares the meetings of the Church Assembly and follows up its resolutions. It may also take the initiative in proposing legislation for the Church and is consulted by the government on its own proposals for legislation. Finally, it prepares the Church's budget proposals (Hugason 1990: 54–5).

In its *International Religious Freedom Report* for 2006 the State Department had previously noted that in October 2004 the Social Democratic Alliance Party had tabled a motion in Parliament on constitutional amendments that had called, inter alia, for consideration of the separation of Church and state, while in October 2003 the Liberal Party had presented a Bill to disestablish the Church. According to the *Report* for 2007, however, the two initiatives had lapsed and had not been revived. Moreover, the State Department concluded that, although surveys suggest that a majority of Icelanders would favour separation, it

> most probably would not support the change if it meant closing Lutheran churches because of lack of funding. According to the State Church Bishop's Office, nine out of ten children are baptised in their first year, more than 90 per cent of adolescents are confirmed, 75 per cent are married in the church, and 99 per cent are buried with church ceremonies. Although few citizens regularly attend services, they see the Lutheran religion as part of their culture and view the closing of a church as losing a part of their heritage.

Norway

The Constitution of 1814, which marked the country's brief period of independence in the transition from Danish to Swedish rule, stated that the Evangelical-Lutheran faith should be the religion of the Kingdom of Norway; and establishment remains embedded in the Norwegian Constitution. In two rather incompatible provisions, Article 2 states that:

> The Evangelical-Lutheran Confession remains the official religion of the state. Inhabitants belonging to the Evangelical-Lutheran faith should raise their children in the same. (Art. 2.1)

> All inhabitants should enjoy the right to free exercise of religion. (Art. 2.2)[7]

Article 4 further states that the king is the head of the Church of Norway, and Article 12 requires that at least half of the government shall be members of the Church. Under Article 27, it is those members of the government who are responsible for Church matters; and the king (in practice, those ministers who are members of the Church) is required by Article 16 to provide statutes governing liturgy and to ensure that the teaching of the Church is in accordance with Lutheran confessional standards (Plesner 2001: 318). The tension over religious education remains; in June 2007 the European Court of Human Rights held that the refusal to allow humanists to withdraw their children from compulsory classes in 'Christianity, Religion and Philosophy' contravened their rights under Article 2 of the First Protocol to the Convention.[8]

During the early part of its history the clergy of the Church of Norway were civil servants; however, the nineteenth and twentieth centuries saw a degree of democratization of the Church; parish councils were established in 1920, diocesan councils in 1933, the National Council in 1969, diocesan synods in 1984 and, finally, the General Synod in 1984 (Church of Norway n.d.).

In spite of the provisions of the Constitution, the Church of Norway was, in effect, disestablished from 1942 until the end of German occupation. Refusing to give legitimacy to the Quisling regime, all the bishops declared their dioceses disestablished and issued the celebrated pastoral letter *Kirkens Grunn* ('The Foundation of the Church') in which they stated that the ministry and worship of the Church could never be a matter for the state and that the only legitimate relationship between Church and state was a concordat. As a result of their opposition to the regime, the bishops spent the rest of the war in prison; and although the Church was re-established after the war, the sentiments expressed in *Kirkens Grunn* continued to have considerable resonance – even though some thought that its ecclesiology was rather un-Lutheran because it characterized the Church as a sacramental fellowship distinct from the state.

In 1981 the Norwegian Parliament (*Stortinget*) voted to retain the state Church with the king as its constitutional head but agreed to grant it more autonomy and established the General Synod, which met for the first time in 1984; a Church of Norway Doctrinal Commission was established in 1987 (Church of Norway n.d.). Legislation concerning the Church still has to go through *Stortinget* and responsibility within government rests with the Minister for Culture and Church Affairs; but under the Church Act 1996 the authority to determine the content of the liturgy and the right to regulate the use of church buildings have been delegated to the General Synod (Plesner 2001: 318). Article 2 of that Act also gave legal personality to the parishes – but financing of activities of the local church, maintaining church buildings and cemeteries and paying those church staff not paid by the state all remain the responsibility of the secular municipal authorities (Plesner 2001: 318–19). Since 1989 parish pastors, who had been appointed by the king since 1660, have once again been appointed by diocesan councils; as in England, however, bishops and deans are still appointed by the Crown (Church of Norway n.d.; Plesner 2002: 265).

The General Synod, which meets once a year, has 85 members: the 80 members of the eleven diocesan councils (including all the bishops) and 5 members representing clergy, the lay employees and laity. The three theological faculties each nominate a non-voting representative. Its main executive is the 15-member National Council, which meets four times a year; but it also has a separate executive on ecumenical and international matters: the 18-member Council on Ecumenical and International Relations, which meets at least twice a year and which replaced the previous Council on Foreign Relations that had been established by the bishops in 1971 (Church of Norway n.d.).

Where Norway differs from the prevailing custom in Scandinavia is over finance. Instead of receiving the proceeds of a separate church tax, the Church is directly funded, partly by the state and partly by the municipalities. This right to state support was extended to non-established churches and other faith-communities by the Act on Faith Communities 1969 (Plesner 2001: 320–1); they receive equivalent per capita funding to that of the Church of Norway (Aarflot 2004: 168).

In March 2002 a commission of the National Council of the Church brought forward a series of recommendations on church/state relations. Its report, *Same Church – New Relations* (*Samme kirke – ny ordning*) recommended changing the constitutional provisions relating to the Church by elevating Article 2.2 to prime position and replacing the rest with a provision stating the responsibility of the state to support faith and 'life-stance' communities (Plesner 2002: 263, 266).[9] The commission also wanted the government to relinquish the right to appoint bishops and deans.

Where the committee could *not* agree was over whether or not the Church of Norway should be given specific mention in an amended Constitution; the majority wanted a reference to the Church but the minority did not, while a sole dissentient wanted the status quo (Plesner 2002: 266). The report of the committee led to the government's establishing a multi-party commission under the chairmanship of Kåre Gjønnes, a former government minister and a Christian Democrat, to look at the issue of church/state relations; it was asked to report in 2005 (Plesner 2002: 263). Andreas Aarflot, until his retirement Bishop of Oslo and *Praeses*, noted while the commission was sitting that

> there has recently been a marked trend, both in church and political circles, to advocate disestablishment and seek new ways of cooperation between the state and all religious societies in an increasingly pluralistic world. It becomes increasingly clear that the commitment to international conventions on human rights and equality are at odds with the idea that any church appears as 'the official religion of the state'. (Aarflot 2004: 162)

The Gjønnes Commission reported on 31 January 2006. Eighteen of its 20 members wanted to abolish the system, while only 2 wanted to keep it. Fourteen members of the majority wanted to see church/state ties loosened rather than completely severed and recommended that the legal status of the Church of Norway should no longer be founded in the Constitution. The Commission therefore recommended that General Synod should assume the powers currently vested in the king and the cabinet, including the appointment of bishops and deans. However, a majority wanted to retain the present arrangement for clergy stipends, wages and the maintenance of church buildings (Østang 2006a).

At its annual meeting at Oyer in November 2006, General Synod voted to change the Church's relations with the state. Out of 85 delegates, 63 voted for a proposal that the constitution should be amended, that the Church should be founded on a new Act of *Stortinget*, and that the Synod should assume all the responsibilities currently exercised by the king and the government (Østang 2006b).

The most likely outcome, therefore, is that Norway will follow Sweden and that in due course the constitution will be amended and a Church of Norway Act placed on the statute-book – though Øivind Østang notes that local church councils are less enthusiastic about the proposed change than is the General Synod (Østang 2006b). But it will in any case be a long process, since Article 112 of the constitution requires a two-thirds majority for constitutional amendments; moreover, Article 112 also provides that any proposal for amendment must be brought forward before a general election and can only be enacted after the election by the new *Storting* – the intention being that the proposal can be taken into consideration in voting for those who are to implement it (Plesner 2002: 270). The last general election (which was won by the Labour Party) was held in September 2005 and the next is due in September 2009 – which means that the process of implementing the Gjønnes Commission's proposals is likely to take several years. The next step is a consultation process by the Ministry of Culture and Church Affairs that is likely to result in a report to *Stortinget* late in 2008 (Østang 2006b).

Sweden

Until the middle of the nineteenth century the Swedish Parliament (*Riksdagen*) consisted of three Houses: Nobility, Clergy and People. The General Synod (*kyrkomötet*) was established in 1863 to fill the vacuum in respect of matters affecting the Church that was created by the abolition of the House of Clergy of the unreformed *Riksdag*; however, the Church was very much part of the apparatus of the state.

In the early 1990s I spent a week at the Parliament in Stockholm and on my host's desk I found a copy of the Swedish *Civil Service List*. Listed in it were all the bishops and cathedral deans and, to my surprise, the rectors of every parish in Sweden. Prior to disestablishment, the Crown (presumably on the advice of the Minister for Church Affairs) appointed to every third vacancy in every parish, and a parish rector in Skåne once told me, tongue-in-cheek, that he was 'the King's man' because he had been appointed when it was the Crown's turn to nominate. In addition, until the early 1990s the parish rector was also registrar of the *civil* parish and was responsible for maintaining lists of residents. Since Swedes pay local tax on the basis of primary residence (presumably because vast numbers of them have little country cottages or chalets), in the event of any dispute the civil registrar decides the place of residence for local tax purposes. In the case of a company with more than one branch, however, this means that the civil parish registrar may decide, in effect, which *kommun* is going to collect rather a lot of tax. The impression was that the Swedish clergy were very happy to be relieved of this responsibility.

Prior to 1 January 2000, dignitaries were appointed, as in England, by the Crown on the advice of the government. When a bishopric was vacant an electoral college, consisting of the diocesan council and parish representatives, voted on the candidates and sent a list of three names to the government. (There was a more complicated system for a vacancy in the primatial see of Uppsala.) The government was not obliged to choose the first name on the list though, unlike the deliberations of an English vacancy-in-see committee, the votes of the electoral college were made public.

The legal status of the Church of Sweden changed radically at midnight on 31 December 1999, though it remains a major player within Swedish society (Gustafsson 2003; Cranmer 2000: 417). Prior to this there was a long series of consultations, culminating in two major pieces of legislation which are regarded as part of the 'fundamental law' of the state: the Religious Communities Act 1998 and Church of Sweden Act 1998 (Persenius 1999: 182–3).

The Church of Sweden Act and the resulting Church Ordinance that came into force on 1 January 2000 put clergy of the Church of Sweden on the same footing as clergy of other denominations. Since the passing of the Religious Communities Act, any religious organization which fulfils a few very basic criteria has been able to register as a religious community and acquire legal personality. The purpose of the change was to enable dissenting churches who wished to do so to formalize their position as *churches*; prior to the Act, the Roman Catholic and

Orthodox Churches had described themselves as 'foundations'. Registration is not compulsory; and those faith-communities that do not wish to register are free to continue as foundations. However, registration is a necessary prerequisite for any church that wants its membership dues collected through the tax system or wishes to solemnize marriages that are recognized in civil law (Friedner 2005: 545). All religious organizations, including the Church of Sweden, are now taxed as not-for-profit organizations (Persenius 1996: 125).

Section 3 of the Church of Sweden Act 1998 has given the Church full legal personality in its own right for the first time: 'The Church of Sweden may acquire rights and assume liabilities as well as plead a cause in court.' The Act sets out a skeleton structure for the new government of the Church, principally by defining it as a religious community with a legal personality, by providing for a parochial and diocesan structure, by establishing an ecumenical church fee, collected by the government, to replace the former church tax, and by making general provision about property and assets. The church fee continues to be compulsory for members of the Church of Sweden, while other churches are now able to have the fee collected from their members.

The new Church Ordinance that came into force on 1 January 2000 (replacing the Church Code 1992 and its associated legislation) put the flesh on the bones. It has five constituent parts: the Confession of Faith, Order of Services and the General Synod (*kyrkomötet*); working structures at the various levels; elections, parish boundaries, church registers and archives; finance and property; and staff, structures of authority and complaint procedures.

Does all this constitute disestablishment? Pointing to the persisting, salient place of the Church of Sweden in the country's constitution, the state's collection of the Church 'fee', and the continuing role of the monarch as the 'first member' of the Church, Paul Avis thinks not: 'Clearly, in English terms, the Church of Sweden is very far from having been disestablished' (Avis 2001: 20).

Lars Friedner would seem to agree, pointing out that 'there are several links between the Swedish State and the Church of Sweden', not least as the custodian of a significant part of Sweden's historic buildings (Friedner 2005: 542–3). Though in terms of constitutional law both the intention and the technical result of the legislation were to put the Church of Sweden on the same footing as other churches, perhaps its practical outcome has been a situation in which, as in Wales (Watkin 1990 passim), Sweden has retained some vestiges of establishment. And a comparison between Swedish and English establishment may in any case be flawed.

The Church of Sweden is still the church of the vast majority of Swedes in a way that is no longer paralleled by the Church of England; and it may be that its position as the 'default' church gives a particular flavour to church/state relations even under the new dispensation.

Conclusion: different but the same?

As noted above, the Scandinavian Lutheran churches have diverged somewhat since the Reformation and are likely to diverge even more widely in future. As we have seen, the Church of Sweden has been disestablished and the Church of Norway seems to be moving slowly in that same direction, while the relationship between the Church of Finland (and, indeed, the Finnish Orthodox Church) and the state may have been subtly changed by the passing of the Freedom of Religion Act 2003. The differences and similarities between the churches may be represented schematically as in Table 9.1.

Institutionally, therefore, no two churches are exactly the same – but they still retain a degree of shared experience and family resemblance, not just in their Lutheran history and theology but in other ways as well.

Perhaps their most striking common feature is the extremely high proportion of citizens in membership, even if their adherence may be largely nominal. But it is difficult to know what weight to place on that kind of semi-detached relationship and there is always a potential danger in the inclusivist approach: that, in the end, the Church may be seen just as another undifferentiated social service without any distinctive message. As Bishop Charles Gore rather tartly observed in the 1920s:

> [T]he sort of Christianity which claims to embrace the whole of society, which it costs nothing to profess and into which children are baptized practically as a matter of course, appears to be as audacious a departure from the method of Christ as can well be conceived. (Gore 1926: 968)

Bishop Andreas Aarflot expresses sentiments that are not dissimilar, even though couched in far more gentle terms:

> For many in the Church of Norway their feeling of belonging to a religious community offering its services and sympathy is more important than the contents or character of the goods that this fellowship delivers. Grace Davie has offered the observation that in Great Britain religious life is often characterized by 'believing without belonging'. In Norway one may well see the opposite position: 'belonging without

Table 9.1 Comparative characteristics of Scandinavian state churches

	Denmark	Finland	Iceland	Norway	Sweden
Membership (%)	85	85	82	83	83
Established?	Yes	Yes	Yes	Yes	No
Final legislative authority	Parliament *Folketinget* (all matters)	Parliament *Eduskunta* (confirmatory only)	Synod *Kirkjupingi* (all matters except constitutional issues)	Parliament *Stortinget* (except liturgy and use of buildings)	Synod *Kyrkomotet* (all matters)
National synod	No	Yes	Yes	Yes	Yes
Parish councils	Yes	Yes	Yes	Yes	Yes
Senior appointments	State confirmation	Church	State confirmation	State	Church
Finance	Church tax and direct government grant	Church tax and share of corporate tax	Church tax and government pays clergy salaries	Direct government and municipal grants	Church fee

believing' ... But this sense of belonging is often not related to the real evangelical and biblical basis of the activities of the Church. (Aarflot 2004: 170)

Aarflot's observations support both the analysis of Jan-Olav Henriksen quoted earlier and the statement by the Church of Sweden that membership is an expression of a desire for fellowship with the Church rather than evidence of faith. And if all this is true for Norway and Sweden, then it is probably true in some degree for the rest of Scandinavia as well.

The Scandinavian model of church/state relations has also rested on an implicit assumption that it is as much a part of citizenship to support the Church financially as to support the state. Moreover, the fact that clergy in some of the Nordic countries have had secular functions as well as pastoral ones has given a particular flavour to the church/state relationship. As noted above, prior to disestablishment the clergy of the Church of Sweden were included in the Swedish *Civil Service List* and until fairly recently acted as civil registrars. Clergy of the Church of Iceland are paid by the state and appear to have been regarded as civil servants for all practical purposes, while clergy of the Church of Norway were certainly civil servants in the eighteenth century. The situation of the clergy in the Church of Denmark is less clear since, though not employed by the government, they still act as civil registrars. To assert, as did the Methodist Faith and Order Committee, that 'Clergy in some European countries, particularly in Scandinavia, are civil servants with standard employment contracts paid at least partly from taxation' (Methodist Church 2004) is something of an oversimplification – but it is undoubtedly true that the idea of the clergy as part of the general state apparatus seems to be deeply embedded in the Scandinavian Lutheran model of governance.

Part III
Policy Analysis

So far this study has examined the background to, and present state of, establishment in the United Kingdom. To give that examination some depth of field, it has also looked at establishment in Scandinavia.

What now follows is an attempt in Chapter 10 to chart the state of religious belief in Great Britain and to explain its greatly changed character in the case of Christian belief and what might be called Christian *un*belief. The statistical data – which concentrate on religious observance – are not without controversy as to some of their detail though at least broadly accepted as an account of a considerable decline in active belief. Much more controversial is how to explain the statistical data. As a way of assessing the material, an attempt is made to offer the kind of conclusions that might be drawn by a current, anonymous statesman.

Chapter 11 moves on to look at how establishment, especially in England, is regarded. It shows that most of the interest in change comes from within the Church of England itself. There is, however, no agreement in the Church about whether and to what extent it should occur. It seems unlikely, however, that Parliament would seek to prevent the Church from achieving change if it were agreed within itself upon what it wanted.

10
The Condition of Modern Belief

It is impossible to discuss how the state should relate to religion without a secure understanding of the forms and significance of religious belief. This chapter looks accordingly at what the available data on religious observance suggest about current religious affiliations, examines the possible explanations for the changes the data expose, assesses the extent to which the changes may be irreversible, and, with particular reference to the established churches, weighs what the political implications of the data may be for approaching the structuring of church/state relations.

Having – or not having – a religious belief is an intensely personal matter. It is therefore inherently problematic to measure. Numerical accounts from individual religious bodies themselves suffer all the drawbacks of self-reporting. Just as Elizabeth I said she did not wish to make windows into men's souls, so she might have gone on to say that assessing what might be found there would be beyond the state's capacity to encompass. In such circumstances, it seems best to concentrate on actual behaviour both for its own sake and as arguably the best available proxy for actual belief. Similarly, measures of observance are to be preferred to measures of membership principally because churches do not follow mutually compatible criteria of enumeration. For example, the Church of England commonly uses baptism as the standard whereas others tend to use measures based on informed, adult choice as more appropriate. No system of church self-defined membership is, of course, capable of indicating actual behaviour, just as surveys have difficulty in pinpointing nuances of belief. Whereas surveys would often offer a reliable means of calibrating behaviour, they have proved unreliable in the case of religious conduct: 'The reason is that people exaggerate their attendance at religious services to a surprising degree' (Voas 2008: 0.3) – by a factor of

Table 10.1   Population of Great Britain by religion in 000s, Census April 2001

Religion	Total population	Non-Christian religious population	
	Numbers	Percentages	Percentages
Christian	42,079	71.8	
Muslim	1,591	2.8	51.6
Hindu	559	1.0	18.1
Sikh	336	0.6	11.0
Jewish	267	0.5	8.7
Buddhist	152	0.3	4.9
Other religion	179	0.3	5.8
All non-Christian religious population	3,084	5.4	100.0
All religions	45,163	76.8	
No religion	9,104	15.5	
Religion not stated	4,289	7.3	
All population	58,789	100.0	

Source: <www.statistics,gov.uk/cc1/nugget.asp?id=293>, accessed 29 April 2005 (Because of rounding, the percentages may not total 100 exactly.)

nearly two in a US instance. Accordingly, attendance has to remain the best available indicator of active membership.

Religious observance

Tables 10.1 and 10.2 from the 2001 Census have to be the starting point for discussion of the available statistics on religious affiliation. The differences between the tables are accounted for by the fact that in Scotland the census distinguished between Christian denominations while that for England and Wales did not.

Granted the differences between the detail of the questions, there was some dissatisfaction with the fact that the census in England and Wales did not seek to distinguish between types of Christianity or, as again in Scotland, between current religious attitudes and the religion of upbringing. The latter data showed, for example, that 7 per cent of Scottish respondents had moved from their religions of upbringing, and at a greater rate for the Church of Scotland than for Roman Catholics (Scottish Executive 2005: Table 1.2). An outcome that could be stated comparatively was that, whereas 77 per cent in England and Wales

Table 10.2   Current religion in Scotland, Census 2001

	Number (000s)	Percentage
Church of Scotland	2,146.3	42.40
Roman Catholic	803.7	15.88
Other Christian	344.6	6.81
Buddhist	6.8	0.13
Hindu	5.6	0.11
Jewish	6.4	0.13
Muslim	42.6	0.84
Sikh	6.6	0.13
Another religion	27.0	0.53
All religions	**3,389.6**	**66.96**
No religion	1,394.5	27.55
Not answered	278.1	5.49
All no religion/Not answered	**1,672.6**	**33.04**
Base	**5,062.0**	**100.00**

Source: Scottish Executive 2005: 6.

reported having a religion, the figure for Scotland (traditionally *more* observant than England) was 67 per cent, and the figure for those reporting no religion was correspondingly higher in Scotland than in England and Wales.

These latter outcomes were surprising and attracted particular comment, especially since the England and Wales figures seemed to be at variance with earlier studies such as the British Social Attitudes (BSA) survey, itself corroborated by other findings. The BSA survey showed Christian affiliation and no religion at 54 and 40 per cent respectively rather than the 72 and 15 per cent shown by the Census.

In their study of the figures, David Voas and Steve Bruce concluded that the Census outcome in England had to be interpreted as indicating anxiety about national identity. In Scotland, in contrast,

> One reason why fewer non-church going Scots may have felt impelled to assert their nominal Christian identity is that there are far fewer non-Christians in Scotland (less than one third of the proportion in England) and they are so concentrated as to be a significant part of the cultural landscape only in one part of Glasgow. (Voas and Bruce 2004: 26)

Moreover, it was likely that differences in the positioning of the religious questions in the English and Scottish census forms influenced responses. In England the question followed questions on ethnicity, whereas in Scotland the question preceded such questions and was likely, therefore, to have been less ' "contaminated" by the desire to make it clear that "we're white and not Muslim" ' (Voas and Bruce 2004: 27).

A review initiated by the Office of the Deputy Prime Minister appeared to show that respondents asked the kind of single question posed in England and Wales were likely in fact to record their religion of upbringing. The review of data concluded:

> Given the nature of the question as asked in England and Wales, the results are best understood as reflecting the broader cultural and religious background of those who responded, within which is nested an active core of membership and belief whose size varies with the particular religions. (Beckford, Gale, Owen, Peach and Weller 2006: 6)

The census data are therefore incomplete guides to actual religious observance even where, as in Scotland, they may be reasonable guides at least to religious affiliation. It is, however, the former – observance – rather than the latter – affiliation – which must be the better test for policy purposes.

Because the concern is with the future of establishment, what follows will concentrate on Christian observance. At the outset, it must be made clear that the available data relied upon are not only imperfect but also merely indicative: attendance figures measure solely those who actually go to church, and do not by themselves measure their beliefs and still less the beliefs of those who do not attend. Further, the extent to which people avail themselves of the ability to mark the rites of passage through life by calling on churches for baptisms, marriages and funerals is connected with larger cultural manifestations of identity and not necessarily religiosity.

It is possible, too, that the numbers themselves seen commonly within a dominant paradigm of secularization may conceal changes in the way in which religious feelings are being expressed: 'The dominance of secularization theory in the sociology of religion has often inhibited study of the nature, survival and transformation of religion in modern societies' (Woodhead, Hellas and Martin 2001: 3). At the same time, attendance and rites of passage data do indicate the extent of on-the-ground support for the churches as institutions, and it is primarily for assessing the

Table 10.3   Past and projected Sunday attendance for England 1979–2015

Year	Sunday attendance numbers	Decline in numbers	% of decline on previous attendance	% attending of England population
1979	5,441,000	N/A	N/A	11.7
1989	4,742,800	698,200	13	9.9
1998	3,714,700	1,028,100	21	7.5
2005	3,166,200	548,500	15	6.3
1979/2005	–	**2,274,800**	**42**	–
Projected 2015	2,474,200		55	(on 1979) 4.7

Source: Brierley 2006: 12.2.

prevalence of such support that the data are deployed in the argument that follows. Fundamentally, what is being assessed in this chapter is the *political* significance of modern religious phenomena.

Data on observance may be found in two principal sources: the unofficial but well-regarded censuses of church attendance conducted over a period of some years by Peter Brierley of Christian Research; and the records of people's behaviour in terms of the extent to which they have resorted to religious authorities to solemnize rites of passage such as childbirth, marriage and so on.

Table 10.3 shows overall decline in attendance both in absolute numbers and as a proportion of the population in England. The numbers are substantial: over a million left in the 1990s. In constrast, the rate of loss slowed from 1998 to 2005 – 'Pulling out of the nosedive', Brierley called it (Brierley 2006) – and some churches (especially charismatic and Pentecostal churches, for which generally see Martin [2002]) are growing as others decline. Notably, the Christian Research 2005 census recorded that 10 per cent of all churchgoers in England are now black and 83 per cent white. In London black churchgoers constitute 44 per cent of congregations with 14 per cent other non-white and only 42 per cent white.

Particularly significant are the changes in the ages of those attending. Between 1979 and 2005, the number of 15–19 year olds declined by 69 per cent, and those aged 20–9 by 61 per cent. In 2005, 29 per cent of all churchgoers were 65 or over as opposed to 16 per cent in that age group overall. Moreover, 12 per cent of all churchgoers were 75 and over. The effects of increasing ageing will be one of the principal factors in what at present appears to be a continuing decline in church attendance.

Table 10.4 Past and projected Sunday attendance of main English and Scottish Christian denominations 1990–2025

Year	Anglican	Roman Catholic	Presbyterian	Baptist	Methodist	All others	Total
1990	1,364,700	1,913,200	523,400	332,200	533,200	928,000	5,595,600
1995	1,218,700	1,661,100	462,300	327,600	456,200	891,400	5,017,300
2000	1,045,100	1,345,400	407,000	318,200	392,700	862,000	4,370,400
2005	945,900	1,145,800	318,000	297,800	306,400	912,400	3,826,300
% decline 1990–2005	31	40	39	10	43	2	32
% decline England only 1979–2005	48	55	N/A	12	53	N/A	42

Source: Brearley 2006: 12.2.

Projected

Year	Anglican	Roman Catholic	Presbyterian	Baptist	Methodist	All others	Total
2015	722,000	812,100	212,200	260,900	208,600	865,700	3,081,500
2025	528,300	503,500	112,000	225,100	108,800	788,400	2,266,100

'All others' includes movements in both directions, for example shrinking United Reform Church (190,000–69,900) and expanding Pentecostalists (228,000–287,600).

Source: Brierley (2008: 12.6). The projections, which proved controversial on publication, are here taken to 2025 rather than 2050.

Among denominations, the swiftest declines in the main denominations during 1979–2005 have been experienced by the United Reformed Church (from 190,000 to 70,000 or 63 per cent) and the Roman Catholics (55 per cent, though with attendances still outnumbering the Church of England) closely followed – from a lower base – by the Methodists at 53 per cent. The slowest rate of decline was that of the Baptists (12 per cent).

Church of England attendances declined by 48 per cent over 1979–2005. However, according to *Church of England Statistics 2006/7*, based on the introduction from 2000 of fresh attendance measures, average *weekly* attendances in 2005 amounted to 1,174,000 as opposed to average *Sunday* attendances of 993,000. The last figure is somewhat higher than the corresponding figures produced by the Christian Research surveys which put average Church of England Sunday attendance at 870,600. Different methods of collection no doubt account for the difference.

The effect of different collection methods can be illustrated further by two attempts to estimate the relative size of the two most important Christian denominations, that is, the Church of England and the Roman Catholic Church. Christian Research has the two churches at a level-pegging share of 28 per cent each of total Christian Sunday attendance. The BSA survey, in contrast, records 27 per cent of the population saying they regarded themselves as belonging to the Church of England but only 9 per cent saying they were Roman Catholics.

The Church of England statistician, Lynda Barley, has pointed out that counting only Sunday attendance underestimates total *weekly* attendance. At a time when the Church of England is responding more flexibly to 'consumer' convenience, attendances on days other than Sunday become more significant. Counting this increment since 2001 is claimed to show the need to add 12 per cent, or one in eight, to national average weekly attendance levels (Barley 2006: 21). Moreover, if individual attenders are counted rather than totals, such a system captures the less-regular attenders (though not perhaps those who appear only at Christmas or Easter) who may nonetheless be regarded as part of the totality of all more regular if not actually more frequent attenders: 'One million are in church on a typical Sunday, 1.2 million over a typical week but over 1.7 million attend over a typical month' (Barley 2006: 24). These figures may be taken to qualify the rate of decline experienced but cannot be said to be evidence of reversal.

Attendance is not, of course, the only measure of observance. Granted, however, the rates of decline observed in attendance, it is not surprising that the Church of England's role in marking the rites of passage through

Table 10.5   Rites of passage and the Church of England

Year	Confirmations 000s	Easier communicants per 1,000 adult population	Baptisms per 1,000 live births	Parochial funerals as % all deaths	No. of Anglican marriages	Anglican marriages per 1,000 marriages
1900	181		650			
1910	227		689			
1920	199		678			
1930	197	80	699			
1940	144	64	641			
1950	142	58	672			
1960	191	65	554			
1970	113	46	466			
1980	98	42	365			
1990	60	35	275		109,369	350
1995	44	32	240		79,616	297
2000	36	29	198	46	61,519	242
2005	30	25	153	43	57,210	224

Source: *Church of England Statistics* at <www.cofe.anglican.org>, accessed 2 July 2008.

life has also changed adversely. In 2005, baptisms constituted 15 per cent of live births in England but approached nearly 70 per cent upto 1950. Since 1960, Easter Day communicants per thousand of the population have declined by more than half. Confirmation rates in 2005 were one-seventh of the total in the twentieth-century peak year of 1910, and one-sixth of the total in 1960. While nowadays 43 per cent of funerals are still marked by Church of England ceremonies, religious marriages have declined significantly for all denominations. Whereas religious ceremonies formerly constituted the majority of all marriages, they became the minority from 1992 (NSO Dataset NePMH38B). While in 1982 the Church of England solemnized 66 per cent of all religious marriages and 34 per cent of all marriages in England, by 2004 the proportions were 70 and 22 per cent: a larger proportion of the remaining religious marriages but a much smaller proportion of all marriages. Indeed, in 2005 the Church of England solemnized only 57,210 marriages, or just over half the number it solemnized in 1982. While some of the trend against religious marriage may have been influenced by the 1994 Marriage Act's widening the choice of civil venues, the Act cannot, of course, have been the cause of the prior general trend towards civil marriage.

One of the more difficult figures to obtain is the proportion of people who have *no* religion. The difference between the census outcomes in England and Wales as opposed to Scotland is noted in Tables 10.1 and 10.2 above where the proportion was higher in Scotland. According to the BSA survey, the proportion of people in Great Britain who have no religion is 40 per cent, a higher figure still (*Social Trends* 2007: 181). As the Appendix to *Social Trends* explains, 'The Census question may suggest an expectation that people would have a religion while the BSA question introduced the possibility that people might not have a religion' (*Social Trends* 2007: 219).

Summarising the evidence brought to her attention, the UN Rapporteur on Human Rights protection in the UK judged that in 2007 approximately two-thirds of the UK population 'either did not claim membership of a religion or said that they never attended a religious service' (Jahangir 2008: 9). This figure no doubt reflected the BSA finding published in 2008 that the category amounted to 69 per cent of the UK population (NCSR 2008).

The most recent comprehensive account of the current state of religious observance is the UK-wide survey published by Tearfund in 2007. This was based on a representative sample of 7000 who were asked about their beliefs and churchgoing (Barley 2007: 1). Its main findings were that for all aged 16 and above in the UK, 53 per cent were Christian, 6 per cent belonged to other religions and 39 per cent had no religion, the last figure endorsing the findings of the BSA survey. After Northern Ireland, London is the most observant region in the UK, a fact associated with its relatively much larger black population: whereas ethnic minorities constituted 8 per cent of the UK population in 2001, they were nearly 29 per cent of London's population and the black component 12 per cent (Bains 2008: Table 3). As recorded in the Christian Research findings mentioned above, the consequence is that ethnic-minority churchgoers are now a majority of all churchgoers in London. Reinforcing the point, the Tearfund survey found that, among adults of black ethnic origin, regular churchgoing (defined as at least once a month) amounted to 48 per cent as opposed to 15 per cent of the white population. Not surprisingly this leads to a situation where the proportion of black-ethnic origin among regular churchgoers (10 per cent) is higher than among all UK adults (3 per cent).

There are also significant gender and class differences within the population overall: women churchgoers (who outnumber churchgoing men 65:35) are overrepresented compared with the 52:48 gender split in the general population; and so, too, are the higher social AB grades who constitute 25 per cent of churchgoers compared with 19 per cent of all adults. The churchgoing population is also more ethnically diverse than the population as a whole. In many ways, however, the most telling finding was less about belief than observance:

Two thirds of UK adults (66 per cent) or 32.2 million people have no connection with church at present (nor with another religion).

These people are evenly divided between those who have been in the past but have since left (16 million) and those who have never been in their lives (16.2 million). This secular majority presents a major challenge to churches. Most of them – 29.3 million – are unreceptive and closed to attending church; churchgoing is simply not on their agenda. (Ashworth, Research Matters and Farthing 2007: Summary)

On the one hand, the findings overall are not consistent with an accelerating, linear decline to a vanishing point. Fifteen per cent (7.6 million) of the population were estimated to go to church at least once a month and, it is claimed, 'there is more, far more going on out of apparent sight in everyday life in Britain today' (Lynda Barley in Ashworth, Research Matters and Farthing 2007: 1) On the other hand, the twenty-fourth BSA Report (NCSR 2008) further emphasized both the decline in religious identity (from 26 per cent having no religious connection in 1964 to 69 per cent) and that even those with a religious identity were less likely to attend services (from three-quarters being likely to attend in 1964 to only one-half).

Also instructive are the differences in intensity of belief/identification between Christians, and between them and the members of other religions. In the Home Office 2001 Citizenship survey, respondents were presented with a list of 15 social factors including their family, their education, income, ethnicity, sexuality and so on. They were then asked to state the 10 things in the whole range that would say something important about them. Religion came ninth overall, tenth for white respondents, third for black, second for Asians and seventh for those of mixed ethnicity. The same question ranked according to the religion of respondents put religion at seventh for Christians, first for Jews, second for Muslims, Hindus and Sikhs, and third for Buddhists (O'Beirne 2004: 17–20).

Explaining the changes

> That it [secularization] represents truth is hardly to be doubted, but what truth is not so easy to define. (Chadwick 1972/I: 423)

There is a continuing debate about how best to account for and understand the decline in religious observance shown by the data. The two main academic disciplines involved – sociology and history – adopt rather different approaches: the former is apt to offer explanations based on large observations of general social trends (for example, the impact of 'modernity'), and the latter to look for more particular event-based interactions albeit in the long timescales apt for religions. In addition to these fundamentally different intellectual approaches, individual sociologists and historians stress different features and events as lying behind the data.

As ever in such controversies, much turns on the terms of debate. The first stumbling block is the notion of 'secularization' itself. This is because it is used both as a description *and* as an explanation of change. Callum Brown puts it as a paradox: 'Secularisation is happening, yet secularisation theory is wrong' (Brown, C. G. 2001: viii). As a description, the term has acknowledged power: no-one seriously doubts that there have been – at least in parts of Europe – great changes in the extent of religious observance over the last century or more which may usefully be described as very considerably increasing the secular character of societies. The state has ceased to be confessional not only in England but also both where it is still theoretically so (Denmark) and where it was in fact though not in theory (Ireland). Only minorities now regularly attend churches, and belief in a personal God has declined significantly.

How most convincingly to account for these changes is, however, another matter entirely. Some sociologists have taken the view that changes in social organization have in the past diminished religious belief and pushed organized religion to the margins of political society with a concomitant reduction in influence – and will inevitably continue in the future. They see this as the consequence of 'modernity'. This concept has no very precise definition but is generally understood to comprehend a complex of social changes wrought by the functional differentiation that has accompanied and continued after industrialization, the growth of individualism and the more autonomous thinking that comes with it, plus globalization which has both intensified the other processes and increased relativistic attitudes towards religion (all religions are much the same and none therefore has unique claims). One of the leading proponents of this view in Britain is Steve Bruce:

A considerable body of evidence on church membership and attendance shows that, unless trends that have held since at least the 1950s are soon reversed, major British denominations are only a generation away from extinction. While we may legitimately argue about the causes or the exact trajectory of secularization, no amount of revisionism will change the fact that, if we can legitimately extrapolate from well-established trends, the religious culture that has dominated Britain for the last twelve centuries is in serious trouble. (Bruce 2002a: 60)

Other sociologists have taken a different view. As they interpret behaviour it is to be understood as showing 'individualization' – a movement away from old to new forms of observance. A thesis advanced by sociologists from Lancaster University as a result of their study of modern forms of devotional/spiritual, 'New Age' practices in Kendal (Heelas and Woodhead 2005) is that old forms of spirituality are being replaced with looser, less-structured activities. In constrast, Steve Bruce and a colleague have used other data to argue that there is no such general process, and that the concern with well-being typical of 'holistic' spirituality is not confined to those who have no conventional church affiliation (Glendinning and Bruce 2006). As Grace Davie has put it: 'The relationship with the religious mainstream is complex: self-spiritualities are both friend and foe of more conventional forms of religion' (Davie, G. 2007: 164). A further study seems to have cast serious doubt on whether any of these changes can be understood as substituting for former levels of observance:

> The relative marginality of non-church religiosity and the fact that it does not pose a serious alternative to traditional church adherence does not justify its emergence to be used as an argument against the secularization thesis. (Pollack and Pickel 2007: 627).

Other intellectual traditions find sociologists' resort to abstract concepts such as modernity both inadequate and unacceptably unspecific. More to the point, it is argued, such very general explanations fail to account for the onset and form of particular changes and are inclined also to attribute certain changes to secularization when other explanations seem more plausible. For example, while the British reforms of the law on homosexuality, abortion and divorce in the late 1960s have been instanced as examples of secularization, all were also supported by religious groups: indeed, the 1969 Divorce Act lifted the phrase 'irretrievable breakdown' directly from a Church of England report (McLeod 2007: 264). Very general theories are also incapable of explaining the contrasting outcomes in church/state relations between different countries such as Germany, France and England:

> The different balance of political forces in the three countries brought about very different relations between church and state. This leads to a recognition that in the nineteenth century there were huge divergences between the patterns of religious development in different sections of society. (McLeod 2000: 29)

Taking standpoints that stress more interactive processes leads perhaps to more nuanced and convincing explanations without, at the same time, entirely invalidating the broader sweep of sociological interpretations. Thus, current historiography presents a more mixed picture of the 'advance' of secularization in the nineteenth century and dates the period of most rapid decline of religious observance in Britain from the 1960s. Whereas one leading commentator attributes great importance to gender factors 'in a cultural revolution in which women reconstructed their identities as sexually active and secular beings' (Brown, C. G. 2006: 14), others have not followed. On the contrary, attention has been drawn to the length of the timescale of decline:

> Thus between about 1880 and 1930 new patterns of life were emerging in most parts of Britain, as a result of which, regardless of individual religious belief, the social importance of the churches had diminished ... As a systematic view of life, Christianity in its various forms remained far more popular than any alternative. But more common was a fluid eclecticism, which owed total allegiance to no single religion or ideology. (McLeod 1984: 65–6)

But, there is fair agreement that the crucial period for a manifest and almost precipitate decline in observance was the 'long 1960s', that is, approximately 1960–73: it was then that there was a powerful interaction of forces and events that saw a marked and so far sustained withdrawal of people in Britain and Northern Europe generally from religious observance and coherent religious belief. Hugh McLeod argues that there was no master factor and identifies six principal causes: affluence, the decline of ideologically based subcultures, theological radicalization, sexual revolution, political radicalization (especially from the Vietnam war), and 'women's search for greater freedom, self-fulfilment, and independence' (McLeod 2007: 15). As already mentioned, Callum Brown has stressed the importance of gender changes even more (Brown, C. G. 2006).

The extent of academic agreement should not, however, be exaggerated. Others have pointed out that the decline in observance should not be thought synonymous with loss of belief – the notion of 'believing without belonging' (Davie, G. 1994) – and that the degree of real belief *before* decline should not be exaggerated (Percy 2001). It has also been maintained that an 'empty church' syndrome is a fallacy: the rate at which Church of England churches were thrown up in the nineteenth century meant that many were never filled even at the peak of attendance (Gill 2003). The causal sequence itself has been challenged:

> Conventional wisdom and common sense suggest that people stopped going to church because they no longer believed what the churches taught them. Perhaps the causal mechanism was really closer to the opposite: they stopped believing because they stopped going. (Green, S. J. D. 1996: 301)

Moreover, it is argued that the general applicability of the socio-logical paradigm is challenged by the fact that it is a predominantly European – and at that Northern European – phenomenon not at all reflected elsewhere, including in North America where similar cultural trends could be expected: the secularization of Europe is a particular, unique and 'exceptional' historical process, not a universal teleological model of development which shows the future to the rest of the world (Casanova 2003: 22). Peter Berger has stated an even more strongly worded refutation:

> [T]he assumption that we live in a secularized world is false. The world today, with some exceptions … is as furiously religious as it ever was, and in some places more so than ever. This means that a whole body of literature by historians and social scientists loosely labelled 'secularization theory' is essentially mistaken. (Berger 1999: 2)

It is suggested that Europeans are 'not so much less religious than citizens in other parts of the world as *differently* religious' (Davie, G. 1999: 65). As to the argument from 'modernity', Grace Davie remains unconvinced of its universal explanatory power, and suggests that it is not a single syndrome inevitably hostile to observance but has to be understood as multiple and with different outcomes in differ-ent places (Davie, G. 2007: 248). David Herbert supports the view that 'the decline in traditional indices does not necessarily indicate a decline in religion but rather that the locus of belief and practice is shifting which makes longitudinal comparisons problematic' (Herbert 2004: 15).

However, to emphasise the fluidity of what is occurring, even in the USA so often instanced to counter a purely European perspective, the degree of observance there does not seem necessarily immutable. A recent independent survey based on interviews with more than 35,000 adults gauged that more than 16 per cent were without religion rising to one-quarter for 18–29 year olds. Significantly, more than a quarter of respondents had left the faith in which they were brought up, with one in ten describing themselves as former Roman Catholics. Whereas nearly one in three were raised in the Roman Catholic faith, today fewer than one in four described themselves as Roman Catholics (Pew Forum Survey 2008).

There is also the point about vicariousness put forward by Grace Davie, namely, that people are content that active others should keep religion in good repair so that they may from time to time avail themselves of its facilities:

> [A] significant proportion of Europeans delegate to their churches, often state churches, what they no longer consider doing themselves ... Churches are asked, for instance, to articulate the sacred at times in the life-cycle of individuals and families, and at times of national crisis or celebration. (Davie, G. 1999: 83)

Davie cites the outpouring of public grief in Sweden turning to religiously marked forms following the *Estonia* ferry disaster in 1994 where 900 people lost their lives, and public grief over the death of Princess Diana. For a somewhat lower level, polling by Opinion Research Business on behalf of the Church of England showed various percentages visiting churches for a variety of reasons, for example, for a concert or community event in addition to weddings, funerals and so on (Church of England 2008a: 3). However, the Tearfund finding that 6 per cent at most of those present non-attenders would consider attending some time in the future (Ashworth, Research Matters and Farthing 2007: 11) does not give the notion much evident real support in the sense of confirming occasional, casual acts as likely to have more underlying or continuing substance.

Similarly, there is the question of how far it is right to look at declines in religious observance in isolation. Grace Davie has pointed out, for example, that there have been contemporaneous declines in association for other largescale organizations like trade unions and political parties (Davie, G. 2007: 93–4), and there have been general concerns about what such declines may mean for 'social capital'. While the observation is certainly arresting and immediately plausible, on closer examination it stumbles. The reasons mostly stem from attempting to compare like with unlike: for example, trade union membership has fallen because of a lack of opportunity (hostile legislation and economic change) rather than a lack of belief. As a champion of direct secularization puts it:

> In summary, the case that declining church attendance is merely or largely part of a general decline in civic engagement (rather than a mark of the declining popularity of Christian beliefs) appears unpersuasive, because *there has not been any great decline in associating* ... The difference between the world of secular voluntary organisations and the world of churches is that in the former, total participation has remained stable, while in the latter, total participation has declined markedly. (Bruce 2002b: 326)

In her rejoinder, Grace Davie did not entirely surrender her position but, even in modified form, it seems to rely too much on equating weak survivals of religious sentiment with a regularity and intensity of former attachment now lost: 'As the institutional disciplines decline, belief not only persists, but becomes increasingly personal, detached and heterogeneous, particularly among young people' (Davie, G. 2002b: 333). Her most recent reflections, though more nuanced, do not quite persuade, though her warning against too starkly dichotomizing possible explanations should be heeded (Davie, G. 2007: 93).

Finally, a specifically North American, consumerist theory should be mentioned. This is the theory of rational choice. Broadly summarized, it hypothesises that the more varied the religious provision on offer, the more people will become religiously observant. A contrast is drawn between the religious diversity of the United States and the uniformity once at least prevalent in Europe as leading to very different levels of observance. However, whatever explanatory power the theory may have for North America does not credibly translate to Europe, and especially to Britain where a considerable degree of religious diversity does not have the same predicted outcome (Voas, Olson and Crockett 2002; Halman and Draulans 2006; Davie, G. 2007: 67–88).

A more relevant fit for the United States and the rest of the world may be a different theory. Pippa Norris and her colleague argue that the secularization thesis is not dead though it needs updating. They have offered a revised version that 'emphasizes the extent to which people have a sense of existential security'. Further, they argue that the United State's less than comprehensive social security and relatively low life expectancy for a developed society mean that it falls into the existential insecurity syndrome where higher levels of religiosity will occur (Norris and Inglehart 2004: 4 and 226).

To conclude this section, it will be appropriate to offer a thought experiment as a way of reflecting on the nature of religious change and its relevance for government. The experiment would be to imagine the circumstances in which a modern British government might itself call on the Christian churches in the UK to declare a national day of prayer for some purpose. These calls were based on an Old Testament view of the rightness of calling for a special visitation of divine providence upon the nation. It was noted in the United States in 1941 that the UK when at war had by then twice sought divine intercession: during Dunkirk in May 1940 and in March 1941 at the time of Hitler's seemingly unstoppable Balkan advance. Moreover, on both occasions the prayers had been answered (*Time* 7 April 1941.) In what circumstances would such appeals be contemplated by a modern UK government?

How irreversible?

While the general applicability of European secularization trends must properly be open to question, we are here concerned only with the situation in Britain, whether exceptional or not. The position in 2008 seems to be that the active Christian population has substantially declined and its age profile suggests that demography at least will not arrest current trends in the immediate future. What other factors assist judgement on the issue, bearing in mind that there is no inevitability of continued decline at whatever pace?

The factor perhaps most singled out by sociologists and others is the relative failure of the Christian denominations to socialize the young. In a word, they have failed to take sufficient steps to renew themselves by that means. The number of child Sunday churchgoers aged 15–19 as a proportion of the English population declined from over 13 per cent in 1979 to 5.2 per cent in 2005. The comparable figures for 20–9 year olds were 9.2 and 3.4 per cent (Brierley 2006: 12.3.4). Hugh McLeod has attributed the decline of Methodist membership – 14 per cent in the 1960s and 22 per cent in the 1970s – to a failure to attract the young, attributing such changes among other things to the improved economic status of the young and the choices they took as a result (McLeod 2006: 45–9). Although recent Church of England research indicated that Christian ideas remained in the background of young people's minds, they were also thought to show 'a great deal of fuzziness and uncertainty concerning traditional Christian beliefs' (Savage et al. 2006: 13–14 and 19). Such fuzziness may have accounted for the Easter 2007 reports of a supermarket publicist who confused whether Easter marked the birth or the death of Christ (*The Times* 6 April 2007). Much has been made of the decline of the Sunday school as an instrument for this purpose. It is no doubt one reason why the two churches with the most faith schools – the Church of England and the Roman Catholics – have been anxious to hold on to their schools and, at least in the former case, jump at the chance the Blair government offered to increase the number of their secondary schools.

Despite the churches' efforts with their schools, the schools do not appear by themselves to have remedied the socialization deficits. An important study of the 'believing-without-belonging' thesis has concluded: 'Religious belief has declined at the same rate as religious affiliation and attendance, and is not even necessarily higher than belonging'; and that this situation derives from weak generational transmission – 'only about half of parental religiosity is successfully transmitted, while absence of religion is almost always passed on' (Voas and Crockett 2005: 13 and 11). So far, these conclusions have not been controverted. Indeed, some of the authors' reasoning behind their suggestion that 'believing without belonging' should go into honourable retirement has been partly acknowledged by its proponent (Davie, G. 2007: 140). More emphatically still, the authors have also dismissed the notion that the older become more religious or that immigration will stem or reverse the tide of decline:

> Short of a dramatic and unexpected reversal among the young the decline will continue well into the twenty-first century as older, more religious cohorts are replaced by younger, less religious ones. The gradual ageing of the population tends to disguise the aggregate decline in religious involvement. As the relative size of older age groups increases, overall levels of participation do not drop by as much as we might otherwise expect. Continued immigration from more religious countries will also slow the future rates of decline, but the effects of immigration appear unlikely to accumulate over time as British-born children of immigrants do not appear immune from the forces of decline. (Crockett and Voas 2006: 581)

Nonetheless, even if the point is made by a Christian believer, projections and prophesy must come with a health warning:

> The possibility of a partial rotation in types of religious situation should at least be accorded the same right to consideration as a

straight line (with intermittent wobbles) to a secular terminus. (Martin 2005: 137)

Finally, against that proper point, is the observation by another Christian observer: 'the brute fact of decline ... There is no getting away from numbers' (Avis 2001: 76).

Implications for church/state relations

General

Numbers are important but they are not everything. Politically, therefore, the precise size of the religiously observant population is less important than the institutional presence it can continue to maintain. Even if regarded as simply optional and voluntary organizations, the Church of England and the Roman Catholic churches are large bodies, the former having nearly 1 million people going through its doors every Sunday. Both churches have important presences overseas, and the heads of both churches are, among other things, global – if ecclesiastical – politicians in their own right, one an elective monarch and a head of state.

Nonetheless, all the Christian denominations have to a greater or lesser extent been in numerical decline for half a century. The tendencies noted above to seek out increasingly marginal manifestations of religiosity and to construct rationalizations which mitigate the apparent message of the statistics seem to reflect anxiety about the decay associated with a concomitant wish to identify causes and act upon counter-strategies.

The position of the statesman

The statesman's current conclusions might be as follows:

- All Christian denominations are weakened though they retain their inherited institutional structures and, mostly, their built estates though the relative cost to the memberships of maintaining them is growing.
- Sharp decline is not the same as extinction which, save perhaps for some smaller denominations (including by amalgamation), is not at present on the cards.
- The growth of unbelief has not been accompanied yet by anticlerical feeling, though a certain scratchiness about faith schools could possibly develop into that in a limited area if it is not contained. Otherwise, if there can be said to be a dominant mood at all, it is indifference.

- It is likely that church leaders will become particularly sensitive to any moves that they feel may affect their status adversely. They will, accordingly, be very defensive among other things about maintaining their institutional inheritance and public positions as intact as possible.
- This is not politically an unmanageable situation. Even if it is no longer an instructed Christian nation, Britain remains culturally Christian. Indeed, it is sometimes said that British secularism is no more than a form of abridged Christianity.
- Much more uncertain is how best to respond to the minority non-Christian religions and how their relationship with the state is to be organized in an environment which gives precedence to Christianity.

The remainder of this book attempts to think through the further political and constitutional implications of these findings.

11
Establishment: The State of Opinion

In Scotland, the continuation of the Church of Scotland's position is hardly a live issue. This is in part because it is not clear in what sense it can be said to be established. This ambiguity has been reinforced by the outcome of the *Percy* case dealt with in Chapter 7.

In England, the establishment is still debated. But there has been an inversion: in the past, those who called for disestablishment came from outside the Church of England; nowadays they come predominantly from within. This chapter explores the reasons for this apparent paradox and weighs the case for and against establishment.

Ancient disestablishmentarianism

Dissent was always opposed to establishment but succeeded against it only during the mid-seventeenth-century Commonwealth. The Restoration reaction that followed imposed an orthodoxy that was never strictly enforced and which became increasingly relaxed. Organized political attack on establishment, however, was not feasible until Dissent could muster a sufficient presence in Parliament. The changed composition of the House of Commons after 1832 opened up the possibility, and the Scottish Disruption of 1843 and the Factories Bill of the same year helped to precipitate a more determined and institutionalized response from English nonconformity: the first because it was a challenge to an established church, and the second because the Bill's education clauses would have uniquely favoured Anglicanism. In the following year – 1844 – the first effective pressure group to challenge Anglican establishment was founded. This was the Anti-State-Church Society, which later prudently changed its name to the more plausible and attractive Society for the

Liberation of the Church from State Patronage and Control, known as the Liberation Society.

Dissent considered it had much to complain about, and this fact was ultimately one of its campaigning difficulties. To achieve change it had to attack specific targets but the more successful it was in doing so the more it eroded its own platform. There is also the point that its more general attack on establishment could be seen as negative and threatening – points exploited by the Church Defence Institute that emerged to oppose the Liberationists. Political action led to political identification, Liberation with the Liberals from 1868 particularly, and Anglicanism with the Conservatives.

Change came but slowly. It speeded up only following the alliance forged by Gladstone between Whigs, Radicals and Dissent that created the Liberal Party. As described in Chapter 2, most old specific rubbing points were gradually removed by the end of the century, and there was a degree of church/state institutional separation over time that mitigated old hegemonies. But successive parliamentary motions in favour of disestablishment failed and the central bastions of establishment remained: the exclusively Anglican character of the monarchy, episcopal membership of the House of Lords, and the Church of England's dominant social status. Irish disestablishment from 1869 did not, as Liberation expected, prove to be the precursor of disestablishment in England. At the end of the nineteenth century, the Liberation Society ran out of money (Mackintosh 1972: 293–6) and, despite determined attacks on ritualism in the 1890s initiated among others by the Nonconformist MP, Samuel Smith (Smith 1902: 386–408), disestablishment in England as opposed to that in Wales did not become revived as a parliamentary issue. As Lewis Dibdin, the great ecclesiastical lawyer of his time, later observed: 'Disestablishment is still claimed by the great Nonconformist bodies, but only languidly' (Dibdin 1932: 1).

Modern Anglican disestablishmentarianism

The defining moment can be seen as Parliament's successive rejections of the Prayer Book Measures in 1927/28. To Anglicans who thought that the Enabling Act 1919 had granted the Church effective autonomy, these reversals were painful in the extreme. Notoriously, the experience made Hensley Henson, Bishop of Durham – previously a fervent advocate of establishment who had doubted the merits of the Enabling Act 1919 – into a leading proponent of disestablishment. This reaction never then or since became a majority Anglican view, and was opposed magisterially and somewhat obsessively perhaps by an archbishop of York (Garbett 1950). All the subsequent Church and state committees (Cranmer, Lucas and Morris 2006: 49–57) subsequently set up by the archbishops, and to this day all votes in the Church of England Synod have come down in favour of continuing establishment, though the last committee – the Chadwick Committee – had an eloquent memorandum of dissent by Valerie Pitt. Against the grain of the majority, she maintained that

> The traditional argument that the link between Church and Crown must be retained for historical and cultural reasons is no longer acceptable because our culture itself, as it grows away from its Christian roots, increasingly compels us to choose an allegiance. (Chadwick 1970: 74)

While specifying the range of legislative and other changes involved, she stressed that her case was 'for the separation of Church and State though not of the Church from the community' (Chadwick 1970: 78). In other words, Valerie Pitt rejected the 'congregationalist' arguments advanced by some Anglican disetablishmentarians.

For the present, not only is it true that Anglican disestablishmentarianism persists but also that it has today a sharp, often polemical, voice. The best-known example is perhaps that of the former Bishop of Woolwich, Colin Buchanan (Buchanan 1994). His argument – not dissimilar from Valerie Pitt's dissenting memorandum – is grounded on the necessity of independence to avoid being unavoidably compromised by association with a secular state, and to remove thereby otherwise insurmountable impediments to ecumenism. The argument acknowledges the difficulties in the way, and canvasses alternative ways of encompassing the desired end. Buchanan leans to the Scottish model as one which would most fittingly preserve a national role without being dependent on the state. He is also open-minded about the implications for the role of the sovereign and how coronations might be conducted. Whether the sovereign (or spouse) should continue to be precluded from being a Roman Catholic would be left to *Parliament* to decide, just as Valerie Pitt would have left it to the *state* to decide whether bishops should remain in the House of Lords.

Avowedly an Anglican polemicist, Theo Hobson argues from the assertion that the original basis of establishment has decayed beyond repair and the gap between the theory and reality means that establishment should be abandoned:

> The disestablishment of the Church does not entail a cultural revolution. It entails being honest about a cultural revolution that has already taken place. Over the past generation or so, Britain has rejected its traditional religious identity. (Hobson 2003: x)

Hobson does not go on to discuss how disestablishment should be achieved or in what form. His purpose is, after all, to make the case in principle. Similarly, though less polemically, Martyn Percy has made the case for disestablishment on 'realistic' grounds, and voices in the Church of England continue to articulate such a case, often with a congregationalist tinge – that is, with the aim more or less explicit of freeing the Church to minister only to its own signed-up members. That approach would, of course, abandon the 'national church' role which is often advanced by other Anglicans, and particularly senior Anglican figures, as the rationale for *maintaining* establishment. David Martin has claimed that 'many churchmen dislike being a part of a Ministry of Ceremonies, decorating the state' (Martin 1984: 134). And William Fittall, although writing in support of the status quo, has not sought in any way to conceal the existence of these and similar feelings (Fittall 2008: 79).

Disestablishmentarianism elsewhere

It is not a burning public issue. Some *Guardian* writers perhaps assume it is one of the staple topics of middle-class dinner-party conversation, but active proponents outside the Church of England itself are few. Current attitudes among nonconformist churchmen (Morris 2008a) seem to show that, while objections of principle remain, there is in practice indifference to agitating for change. It is a policy of the Liberal Democrat Party, of whose persuasive power no more need perhaps be said.

Stewart Lamont, a Scottish journalist writing a few years ahead of Buchanan, similarly favoured the Scottish model and after reviewing the character of church/state relations in a number of countries argued more from the need to adjust to changed realities: 'On the twin horns of multi-culturalism and secularism, the Church of England has been gored and is slowly bleeding to death' (Lamont 1989: 174). A Fabian Society study did not recommend disestablishment as such but did think that the

Supreme Governor role should be ended and the sovereign be permitted to have any religious faith or none:

> If the Head of State is to perform the role of unifying the diverse communities of the UK, and to act as the representative of contemporary Britain, we believe that Church and state need to be distanced, both symbolically and institutionally. (Fabian Society 2003: 71)

The Fabian Society's preference for something on the lines of the 'Scottish model' was shared also in a later New Politics Network study which, while similarly rejecting outright disestablishment, was thought – with its preface by Colin Buchanan – to go a considerable way in that direction. Maintaining that what it sought was 'not technically disestablishment, as it proposes maintaining the Church's status as the national church in England', the study advocated taking the bishops out of the House of Lords and 'removing political control over Church affairs, and allowing it the same degree of self-governance that the Church of Scotland enjoys' (McLean and Linsley 2004: 1).

Much less restrained is the position of the National Secular Society (NSS) which, over a long life stretching from 1866, has consistently called for

> disestablishment of the Church and for its privileges to be withdrawn. The State should be entirely neutral in dealing with the philosophical or belief systems of its citizens. The NSS seeks to secure equal rights for the non-religious. (Wood 2008: 59)

The NSS case is based on its view that the state should not in principle be involved with any form of religion. Accordingly, its recommendations envisage (Wood 2008: 73) the most thorough severance conceivable between the Church of England and the state, if not actually to the point of disendowment.

The British Humanist Association takes a similar if, it is claimed, more nuanced view:

> The uncoupling of church and state is a priority for most humanists. The basis of this is not anti-Anglican animus, but a commitment to the open society that recognizes the privileging of any one religious denomination (especially against a social backdrop of massive heterogeneity) as a real inequality ... Secularism is not atheism and it is not anti-religious – in fact it benefits both the religious and the non-religious in their aspect as members of a single society. (Copson and Pollack 2008: 58)

One of the themes running through some of these approaches is argument from the multi-faith and multi-ethnic character of modern Britain. While the public at large could reasonably be thought to share that understanding of the changed character of British society, it would be quite wrong to say that there is any head of public steam behind disestablishment in consequence. It is in no way a salient political or religious issue. Within the Christian community, even a study by the Evangelical Alliance – many of whose members have been historically opposed to establishment – stopped short of recommending disestablishment. No doubt in deference to its own Anglican members, the Alliance report accepted continuing establishment in England if merely on expedient grounds: 'wholesale disestablishment would involve longstanding and complex constitutional challenges, and [it is accepted] on this basis that government and churches should not divert significant resources to such a project' (Evangelical Alliance 2006: 169).

Parliament and establishment

In the end, all major changes in the governance of the Church of England have to come to Parliament for approval as Measures. In both Houses there is a mixture of views on church/state links, and no settled agreed view on whether current arrangements should continue. As might be expected, it is voices calling for change rather than maintaining the status quo that are heard.

Thus, in addition to the Liberal Democrat views mentioned above, there are other views sympathetic to disestablishment. At the time of writing, for example, there is a House of Commons Early Day Motion (No 666 – the mark of the beast) calling for disestablishment. If it includes Labour as well as Liberal Democrat signatories, the fact that after six months it had attracted only 20 signatures suggests that the cause of direct intervention has at present but limited support. The principle of establishment was last debated in 2002 on a motion by the Liberal Democrat peer, Lord Maclennan. It elicited no perfervid support. On the contrary, the then Lord Chancellor was frankly dismissive:

> I conclude as unequivocally as I may. As matters stand now, in the Church and in the Nation, the Government believe that our collective time can be better spent in pursuing other priorities. (HL 22 May 2002, col. 815)

However, this would be to overlook other, perhaps less-direct expressions of parliamentary opinion in practice hostile to establishment.

Avowed secularists are raising their voices. In 2006 Graham Allen, Labour, introduced a Westminster Hall debate – 'Admissions Policies (Faith Schools)' – directed at drawing attention to the claimed disabilities suffered by non-believers in a schooling system that included schools that could select pupils according to religious criteria (HC 14 February 2006, cols 367–390WH). Lord Harrison, a Labour peer, initiated a Lords debate in 2007 – 'Religion: Non-Believers' – when he drew attention to a series of disabilities from which he felt non-believers suffered, mentioning the desirability of disestablishment almost as an aside (HL 19 April 2007, cols 331–4). Rather more support for his positions was voiced on that occasion than in the Lords disestablishment debate in 2002, though the responding government minister stuck to explaining the government's non-discriminatory policy and avoided commenting on disestablishment.

More oblique still have been attempts to introduce legislation on the face of it directed solely at dealing with what are seen as outmoded or discriminatory constitutional provisions but that would nonetheless inevitably impact on establishment. The most common of these initiatives have been concerned with amending the Act of Settlement 1701 to permit Roman Catholics to succeed to the throne and remove the bar against a sovereign marrying a Roman Catholic. Lord Forsyth of Drumlean, Conservative, introduced a motion to that effect (HL 2 December 199, cols 917–19), Lord Dubs, Labour, a Succession to the Crown Bill (HL 14 January 2005, cols 495–513), Edward Leigh, Conservative, sought leave to introduce a Marriages (Freedom of Religion) Bill (HC 8 March 2005, cols 1392–4), and John Gummer, Conservative, similarly sought permission for a Catholics (Prevention of Discrimination) Bill two years later (HC 20 February 2007, cols 154–6). None of these initiatives either was allowed to or could make progress. All would in effect imply a substantial degree of disestablishment because it would be intolerable to the Church of England to have as Supreme Governor a person whose religious authority recognized neither the validity of Anglican orders nor the validity of the Church of England. That a later Lord Chancellor appeared to indicate (HC 25 March 2008, col. 25) greater sympathy for tackling the 1701 Act's discriminatory character was therefore surprising and, almost certainly in any committing sense, unintended.

Finally, it is relevant to bear in mind that there has been in the past at least a strand in parliamentary thinking which has challenged the autonomy of the Church of England's institutions and sought to restate the extent of Parliament's ultimate control. As mentioned in Chapter 2's discussion of Parliament's role vis à vis the Church, although the important

Worship and Doctrine Measure 1974 sailed comfortably through the House of Lords (on Archbishop Ramsey's last day in office), a division was forced in the Commons debate (HC 4 December 1974, cols 1567–1698). The argument of the dissentients (who lost 145:45) was that the General Synod did not represent 'the man in the pew', that the Measure would make the Synod 'infallible', and that the Church was trying to cut itself off from outside control – 'how soon will the Church demand the right to appoint its own bishops'. A Roman Catholic was particularly critical. The Church was asking the House

> to retain the status of the Established Church while taking away from this House the power and responsibility for its existence ... We are being asked, to all intents and purposes, to disestablish the Church of England and yet retain it as the official Established Church ... (Hugh Fraser, cols 1612–13)

Two decades later, the Commons Social Security Select Committee intervened in the aftermath of the Church Commissioners' property losses ostensibly to express concern about clergy pensions, but in fact to try to influence changes then contemplated in the Church of England's internal governance structures:

> The Church of England remains a national Church, and Parliament has a special responsibility for its worldly endowment with part of the national patrimony, built up over generations. We are anxious that proposed changes in the position of a major part of the constitution should be presented in a form which Parliament is not prevented from amending if after debate it wishes to do so. (Social Security Select Committee 1996, para. 1)

A Commons debate (HC 11 May 1995, cols 910–61) did not see that view generally supported. The government spokesman taking strongly the opposite view: 'It seems entirely right that the way forward for the Church of England should be led by the community of that Church' (col. 928).

On both occasions, the dissentients espoused what were clearly minority views. However, it could not be entirely ruled out that such voices might seek to reassert themselves in certain circumstances. To take an obvious example, they might do so where it was judged that the consecration of women bishops would create an avoidable threat of Anglican schism within England from which it was Parliament's duty to preserve the Church. If so, it is unlikely that the outcome would be to strengthen establishment but, rather, the reverse. If past experience be any guide, Parliament would be more inclined to let the Church have its way than seek to assert its own. If not in the sense or with the effect then intended, the 1931 statement of Thomas Inskip (then Solicitor General) to the Cecil Committee could indeed remain true: 'I regard the House of Commons as speaking for the nation . . . ' (Cecil evidence, 15 December 1931, p. 301).

Establishmentarianism

Non-Anglican

An initial surprise to the newcomer to this subject is that establishment is not favoured only by Anglicans: it is supported also by members of non-Christian faiths. The reason for this support is that establishment can be viewed not only as the privileging of one particular Christian denomination but also as a state of affairs that elevates – particularly but not only in episcopal membership of the House of Lords – the place of religion in national cultural and political life. The Chief Rabbi has expressed such a position as follows:

> The task of representing shared values traditionally fell, in England, to the established Church. Our current diversity makes many people, outside the Church and within, feel uneasy with that institution. But disestablishment would be a significant retreat from the notion that we share any values and beliefs at all. (Sacks 1991: 68)

Discussion of how the state and non-Christians should relate to each other has invariably had to address how those relations should be structured. Bhikhu Parekh has characterized the secularism of the state as having two forms:

> In its weakest version it separates *state* and *religion* and maintains that the state should not enforce, institutionalize or formally endorse a religion, be guided by religious considerations in its policies and treatment of citizens, and in general should retain an attitude of strict indifference to religion. In its stronger version it also separates *politics* and *religion* and maintains that political debate and deliberation should be conducted in terms of secular reasons alone. (Parekh 2006: 322)

The Commission on the Future of Multiethnic Britain – established by the former Commission for Racial Equality (CRE) – that he chaired noted in its report those areas where the law or custom privileged the Church of England but stopped short of calling for their abolition. Instead the report concluded: 'We recommend that a commission on the role of religion in the public life of a multi-faith society be set up to make recommendations on legal and constitutional matters' (Parekh 2000: 243). While this recommendation was not acted upon, in his *Rethinking Multiculturalism* published originally in the same year, Parekh thought aloud about how religious communities might be drawn into the mainstream of political life, suggesting a 'national interreligious forum' as a possibility but, again, without going on to argue that such devices should replace establishment (Parekh 2006: 331).

Tariq Modood, a Muslim and a sociologist, has written extensively from a multiculturalist perspective on the place of religion in British public life: 'I have to state as a brute fact that I have not come across a single article or speech or statement by any non-Christian faith in favour of disestablishment' (Modood 1994: 61). His aim has been to explain the limitations as he sees them of a purely secular state from the point of view of the minority non-Christian religions:

> [A] further advance for secularism is likely to be at the cost of the new as well as the old faiths. On the other hand, the minimal nature of an Anglican establishment, its proven openness to other denominations and faiths seeking public space, and the fact that its very existence is an ongoing acknowledgment of the public character of religion, are all reasons why it may seem far less intimidating to the minority faiths than a triumphal secularism. (Modood 1994: 72–3)

Moreover, he has gone on to explore what mechanisms might be feasible to ensure that minority non-Christian religions have a recognized place in British political life. While some forms of multiculturalist discourse have fallen recently out of favour, the perspectives he has been exploring have been in no way invalidated even if they may not secure universal acceptance:

> an alternative to disestablishment is to design institutions to ensure that those who are marginalized by the dominant ethos are given some special platform or access to influence so their voices are nevertheless heard ... In the British context, this would mean pluralizing the state-religion link (which is happening to a degree), rather than severing it. (Modood 2005: 145)

This gets close to advocating 'concurrent establishment' which existed in a weak form in eighteenth-century England and Ireland, and was toyed with by the House of Lords during the debates on the Irish Church Disestablishment Bill in 1869. As Edward Norman has pointed out (Norman 2008: 11), present governments have shown a tendency to revive such policies in its pursuit of 'social cohesion' agendas. However, this is not to say that Tariq Modood has advocated any particular *form* for how the goal of this kind of pluralization may be realized, a topic to which this chapter will return later.

Interestingly, one of the subtler defences of establishment has come from a Roman Catholic. In a collection of views on the subject edited by Tariq Modood, Adrian Hastings argued:

> The Church of England is, today, clearly distanced from the state. While a strong establishment is bound to be erastian, a weak establishment may well be the best basis for the maintenance of a constructive dualism ... The bishops in the House of Lords cannot really be there as Anglicans but rather as representatives of spirituality, a voice of Christianity and indeed of religion even wider than Christianity. Maybe they do not do it perfectly and it is certainly something of a chore for busy men. But it remains in principle right, even wonderful, that it should be done and be part of our constitution. (Hastings 1997: 41–2, 46)

Anglican positions

By definition, unless they explicitly renounce the position as has Colin Buchanan, all Anglican clergy and laity must be judged as favouring establishment. This they indeed do but with marked differences of tone from the language of the nineteenth century. For example, while successive twentieth-century archbishops' commissions on Church and state came down in favour of continued establishment, they did so in changing language. Not specifically concerned with the merits of establishment rather than its working, the Selborne Committee's report in 1916 nonetheless displayed the closest possible interest in the position of the Church of Scotland (Selborne 1916: Appendix V). The Cecil Committee of 1936 rejected the Scottish model, and on this occasion looked explicitly at disestablishment but declined to recommend it:

> The history of the Church and nation is, in England, so closely intertwined that the separation could not be effected without injury to

both of a kind impossible to forecast or forestall, which could only be fully appreciated when remedy is out of the question. (Cecil Report 1936: 49)

In an earlier passage, the committee claimed that the Church of England continued

to represent the Christian faith of the nation as a whole. Its primacy has been maintained by the essentially conservative English mind as a primacy of age and honour and comprehensiveness as the acknowledged position of a body which at crucial moments in the spiritual history of the nation has the right to speak for all, however sundered its religious tenets may be. In this sense the Christian State of England may be termed a Church of England State. (Cecil Report 1936: 17)

In what might now be taken as hyperbole, the Moberly Report of 1952 claimed that disestablishment 'would be a shock to opinion throughout the world because it would be taken as the British People's repudiation of continuous Christian tradition' (Moberly 1952: 10). Nearly twenty years later, the Chadwick Committee took a cooler line:

We want to make it clear . . . that we are not blind to the plural nature of English society. The Church of England is one Church among several. So far as it is called a 'national' Church, it professes a mission to all the nation. It does not claim to cast its shadow over men and women who repudiate it. (Chadwick 1970: 10)

Forestalling Grace Davie's later theory of vicariousness, the committee recommended against a total severing of the historic church/state links:

The people of England still want to feel that religion has a place in the land to which they can turn on the too rare occasions when they think that they need it; and they are not likely to be pleased by legislation which might suggest that the English people as a whole were going unchristian. (Chadwick 1970: 65)

Naturally, how best to regard, explain and defend the form of establishment existing in England has remained of great concern to Anglicans as they respond to the changes occurring in British society. A dean of Westminster has spoken of a 'developing establishment' accommodating itself to these changes (Carr 1999), and of distinguishing between 'high' and 'earthed' establishment where an established church 'remains a reminder to the Christian of this profound spiritual truth: there is no privilege which does not bring commensurate responsibility' (Carr 2002a).

The Anglican theologian Paul Avis has sought to restate the theological and ecclesiological arguments that underpin the notion of the establishment of a national church:

> The idea of a national church ... is of a church that is concerned with a nationwide mission of the gospel and nationwide service to the community. A national church understands that its mission is to the whole nation, to the whole population considered as a great community (or community of communities). (Avis 2001: 15)

By the same token, Avis argues, should the Church of England ever renounce its mission to the whole nation, 'it will have abdicated the very role that secures its special position in the nation and facilitates its distinctive mission' (Avis 2001: 82). This is a position which the present Bishop of Durham, Tom Wright, has also strongly supported:

> To cut the link, to insist that the church is only there for its fully paid up members, would be to send a signal to the rest of the world that we were pulling up the drawbridge, putting mirrors around the light to keep it in instead of windows to let it out. (Wright 2002)

Granted, Avis maintains, that there is now little or nothing in the established status of the Church of England to which other Christian denominations (including Roman Catholics) could 'reasonably' object, 'The established status of the Church of England remains a constitutional defence against the complete secularization of the state' (Avis 2001: 78).

Another important strand in Anglican approaches to establishment is the link that is made between the idea of a national church and the monarchy. A representation of this view is a recent essay by the Bishop of Derby:

> This essay will argue that the royal prerogatives and the established Church are essential to the wholeness and well-being of our nation – not as identifiable systems with clear functions and boundaries, but as entities that are often notions in the mind, frequently ignored, always shrouded in ambiguity, and yet available to provide a vital perspective on the human enterprise of organising society creatively

and justly ... In theological language, the role of Crown and Church is thus to consecrate public life: to make it holy or whole, by providing engagement with a greater reality. (Redfern 2007: 38, 42)

It is a linkage stressed also by Paul Avis, and to the extent that they are mutually dependent. Not only would disestablishment leave the monarchy isolated and exposed, but as to a secular monarchy

what would the constitutional rationale of a secular monarchy be? As things stand, Crown, church and constitution are bound up together in a delicate constitutional ecology. It is to the benefit of constitution, church and Crown that they should remain so. (Avis 2001: 31)

A speech by Lord Carey, when Archbishop of Canterbury, on St George's day 2002, put forward the following overview:

From the perspective of the Church of England, establishment helps to underwrite the commitment of a national church to serve the entire community and to give form and substance to some of the deepest collective needs and aspirations ... Part of the Church's service – born out of establishment – must be on behalf of faith generally. That is the basis on which bishops in the House of Lords have interpreted aspects of their role ... We are committed to what I would call a 'hospitable establishment'. So, it is part of our role ... to seek to provide space and access, opportunity and the right atmosphere for the many dealings and interactions between faith communities and the wider society, however and wherever we can. (Carey 2002)

Lord Habgood, a former Archbishop of York, when speaking a few weeks later in the House of Lords disputed the term 'hospitality' as unfortunate and preferred 'partnership' as a more apt description, but voiced one of the classic defences of establishment:

These days, established churches place few constraints on government. However, they are valuable reminders that the state itself is not absolute. They point to a moral authority that transcends us all. In this Chamber we begin our day with prayer, because we are a Christian country. The established Churches hold in trust for the whole of the United Kingdom the belief that sovereignty is to be exercised as a God-given responsibility and not as a manifestation of arbitrary power. (HL 22 May 2002, col. 782)

And, indeed, as remarks by the then bishop of Guildford show, the bishops do claim in Parliament the wider role of which both the former Lord Carey and Adrian Hastings have spoken:

The bishops are here not primarily to speak for the Church of England, narrowly conceived as a denomination, but for the spiritual and moral needs of the whole community. That is why we have stood for holding on to the best of our inheritance as we seek a more representative and inclusive shape to the whole House, including its spiritual aspects. (HL 4 July 2002, col. 357)

The same relatively new claim infuses a recent religious think tank study (Partington and Bickley 2007).

At the time of writing, there is no 'official' view from the Church of England itself about establishment. Indeed, its own dispersed structure makes the formulation of such an authoritative statement virtually impossible to achieve in the sense of a single, unambiguous pronouncement. Debates in Synod may constitute some approximation, and they have disclosed no majorities in favour of disestablishment. However, a recent overview has been offered by the Secretary General of the General Synod and Archbishops' Council with every proper qualification by him as to its status and was composed *before* the Prime Minister's initiative over senior appointments. It may be taken to reflect, if not actually represent, the views of the majority leadership. Referring to past governments' views that disestablishment would not become an issue unless and until the Church requested it, the Secretary General went on

The Church has shown no such inclination, nor does it seem likely it will do so over the coming years. Any move on the part of the Church would be more likely to be prompted by events and particular problems than any fundamental change of view about the value of Establishment. So, a special relationship between the Church of England and the State has every prospect of continuing, unless the view of Government changes ... The probability is that there will be further evolution ... A cutting of the cord would, however, be seen by many in the Church of England not simply as the end of an era but as a sad day for the Christian faith, and indeed for religious faith more generally in this country. (Fittall 2008: 79–80)

The Prime Minister's initiative may, of course, have caused some subsequent modification of such views. It certainly precipitated some

'evolution', and a subsequent 'semi-official' Church of England publication has sought to refute anti-establishment arguments head on
(Davie, M. 2008: 67–72). Selecting but three of the anti-establishment
arguments, Martin Davie contends (if at times with some circularity)
that, if there is to be some special relationship between church and
state, then in a divided Christendom one church has to be selected
and in England it is 'for historical reasons' the Church of England; that
the constitutional discrimination against Roman Catholics is caused by
their own refusal to accept the Church of England's validity; and that
objection to the Crown appointment of bishops is misplaced because in
practice they are nominated by the Church of England itself.

For the present, the last word from the Church of England might
reasonably rest with the present Archbishop of Canterbury, Rowan
Williams. Unprecedentedly, he has had the experience of serving as a
bishop and archbishop in the disestablished Church in Wales before
becoming Primate of the Church in England. This has, understandably,
influenced his approach. Responding to a question about disestablishment following a 2008 Holy Week lecture, he thought the case for
retaining establishment rested on two things. First was 'the recognition
by the state of some element in its life answerable to more than narrowly
political interest'. Second was the 'state's recognition that everyone in the
nation has a right to access some kind of spiritual service'. He continued:

> Quite a lot of both of those can be met in ways other than the
> establishment as we now see it. I had ten years as a Bishop in a dises-
> tablished Church in Wales without noticing a great deal of difference
> a lot of the time. So I don't believe in the general principle that dises-
> tablishment is lethal for the Church, or that the establishment in its
> present form is a ditch the Church would have to die in. I have more
> faith in the Church than that. (Williams 2008)

Finally, rarely mentioned out loud, is the belief that establishment has
helped to hold the ring for a church that some feel would be in danger of
fragmenting if government and ultimate parliamentary oversight were
withdrawn. On this view, establishment helps to keep the high church
and evangelical factions in balance, episcopal pretensions restrained and
the Synod in its place as but one element rather than the dominant legislature it could otherwise become. As one distinguished ecclesiastical
lawyer has put it: 'There is still a feeling that the State has a responsibility to "hold the ring" and ensure that neither one group nor party
acquires control of the Church' (Kemp 2003: 49). Whether these *ur* fears

of self-government are credible or not, they retain a presence in Anglican appreciations of the case for establishment. Reflecting on the events of 1927/28 in his written evidence to the Cecil Committee, Maurice Gwyer (Treasury Solicitor) said

[I]t is at least a possible interpretation of recent events that the bonds which today unite the Church to the State are also the bonds which preserve the unity of the Church. (Cecil Report 1936: 188)

Part IV
Establishment Futures

This part looks at the options for adjusting the constitutional position of the Church of England and, to a much lesser extent, that of the Church of Scotland. The argument starts from the contention that establishment in England is not an all-or-nothing concept (Morris 2006). On the contrary, it is best regarded as a web of connexions between the Church of England and the state which may be amended selectively as alternatives to the rupture of total, climactic disestablishment. Changes of a less final kind deserve examination, particularly if they seem likely to achieve the benefits of substantive alteration in the direction of equality without the evident costs of disestablishment. A further assumption is that the merits of particular courses have to be viewed from the separate standpoints of the Church itself, the sovereign and that of the state: the standpoints and interests are not necessarily the same. It is also argued that such an approach facilitates change because it can be accomplished incrementally taking advantage of particular opportunities as they arise, for example, changes of government and of archbishop as well as of sovereign. Everything does not have to be done at once: it follows that the impossibility of attempting everything simultaneously cannot be urged as a reason for attempting nothing at all.

12
The Higher Architecture

By way of presenting it as a yardstick for comparing lesser measures, the chapter begins by considering full-blown disestablishment. From there it analyses the position of the sovereign, and the case – together with the means – for separating the headship of the state from the headship of the Church of England, and from the ancient obligation to uphold the Presbyterian form of the Church of Scotland.

Disestablishment

Although frequently and glibly mentioned, disestablishment is rarely analysed with adequate rigour – an exception is Professor Robert Blackburn (Blackburn 2006: 108–38). Too often commentators refer to it as a sort of shorthand for abolishing the feature of present arrangements that they dislike most. It has, therefore, to be said straight away that disestablishment is not by itself a route to a British republic. Neither will it abolish faith schools. It would not even get rid of bishops, still less the Church of England itself.

Disestablishment may be defined as the abolition of all privileged links between the Church of England and the British state to place the Church of England in the same position as any other religious body in the UK. Some of the necessary changes are obvious, but many others are obscure and not easily realized. Many features would call for awkward judgements on what exactly should be the right technical solution, for example, as to the management of the legacy of past primary legislation, and the whole question of whether disendowment should be an essential concomitant of disestablishment and, if so, to what extent and in whose interests.

It should also be borne in mind that no-one has yet canvassed a form of disestablishment that would put a church *outside* the law. As one of the early archbishops of the Church in Wales put it:

> There is not a religious body in this land, however loudly it protests its freedom from state control, that is really outside the law: the law conditions and protects its existence. In this sense, Welsh Disestablishment substituted one form of establishment for another. (Green, C. A. H. 1937: 11)

It has been the declared policy of successive modern governments that the question of the future of establishment should be for the Church of England itself to determine: 'any profound change in the status of the Church must be in the first instance for the Church itself' (Government Papers Cm 7027). That was the theory in February 2007. However, the theory did not restrain the government from unilaterally deciding in its July 2007 White Paper, *The Governance of Britain*, to withdraw from active involvement in all ecclesiastical patronage, including of course the appointment of bishops.

The result nonetheless is that there has not been in modern times any authoritative study of how disestablishment might be carried out. So far as is known, the Church of England itself has not engaged in any contingency planning. The sole attempt within government to look into the subject seems to have been a fairly perfunctory reconnaissance by a committee of officials during Whitehall's consideration in the 1970s of the implications of the Chadwick Report's recommendations. Officials having reported to ministers that, on certain interpretations, some of the recommendations could imply disestablishment, the Prime Minister asked for an account of what disestablishment might mean (Heath to Allen 30 August 1973 TNA HO 304/43).

Granted the time available for the exercise and, because of its secrecy, their inability to consult outside Whitehall, officials explained that they could offer only a conspectus of issues which, they thought, would require a great deal more consideration probably by a Royal Commission. The committee of officials was chaired by Philip Allen, the recently retired Permanent Under Secretary of the Home Office. Its members included the Treasury Solicitor, the Home Office Legal Adviser, the Prime Minster's Appointments Secretary, and representatives of the Home Office, the Lord Chancellor's Department and, especially for the disestablishment study, the Welsh and Scottish Offices.

For working purposes, the committee adopted the following definition of disestablishment:

> a complete severance of all obligatory and exclusive official relations between Church and State. This should create complete freedom for the Church as respects discipline, doctrine, finance, appointments and promotions and general administration. It should also entail the abolition of any precedence officially accorded at present to the Church at all official, National, civic and legal ceremonies and of any limitation to officers or members of the Church in connection with official appointments. (TNA HO 304/45, PA(74)1, para. 3)

In the event, the officials' report was more a list of problems than of solutions. Broadly classified they fell into four groups:

- How to treat church law, church courts and church property – the latter extending beyond that administered by the Church Commissioners. Citing the Irish and Welsh experiences, decisions would have to be made about what was to be secularized, and with what compensation/commutation. The Church would have itself to be empowered to reorganize itself to the extent necessary and to administer its property.
- The consequences for the Crown, executive and legislature – what if any links with the Crown would continue and in what form; what consequences thence for the Act of Settlement requirements, Royal Marriages Act and Defender of the Faith title (already by then dropped in some of the Commonwealth monarchies who, under the Statute of Westminster 1931, would all have to be consulted about such further changes); and what consequences also, for example, for the Ecclesiastical Committee, the 1919 Enabling Act machinery and episcopal withdrawal from the House of Lords?
- A host of lesser order issues – fate of the Royal Peculiars and Visitation, position of chaplains in public departments, dissolution of cathedral and all other ecclesiastical corporations, status of burial grounds, marriage law exemption from registrar attendance, charity law status, possible consequences for universities and public schools.
- What officials called 'interesting general questions' – would the state become entirely secular; would any form of national ceremony continue to have a religious aspect; while personal Royal events such as marriages might be celebrated by the Church of England for so long as sovereigns remained members, what should be the position

for jubilees, the cenotaph ceremony and services of the Orders of Chivalry: and to what extent would the current legal obligations of incumbents to their parishioners fall to be altered? (TNA CAB 165/1047 Memorandum CE[74]4 20 November 1973)

No record of any ministerial discussion has survived. Implicitly, the ministerial committee can be taken to have agreed perhaps with officials' conclusions in their first discussion of the remit:

> This confirms our view that the Government should not grasp this nettle unless it is forced to; on the contrary, it should go out of its way to explore ways and means of satisfying the present aspirations of the Church for lesser changes in the relationship between Church and State. At the present time these fall a good way short of disestablishment ... but, if they are not met, there is likely to be pressure for more radical changes. And once more radical proposals have been developed, it may be difficult to find any satisfactory half way house. (TNA HO 304/45 PA[74]1, para. 7)

Thirty-five years later these problems have not evaporated. If anything, the appraisal gave prominence to the problems for the state without giving proportionate weight to the problems for the Church of England. The main one is that, because it is not a corporate body and does not have a corporate legal personality (Leigh 2004), it would have to determine its future structure and thereby confront latent problems of balance which, under present arrangements, are strung between the Synod, the Archbishops' Council, the Church Commissioners, dioceses and parishes – all bodies with considerable autonomy. Achieving a new, workable structure could not be a neutral process because it would involve defining new relationships and redefining old ones. What may now be blurred would have to become explicit. Major issues of authority and process would have to be faced. A Church which now has a legislature would also then have to create a single executive which, despite its name, the Archbishops' Council is not. (The complexity and bewildering character of Anglican structures of authority was illustrated by a diocesan motion seeking clarity on the subject and debated at the July 2008 Synod.) Moreover, a new constitution could hardly slavishly follow the Westminster/Whitehall model. There, the Opposition is permanently an alternative government in waiting but no feasible ecclesiastical model could follow democratic principles in the same way: there are no 'shadow' Archbishops of Canterbury or York.

Moreover, behind the managerial task would be tensions derived from significant internal differences over doctrine, ritual, ecclesiology and discipline. At the time of the Cecil Committee, the Treasury Solicitor, Maurice Gwyer, was doubtful whether the Church of England could move, or be permitted by Parliament to move, to a condition of establishment closer to that of the Church of Scotland precisely because it lacked the latter's fundamental agreement on doctrine as embodied in the *Articles Declaratory* appended to the Church of Scotland Act 1921 (Cecil evidence 16 April 1931: 490). As noted in Chapter 11, what Gwyer appears to have had in mind is that the Church of England was itself internally pluralized in such matters and it was the existing form of establishment that rendered coexistence possible. The implication of this view was that disestablishment would cause the Church to fragment, the *ur* fear then – as now – of many of those Anglicans who wish to retain establishment.

Officials in 1974, although quick to scent the possibility of disestablishment in the Chadwick proposals, did not apparently discern a direct danger to the Crown. Others, however, have. Paul Avis has put it very directly:

> [P]eople who wish to remain loyal to the institution of the monarchy will be extremely cautious about calling the establishment in question. It has been recognized for centuries that the destinies of the monarchy and the church are bound up together. In our constitutional ecology, the monarchy needs the church just as the polity of the church involves the monarchy. (Avis 2001: 31)

Avis goes on to quote Vernon Bogdanor's comment that, were disestablishment to come 'the position of the monarchy would be radically affected' and a secular monarchy would ensue (Bogdanor 1995: 239). Avis's conclusion is 'In that event, one might ask, what would the constitutional rationale of the monarchy be?' (Avis 2001: 239). This is to suggest a mutual dependency between Church and throne where disestablishment would be fatal to the monarchy but not, actually, to the Church. Ian Leigh has claimed that 'In Britain a hereditary monarch without an Established Church is inexplicable: the two stand or fall together in terms of historical rationale' (Leigh 2004: 269). William Fittall has voiced similar sentiments:

> If the monarchy were to end we would be a different sort of nation. Similarly, if the monarchy continued but the sovereign were no longer

Supreme Governor of the Church of England and no longer symbolically received authority at the hands of the Archbishop of Canterbury,
we would have become a different sort of society. (Fittall 2008: 78)

These are very high claims and will be dealt with at greater length
below. Here it is necessary only to remark that, in a world where other
monarchies exist without established churches, the claims are by no
means beyond question. Interestingly, such claims did not seem to register with a modern Secretary of State at all. When invited to comment on
recent projections of religious observance, the Communities and Local
Government Secretary, Hazel Blears, was reported as saying that Britain
was a 'secular democracy' (*The Times* 8 May 2008). It is the fact that the
UK is, of course, neither of those things formally that underpins the case
for reconsidering those formalities now.

Concentrating on the 'higher' aspects of establishment should not prevent bearing in mind the Church of England's pre-eminence in state
ceremonial – a role that is taken for granted and neither easy to set aside
nor replace. On the strictest interpretation of disestablishment, this function would be abolished. At the same time, it is difficult to see that there
would be a parliamentary majority for going quite so far. And, if that is
the case, then such a conclusion must underline the necessity to define
what kind of disestablishment it is that should be required in the first
place and why.

There is also the point that looking at disestablishment as a series of
technical, legal and management problems does not exhaust all the relevant perspectives. One of the lingering objections of Christian dissent to
establishment is resentment at what might be called the Church of England's *cultural* and *social* status (Roper 2008: 25). Although the Chadwick
disestablishment could be thought in some respects to extend to such
fields, its effect would not be explicit or certain. What is at issue here is
a spectrum of features not themselves crucially dependent on the legal
architecture of establishment but which accord to Anglicanism a degree
of social[1] and civic pre-eminence. Examples include Anglican prayers in
both Houses of Parliament, the tradition of Anglican-led civic services,
Anglican-dominated chaplaincies in the health, military and prison services and, at the most general level, the expectation that those from the
highest social strata will identify themselves with Anglicanism. Legal disestablishment by itself will not alter these behaviours and expectations.
If it did not do so in Wales after 1920, then it is even less likely to do
so in England. As explained at Chapter 8, Welsh disestablishment can
at one and the same time be viewed both as disestablishment for the

Church of England *and* an entirely fresh establishment of the Church in Wales.

In the end, the problem of defining the limits of disestablishment stem from the very plasticity of the term 'establishment' in the first place (Morris 2006). As Frank Cranmer explains in Chapter 9 above, ambiguities in the concept mean that the outcome of the very substantial changes made to the status of the Church of Sweden can be described as resulting both in a disestablished and a still, if in different ways, established church. 'Establishment' does not describe a fixed, unfaltering entity but, rather, a series of fluctuating and mutable links between the Church of England and political authority, itself constantly adjusting to changed social and economic circumstances. It may be possible to take a snapshot of establishment but it cannot be bottled. Every age that wishes for disestablishment must first take an inventory of the goods that are actually there.

In that sense, officials in the 1970s were not far wrong to suggest that a Royal Commission had to come first before the choices may be made. Such a body would need to reconnoitre the separate interests of Church and state with especial care. Whereas, for example, the Church might prefer as clean a break as possible, the state would need to ponder how, if at all, the ceremonies of civic religion might be conducted and the extent to which the Church should be permitted to walk away with its historical patrimony intact where the Church's former pastoral obligations (for example over marriage and burial) were abolished. While the ecclesiastical lawyer Lewis Dibdin was probably right to opine during the Cecil Committee's proceedings in the 1930s that 'the general trend ... in favour of disendowment was far less than it had been' (Cecil Evidence 1931: 283), that did not mean then or now that disendowment would not need to be dealt with. Of course, the legal environment has changed since 1931, and it might be argued that disendowment could never come onto the table because of the prohibition against religious discrimination in Article 14 of the European Convention on Human Rights. Whatever the case, the state would no doubt wish to consider what mechanism would be necessary to ensure that the former pastoral obligations would continue to be observed by the Church.

The position of the Crown

As recorded above, some analysts maintain that breaking the link with the Crown is bound by itself to precipitate disestablishment and, in more extreme forms of the argument, imperil the moral basis of the state. Such positions are fundamentally the views of those within the Church of

England most desirous of preserving the current higher architecture. It is argued that such positions – by no means always as self-interested as they may seem – exaggerate the downside of feasible changes, partly in some cases perhaps to discourage their being contemplated at all. Moreover, they usually fail to consider the possible upside of changes which may be seen to benefit the polity at large as well as help the Crown – bound in to a form of establishment which, among other things, restricts its own religious freedom – to appear to be more open to the consequences of the social changes of the last century. In this context, the questions here are how far the constitutional settlement should be revisited, in what way and with what implications.

Credal requirements

Any significant change in this area cannot avoid revisiting the 1689–1701 constitutional settlement, and dealing with the requirements of the Statute of Westminster 1931. A preliminary question is with what kind of seriousness such questions are to be approached. Does it involve at one extreme addressing the moral basis of the state or, at the other, merely a technical question of modernization? If the former, then the subject would fall to be approached only with due fearfulness and awe; if the latter, a degree of determination somewhat short of levity would suffice. The standpoints of the Church and of the state could be very different: whereas the former could adopt complete self-government regardless of the effect on the Crown, the government of the day could not be indifferent to the consequences for the monarchy – and nor, presumably, would the monarch.

Although, like every other statutory provision, the 1701 Act is not and cannot be entrenched, in practice it has operated substantially with that effect. That is because of the way in which people manage expectations: those in the line of succession where actually succeeding is a credible possibility have been careful not to disqualify themselves; and those without such proximity have not felt the necessity to remain qualified. Apparently, the former holds good even so far as to someone eleventh in line where, in a recent example, a remoter heir's fiancée has sought to enter the Church of England with the effect of preserving her spouse's entitlement. A situation therefore obtains where, although the restriction is evidently and nowadays admittedly discriminatory, no-one appears disadvantaged. That is, the practical and personal drawbacks of the restriction do not manifest themselves. However, as explained above, the discriminatory character of the Act is felt by Roman Catholics at large just as they found offensive the Accession Declaration Oath before its reform in 1910.

Whereas at first sight it might seem feasible to treat the requirement to be in communion with the Church of England and the prohibitions hostile to Roman Catholicism separately, they are in fact indissolubly linked in practice. For example, to allow sovereigns to be married to Roman Catholics and permit them to adopt the faith themselves conflicts with the requirement to 'join in communion' with the Church of England. Conversely, to remove the latter requirement must contemplate the possibility of a Roman Catholic sovereign and/or one who is married to a Roman Catholic. It follows that, in the absence of any special provision, a Roman Catholic sovereign would become Supreme Governor and Defender of the Faith. While assumption of the latter title (conferred after all by the Pope in the first place) would have no practical meaning, assumption of the former would be likely to be unacceptable to the Church of England (and, for different reasons, to many in Northern Ireland) especially but not only because the Roman Catholic Church does not recognize the validity of Anglican clerical orders.[2] A former dean of Westminster has pointed out that Roman Catholic monarchs would not be able to receive communion at their coronations, or to receive the archbishop's blessing, and would have to bring their children up in the Roman Catholic faith. In circumstances where it was highly unlikely that the Roman Catholic Church would do so, the dean nonetheless concluded that it was 'a prerequisite of any such repeal [of the 1701 Act] that the Roman Catholic Church recognize Anglican sacraments and orders and the legitimacy of churches other than its own' (Carr 2002a).

Conversely, there is no absolute unanimity on this point even among Anglicans. The Prince of Wales is said to have expressed an open mind on whether Roman Catholics could sit on the throne (Blackburn 2006: 119, quoting from Lord Ashdown's memoirs). Whether there are arguments that would make it impossible for a Roman Catholic monarch to be Supreme Governor has been contested by a former bishop of Worcester:

> There is no reason why a Roman Catholic, advised by Ministers, who can be of any religious persuasion or none, could not be supreme governor of the Church of England. There is no truth in the contention that a change of this kind will unravel the constitution. (HL 14 January 2005, col. 502)

What this difference of opinion does is focus attention on whether there is any case for retaining the title at all. If the Church of England is now to be understood as in fact making all the appointments to all the senior posts nominally reserved to the sovereign, then it is not clear what if anything is left of the Supreme Governor role or what mischief – apart from resetting coronation formulae – could conceivably be perpetrated by a Roman Catholic or any non-Anglican sovereign. Abolition of the Supreme Governor role would not, therefore, be a fatal blow to anything now existing. As has been pointed out, abolition would merely return the monarchy to where it was before the Reformation: 'There is no sense in which its constitutional legitimacy would be diminished or the case for its own abolition be advanced' (Norman 2004: 83). Moreover, as a Scottish observer has put it:

> Although the Queen displays publicly a strong sense of religious voca-tion, the future of the monarchy is not well served by inflating its metaphysical significance. In any case, it is not clear that its defence needs to be protective of church establishment as it currently stands. (Fergusson 2004: 178)

What kind of legislation – Statute or Measure?

Although addressing these issues would get as close to core constitu-tional matters as the UK constitution's dispersed character allows, it does not follow that their resolution would involve awesome and threaten-ing seismic shifts. While there is a tendency to proceed with particular circumspection in respect of that divinity which hedges the Crown, it is possible to conceive of it as a low-intensity rather than high-wire operation. In particular, there would be a choice about how to proceed depending on whether the government or the Church of England took the initiative.

On the one hand, changing the law could be conceived of as the most important constitutional alteration since 1701, necessitating a referen-dum in the UK and solemn exchanges with the Commonwealth states. The position may be talked up into a condition of high seriousness on the lines, for example, of Lord Habgood recorded in Chapter 11 above.

On the other hand, such changes could be taken simply as rather belated adjustments to the plural facts of British life, themselves lat-terly deepened by the growth of non-Christian religious communities and degrees of unbelief. Many supposed difficulties – Commonwealth monarchies ending up with different monarchs because of altered suc-cession rules, obscure disturbances in the constitutional ether and so on – can be avoided even where not bogus. As Robert Blackburn has pointed out, while the provisions of numerous ancient and not so ancient statutes might have to be addressed depending on the paths of change chosen 'this complication would hardly bother the government's legislative draftsmen' (Blackburn 2006: 126). In other words, the technical problems are not insurmountable if the will exists to make changes. At the same time, Commonwealth governments could be expected to be sympathetic rather than averse. On the one hand, it could be argued that nothing in the 1931 Act would prevent the UK government proceeding because removing the provision of 'Supreme Governor' in the preamble to the Thirty-Nine Articles and repealing s. 8 of the Act of Supremacy 1559 would not involve a change to a royal 'style or title' or succession, though proceeding to remove the 1701 Act's prohibitions would. While advantage might be taken of the non-compulsory character of the 1931 Act, the better view would probably be to consult at the very least as a matter of courtesy whatever changes were envisaged, especially if the timing coincided with managing a change in the headship of the Commonwealth.[3]

Moreover, there is the position of sovereigns to consider: it is not at all clear that they should be the one inhabitant of the UK unable to choose their own religion. As in Sweden where the king – despite disestablishment – remained a Lutheran so British sovereigns might remain Anglican, but then it would be by choice. In such cases, the head of state could be invited if it wished by the Church of England to serve as its patron, and, where not, not. The arguments sometimes advanced that there is no discrimination because a potential heir is not prevented from practising Roman Catholicism, or that there is no *visible* likelihood of disqualification arising for current heirs seem neither reputable nor convincing. The fact that there is still feeling in the Roman Catholic community on this subject is evidenced by the recurrent attempts to raise it as recorded in Chapter 11. When successive governments have been devoted to combating discrimination everywhere else, it is not at all clear why it should be allowed to persist at the apex of the constitution. Finally, the possibility has to be faced that a future sovereign might have no faith, a far-from-implausible eventuality and one which reinforces the case for making such issues of conscience unrestrained by laws originally directed at ancient and long-gone foreign political threats.

Pursuing a 'low-intensity' approach, the changes could be achieved by Measure. In the case of the sovereign's religion, it has even been argued that legislation would not be necessary. This is because of the presumed effects of arguments recently used by the Lord Chancellor and the House of Lords in what could be regarded as analogous circumstances. In the first case, the Lord Chancellor justified the legality of the civil marriage of the Prince of Wales to Mrs Parker-Bowles in 2005 by reference to the effect of the Human Rights Act 1998 when it had hitherto been understood that the Marriage Acts in England required that lawful royal marriages could be effected by the Church of England alone (HL 24 February 2005, col. WS87). Similarly, in a case involving an 1848 Act's prohibition of the advocacy of republicanism, the House of Lords made it clear that they did not think that the Act could survive scrutiny under the Human Rights Act. How much the less, it is argued, could the older provisions of the 1689 Bill of Rights survive similar scrutiny (Dwyer 2005).

That interesting, and not entirely fanciful, speculation aside, resort to Measure for these and related purposes is not to be ruled out. Though it might be assumed that primary legislation should be preferred and that Parliament would resist any other approach, it is by no means automatically or unarguably so. This is not to urge, of course, that the Church might consider taking unannounced or un-negotiated initiatives especially where government co-operation was required, for example, in dealing with Commonwealth states. As the government itself has envisaged, such matters would be 'in the first instance' for the Church.

Who should take the initiative?

Raising here the prospect of proceeding by Measure is also a way of intruding an important general point. That is, a Measure would be viable in the first instance only if the *Church of England* took the initiative. It would itself be well placed to work out the legislative requirement not only in respect of the 1689 and 1701 legislation but also, for example, in removing the need for royal involvement under the Submission of Clergy Act 1533, the summoning of Synod and so on. Parliament would still retain ultimate control because it alone could approve any resulting Measure, and the government of the day would remain the ultimate custodian of the sovereign's position.

Moreover, for that Church there is at the heart of these issues an important question: that is, how far it wishes to mould its own future and take the initiative even if, or indeed especially where, the government does not wish to do so. (The same point is implicit, of course, in the fact that bishops could simply on their own motion withdraw from the House of Lords.) The reluctance of governments to act is not to be seen merely as polite, benign passivity or an unwillingness to shoulder a tricky burden. It also at a deeper level betokens indifference to the Church of England's fate: the Prime Minister's unprompted 2007 initiative to withdraw from active participation in ecclesiastical appointments almost certainly fell into that category. Similarly, not to take the lead itself would betoken the

Church of England's own indifference to the inferior position of other denominations and religions.

There is, of course, room for a different view. If it be accepted, for example, that the destinies of the monarchy and the Church are so bound up together that severance would leave the monarchy isolated, then it could be asked, as Paul Avis has asked, what the remaining rationale of the monarchy would be. Reformers of a very different stripe share a similar attitude if with different motives. Deprecating the Goldsmith Citizenship Review's settling on the monarchy as the single most meaningful symbol of Britishness, Madeleine Bunting said of the monarchy 'It's an institution, like that other great symbol of the nation, the Church of England, teetering under the weight of its own compromised authority and internal contradictions' (*Guardian* 7 April 2008). On the Avis view, these matters are so central to the nature of the UK state that change could be contemplated only by government-managed primary legislation. Whereas the appointment of bishops could be regarded as internal to the Church of England, altering something as fundamental as the Act of Settlement would have to be a matter for the government of the day to espouse. If so, in cold blood, it would be bound to be controversial and very likely could be contemplated only in exceptional circumstances, for example, where a highly regarded sovereign or heir apparent wished to marry a Roman Catholic who did not intend converting, or had principled and clearly genuine reservations about entering into, or remaining in, communion with the Church of England. There could also be changes following some quite seismic alteration in the constitution where the question simply fell away in circumstances where old landmarks were obliterated.

The risks of proceeding exclusively on government initiative are evident. Taking a high view of the interdependence of church and monarchy not only raises the game, but also has its dangers. While, on the one hand, it may, and be intended to, frighten off prospective players from contemplating change by making it all seem too difficult, on the other hand, it seeks to yoke the fate of the monarchy with that of a single institution with which monarchy does not *have* to be associated and upon which monarchy is *not* ultimately dependent. But that overheated route does not have to be followed. And, of course, contemplating it at all has the effect of making proceeding by Measure attractive: the Church itself would be volunteering the case for change, and in a form which could only be accepted or rejected by Parliament. A carefully prepared approach would not necessarily risk rejection, and it could be seen as a statesmanlike gesture by a Church confident of itself and open to the interests of others. Parliamentary control of the succession would remain: the discriminatory rules would go.

Although the first instinct of lawyers and Parliamentarians might be to rule such an approach out, it should receive more than momentary consideration. It is not an objection that such a proposal has not, so far as is known, been made before. Granted that there has been relatively little discussion of the issue and that such discussion has assumed that the Church of England would oppose any alteration, then examination of the means of effecting it has also had to assume that the change would have to be forced upon an unwilling Church from outside. The point here is simply that in this respect, as in some others, the Church of England could itself take the initiative should it wish to do so and, if not actually by Measure, then by other means. While the Church may not be an entirely free agent, it is not without resource and is quite capable of initiating a process of change should it wish to do so.

There is undoubtedly room for argument here, though perhaps rather less than interested parties might allow. It has to be remembered that the weight of evidence about the state of religious belief and its plurality beyond Christianity render the surviving late seventeenth-century settlement in principle indefensible even if its increasingly emaciated formal remnant may stagger on. The problem is how to identify the routes out which do as little damage to existing institutions as possible. They include the Church of England becoming regarded more explicitly as a national rather than a state church or a church *for* the nation, and accepting that the removal of a religious test for monarchy means that it will become a secular monarchy even if monarchs themselves remain religious and, indeed, Anglican. As Vernon Bogdanor has hazarded

> There can be no doubt that a secular monarchy would be a very different type of monarchy from that to which we have historically been accustomed ... But a secularized monarchy might nevertheless prove to be a monarchy more in tune with the spirit of the age. (Bogdanor 1995: 239)

None of this is to be enterprised lightly or inadvisedly, and the lack of enthusiasm on the part of the government may be imagined. But in the end there seems no avoiding the reshaping of the church/state architecture. To be clear, what would be involved would be the repeal of all provisions in the 1689 and 1701 legislation governing the religion of the sovereign, the repeal of the Tudor statutes regarding the sovereign's Church-governing status (including powers of appointment), and the repeal of the Accession Declaration and Coronation oaths – the latter at least in their present form. To repeat, these are all matters within the *vires* of the Enabling Act 1919. In addition, though it would not be a necessary part of ecclesiastical reform, opportunity might also be take to make the law of succession gender neutral – as suggested by the Solicitor General, Vera Baird, in the context of a proposed Equality Bill.

Defender of the Faith

This is the title originally conferred by the pope on Henry VIII before the English Reformation in recognition of the king's supposed authorship of a tract defending the Papacy. Its perpetuation since as one of the formal titles of the sovereign gives it, of course, an ironic ring though the title has long since come to be regarded in practice as a statement consistent with the sovereign's headship of the Church of England.

It is well known that the present Prince of Wales has reservations about the title's wording (Dimbleby 1994: 528). Arising from his feeling that the monarchy should not be seen defending one particular interpretation of faith, he has mused out loud about the possibility of his being the 'Defender of Faith' as a better way of describing the proper role of the monarchy in a pluralized faith Britain. While this approach has generally evoked sympathy with and support for his position, change on such lines would not only be a break with tradition but also be seen as a measure distancing the monarchy from the Church of England. When asked about this in 2008, the Archbishop of Canterbury gave a two-part reply. First, it should be borne in mind that the title has a very specific historical setting and he did not believe in revising historical titles on the hoof. However, second, he went on to add:

> But that the British Monarchy should, as part of its responsibility for the cohesion of our society, take seriously the reality of corporate faith and, in certain circumstances speak on its behalf in the most general way, yes. (Williams 2008)

It does not seem necessary to add to that: the important thing is what current meaning is reasonably given to the title rather than its wording.

Nature of the coronation

The coronation above all other events ceremonially fuses the personal and institutional roles of the sovereign. This fusion is rare in modern societies, and is the source of real difficulty in plural societies. Whereas in the past it could be said that the monarchy – Christian, manifestly and culturally European – has been the one institution unifying the still in many ways very separate parts of Britain, the model's association with one particular Christian religious tradition is challenged by the diversity of British society.

No-one seriously would dispute that life has moved on since 1953 and that the ceremony at the very least needs to be looked at again. A form of coronation which in retrospect appears as the last imperial flourish could, if repeated unchanged, all too easily seem triumphalist and over-representative of the white population as well as wholly Anglican. As one study of religious discrimination has pointed out,

> Coronations are state events which, historically, have expressed the close, symbolic relationship between Established religion and the state. The religious composition of society has changed significantly since the last Coronation and the next Coronation will therefore high-light a series of very important issues and complexities, which it would be best to begin giving consideration to as soon as possible. (Weller and Purdam 2000: 112)

Unchanged, a ceremony which formerly helped unite British society could instead emphasize division. That was why the Accession Declaration Act 1910 radically altered the declaratory formula so offensively hostile to Roman Catholicism. The considerations that held sway in an ethnically homogenous and Christian society in 1910 apply with equal if not greater force in the substantially more plural society of today. In addition, the numbers who still regard the sovereign as providentially chosen (that is, put there by God) must be very small indeed. For the public acknowledgement and celebration of a new sovereign's accession to rest entirely on a wholly Christian, and at that Anglican, ceremony does not seem defensible. As well as excluding non-Anglican Christians, such an event would seem to qualify the extent to which all other religious groups were to be regarded as full members of British society and to be so recognized by the head of state. Some kind of real multifaith inclusion seems unarguable.

All that said, it is by no means apparent exactly what changes might be considered. Not only is there greater diversity in the population but devolution has also altered the constitutional structure of the UK. Account would have to be taken of those changes, too.

Options could include the following:

1. Minimal alteration – Retain the 1953 model, reserving the eucharist for a private, possibly quite separate, occasion, and revising the

Coronation Oath to excise the special position accorded to the protection of the Church of England. This could be justified on the basis that the event celebrated the long historic Christian tradition of the UK, and in terms which emphasized the equal value of other traditions of, and nowadays represented in, the UK.

2. Explicit pluralism – the object would be to recognize and somehow incorporate all religious traditions, not necessarily in the *conduct* of a coronation ceremony but in their association with/presence at such a ceremony *and* by means of a new, separate, representative act of recognition/homage. The latter might take place, for example, in Westminster Hall as a way of linking the legislature (which has no place in the traditional coronation), communities and the monarchy more emphatically than could be achieved by a coronation alone.[4] (The basic idea is not, of course, new. It is the reason why certain religious groups – for example, the Society of Friends and Jews – have long been among the 'Privileged Bodies' with the right to present Addresses to new sovereigns.)

3. Radical pluralism – The sovereign does not accede by right of coronation: the latter only recognizes accession and in a Christian theology which celebrates the visitation of God's grace upon the anointed monarch. For traditional reasons, a Christian coronation ceremony might remain (presuming the sovereign's continuing membership of the Church of England) but more as a secondary and personal rather than institutional event with the main public emphasis placed on the kind of recognition ceremony canvassed at (2). This could also facilitate a situation where, if the Act of Settlement's requirement were repealed, a new sovereign chose not to be in communion with the Church of England or, indeed, a member of any religion. In that case, the old form of coronation could give way entirely to a Westminster Hall style event and, if desired, sovereigns could arrange such private service of blessing or none according to the state of their belief. In the Netherlands apparently the sovereign merely touches the Crown in a non-religious enthronement ceremony, and that symbolism could be sufficient without the extended traditional theatre.

These indicative options hardly, of course, exhaust the possibilities for change which are already being considered out loud in the Church of England, if still within traditional forms (Carr 2002b). In so far as it were desired to alter the coronation oath, legislation (which could be addressed as in 1910 in the interval between accession and coronation) would be necessary if no earlier opportunity presented itself. The same legislation could in fact do away altogether with the requirements of the Accession Declaration Oath Act. As already mentioned, Asquith thought it redundant in 1910 and nothing occurring since has done anything to call his judgement into question. In practice, however, such incremental changes are likely themselves to suggest their own inadequacy and encourage more radical challenges to past forms. In that case, accession could be marked by more modest ceremonies of public investiture or enthronement without sacramental ceremony. Indeed, if the present sovereign abdicated, an old-style coronation of her heir during her lifetime could hardly be contemplated.

The Scottish oath

There would remain the issue of the Scottish oath under the English Act of Union. This requires the incoming sovereign to swear to uphold the Church of Scotland, that is in the same way as the sovereign is required to swear in the coronation oath to uphold the Church of England. Traditionally, the Scottish oath has been taken immediately on accession, that is at the accession Privy Council. Changing the requirement would also require legislation, but if the traditional interval between accession and swearing were followed there would, of course, be no time to legislate. However, it is not inconceivable that the wording of the legislation is consistent with a more relaxed time frame which would allow space for legislation.

While no difficulty would arise at all if new legislation were introduced in advance of demise, it would seem better to reserve making changes until it were possible to do so as part of a thoroughly considered response to all the questions raised following accession.[5] It would also no doubt be desirable to consult the Scottish Parliament which, although formally without legislative locus, must be regarded as properly representative of Scottish opinion, and might also have views about how accession should otherwise be marked in a devolved Scotland itself. (It follows that the devolved institutions in Wales should also be consulted about how the accession should be independently marked, if at all, in the Principality.)

The *content* of the legislation would need careful consideration. Whereas in 1706/07 it was feasible to regard the sovereign as also chief executive of the government of the kingdom(s), that has long since ceased to be the case. It follows that, even if its assurances are annually renewed for the meeting of the General Assembly, the oath can have no real purchase any more than their coronation oaths prevented Victoria and George V giving their assent to disestablishment in Ireland and Wales. In practice, the Scottish oath shares the same redundancy, and all the more so following the Church of Scotland Act 1921. If the oath is not to be abolished entirely, there may be a case for transforming it into a modern declaration recognising Scottish continued nationhood and cultural distinctiveness if, as with defining 'Britishness', that be easier said than done. Any legislation would have to be government legislation, and this fact could tell against resort to Measure for tackling the English aspects of the early eighteenth-century Acts.

Conclusion

What this chapter shows is that changes in what it calls the higher architecture of church/state relations cannot be sensibly confined to considering only the cases for and against establishment. Disestablishment is not itself a term of art for the same reasons that establishment is an ambiguous catch-all for a complex of relations themselves constantly changing over time, informally as well as formally. In disestablishment's most extreme form – total severance of the state from Christianity – it is impossible to see what good would be done unless the aim were to punish an institution that has contributed to the life of our society for longer than the state itself. The argument has therefore been that the subject is best approached by considering the range of feasible measures that would do most to produce religious equality. Religious *freedom* (except for the sovereign) we have already but the present form of establishment remains blemished by the remaining exclusionary forms of defence constructed at the turn of the seventeenth century. While at first sight detaching the sovereign from the religious supremacy may seem revolutionary, it is but to recognize that the head of state's role changes when society changes and it is undesirable for it to be so intimately associated with one particular religious form whether in England or in Scotland. There could still be coronations, Lord High Commissioners could still hold court during the General Assembly in Edinburgh, and sovereigns could still be members of the Church of England if they wished. However, the meaning of such things could be adjusted to sit more happily with what we have become, and the more they were adjusted the more the old forms themselves would fall to be questioned.

13
The Political Representation of Religion

This chapter considers how from a constitutional point of view the state should regard the institutional presence of religion in formal political structures. It starts by examining whether recent discussion has revealed any principles arguing for a special place for religious representation in the legislature, turns to consider whether the actual performance of the bishops in recent years discloses special or practical reasons for their remaining in the House of Lords, and then looks at how they might be removed.

Religion and the legislature – general

At present, the sole ex officio representation of religion is the 26 bishops in the House of Lords. Since the creation of life peers in 1958 made it possible, there have been occasional appointments of people regarded at least in part as representative of other denominations and faiths. These have included Muslims, a former President of the Methodist Conference and former Chief Rabbis. In addition some former archbishops and bishops have been appointed on their retirement when their ex officio membership ends. Examples include former archbishops (Carey and Habgood) and former bishops (Shepherd and Harries).

The Wakeham Royal Commission recommended that a reduction in the number of bishops should be accompanied by more explicit representation of other denominational and faith interests (Wakeham 2000: 152). As against this, of all the written submissions to the Wakeham Commission that discussed religious representation, over 80 per cent opposed the continuation of bishops as ex officio members. The Public Administration Select Committee subsequently recommended against the continuation of any explicit religious representation (PASC

2002: 34–5). Iain McLean has pointed out that there would be no viable basis for religious representation as recommended by Wakeham which did not severely distort membership of the House because of its resulting disproportionate size (McLean and Linsley 2004: 14–15).

At a time when membership of the second chamber continues to be up for review, it follows that the case for religious representation first has to be made before the practicalities of its selection are addressed. The principal arguments for continuing that representation seem to be twofold. First, even if bishops first entered the House of Lords because of their temporal possessions, it is a constitutional tradition that the Christian religion is represented in the legislature and that it has thereby direct means of participating in national deliberations at the highest level, including as to legislation affecting the Church. Moreover, its representatives can ensure that moral issues are fully addressed, even if Wakeham did not give the Church or, indeed, any religion a unique status in that regard (Wakeham 2000: para. 15.6). The Archbishop of Canterbury, Rowan Williams, has phrased the latter case more modestly as where the legislature 'allows that there are people in it licensed to ask awkward questions on a religious basis', foreseeing that other religious bodies might also come to be represented. But:

> simple removal of the Bishops from the Lords might well be the amputation of a genuinely useful part of the polity: not because the bishops are clinging to privilege, but as a matter of witness to that more than political dimension that I touched on. (Williams 2008)

Secondly, granted the greater contemporary plurality of religious life, it is only right that representation should be widened to include all major Christian denominations and other faiths. As already pointed out, many of the latter also take the view that the *present* form of establishment in this respect is better than none because it gives a recognized place to a religion, even if not their religion, in the legislature (Modood 1997). This is not, of course, the view of nonconformist denominations in England who, without the stridency or vehemence of old, nonetheless contest the principle of establishment still. Examples include Baptist opponents of establishment (Weller 2000; and Wright, N. G. 2008) and other nonconformist participants at the Constitution Unit 2006 seminar from the United Reformed Church (Roper 2008), though the contribution from a member of the Society of Friends emphasized how far interest in the topic had declined (Sims 2008). As also recorded above, spokesmen of the Church of England have developed the notion of the bishops' having a representative role in the legislature for *all* religious life even if no-one has, as it were, asked them. (How far it is possible or desirable to speak out publicly in the supposed interests of others is a topic no doubt being reconsidered by the Archbishop of Canterbury following his 7 March 2008 lecture speculating about even a modest degree of recognition for limited aspects of *sharia* law.)

Against these arguments are a number of considerations. First, it is not clear what exactly is meant by religious representation. Wakeham did not distinguish between people who belonged to a particular religion and those who might in some other sense be said to represent it, for example, because of their priestly or office-holding status. These and other ambiguities would need to be faced:

> Even if it is accepted that representatives of religion must act in some sense as representatives of their faith, the extent to which they must be merely the mouthpiece of their religious organisation, holding to the official line of that organisation or, in contrast, to represent the different voices within its membership remains unclear. (Smith 2003: 675)

Judging from a recent study of bishops' views on their membership of the House of Lords (Harlow, Cranmer and Doe 2008), they seem uncertain at present whether they are independent-minded representatives in the Burkean sense or some species of ecclesiastical delegate. On the basis admittedly of a limited range of questions relating to a twelve-month period only and to which only 14 of the 26 bishops replied, the bishops as a group could be described as unclear on their function, sporadic in their attendance and not in fact concentrating on the issues they say they would prefer. Two questioned whether they should be in the House of Lords at all.

Nor is it clear on what basis religion can claim unique consideration for a corporate privilege as opposed to other interests, for example, employers' organizations, trade unions, academia, major professions and so on. The special representation of universities in the Commons was, after all, abolished over fifty years ago and there have been no moves to revive it. There is also the practical point that, the more the second chamber is constituted on an elective principle and, especially if its numbers are reduced, the more any corporate basis – let alone a uniquely privileged one – would be difficult to sustain.

Secondly, the existence of greater religious plurality adds by itself nothing to the case for either extended representation or the principle of religious representation of any kind in the first place. It seems very likely that similar considerations, though not explicitly acknowledged, may have influenced the approach of the Evangelical Alliance's *Faith and Nation* report of 2006. It chose to look at the question of religious membership of the House of Lords tactically and consider not so much the questions of principle as the extent to which it would be right for the Church of England to resist certain possible reforms. The report's overall tone about the bishops' presence in the House of Lords was cool:

> It is possible that their presence in the House adds to the mission effort of the Church of England, but it is a very moot point. We are concerned that too great an importance is being invested in some quarters in this matter. Our conclusion is that no initiative should be taken by the churches to remove bishops. To do this would send out quite the wrong signal to society in general because it would be understood as a diminution of Christian involvement in society. (Evangelical Alliance 2006: 57)

Thirdly, as Wakeham acknowledged, there is no agreement that religious representatives bring unique authority to the consideration of moral issues. Indeed, this claim is fundamentally disputed by non-religious groups (Wood 2008; and Copson and Pollack 2008). Even in Scotland where the Church of Scotland was active in support of a new Parliament it did not dream of arguing for representation in the devolved assembly. Neither that Parliament nor the Welsh Assembly has any institutionalized religious representation or formularies. Above all, some Church of England apologists in effect question their own case. For example, when referring to the House of Lords debate on the Assisted Dying Bill, *Theos* think tank writers referred to the difficulty of registering purely religious considerations in debate:

> For some this would raise the question of what, if anything, the Lords Spiritual contributed to House of Lords debates which could not have been delivered with greater authority and insight by Lords Temporal where a view from a religious community is required. It need not come from a specifically religious bench. (Partington and Bickley 2007: 42)

It cannot be said that government attempts to analyse the issues have been logical or cogent. The 2007 Government Paper (*The House of Lords: Reform* Cm 7027) started from an unexamined assumption 'that the range of religious opinion in the country should also be reflected in the membership of the Lords' (para. 2.8); and equated removal of the bishops from the Lords with disestablishment (para. 6.22) – a point rightly denied by the *Theos* think tank: 'the presence of the bishops in the House of Lords is not an element of establishment' (Partington and Bickley 2007: 16). Not even Roundell Palmer thought so in his magisterial Victorian defence of establishment (Selborne 1887: 76), though a former archbishop, Lord Carey, has argued otherwise (*The Times* 28 March 2007). The Commons vote on 8 March 2007 in favour of a 100 per cent elected second chamber would, as the White Paper pointed out, have the effect of altogether excluding bishops as of right *and* other religious acting in that capacity. That said, it is impossible, of course, to regard the vote on that occasion as anything more than a tactical episode in what seem likely to remain drawn out and uncertain proceedings.

It is therefore not at all surprising that the ensuing White Paper of July 2008 – *An Elected Second Chamber* (Cm 7438) – was unable to identify any basis of inter-party agreement on how further second chamber reform might be designed. Instead, the government settled for composing a list of questions to which it invited answers from the world at large. At the same time, one of its firmer positions was to repeat the unexamined assumptions about religious representation of the White Paper's predecessors. Declining as a matter of principle to list occupational categories to which an Appointments Commission should have regard, the White Paper nonetheless alluded to 'the possible exception of faith' representation (para. 6.27). However, the next paragraph then stipulated the one condition 'faith' representatives (unless superannuated) would be unable to fulfil, that is, that they 'should take part fully in the work of the chamber, in general terms devoting the same amount of time to this work as elected members'. Views were sought (para. 6.54) on whether the Appointments Commission should be given a specific remit in respect of 'other church' (that is, non-Church of England) and faith appointments.

The government's problem is that, for so long as it supports continued Church of England representation in the second chamber, it cannot avoid opening the possibility of offering representation to other religious groups. No doubt it feels forced to play its cards this way because, among other things, the last thing it wants to do is needlessly to upset the Anglican Church when there is in practice now no question whatsoever of any long-term 'reform' solution to second chamber composition making it successfully on to the statute book. Apart from observing again that a 100 per cent elected house would leave no room for appointees whether bishops or anyone else, the government has to persist in maintaining that faith should be the sole exception to the general rule of merit criteria. Moreover, to head off Anglican alarm, the government resorted to heady language:

> The relationship between the Church and State is a core part of our constitutional framework that has evolved over centuries. The presence of Bishops in the House of Lords signals successive Governments' commitment to this fundamental principle and to an expression of the relationship between the Crown, Parliament and the Church that underpins the fabric of our nation. (para. 6.45)

Responding to the ministerial statement in the House of Lords, the Bishop of Exeter repeated the Church's view that it needed a minimum of twenty seats to maintain an effective service to the House (HL, 14 July 2008, col. 999). This was maintained even though the White Paper made it clear (para. 6.49) that, because it was envisaged that a new second chamber would be smaller than the old, it would be 'logical to reduce the number of seats available for Bishops'. Most tellingly of all, however, was the way in which the government's attempt to present religious representation as a matter of constitutional principle was challenged by Evan Harris MP:

> Even the government accept in the White Paper that there is no place for bishops in a 100 per cent elected House, so in their view there is no fundamental constitutional principle in having bishops. (HC 14 July 2008, col. 33)

Quite apart from the questions of principle, there are also *practical* problems in the way of arranging a wider religious representation. Although logically of a second order, they are so substantial in themselves that they would render the presence of religions on any representative principle unfeasible.

First, there are difficulties in agreeing a common basis upon which the size of *membership* may be enumerated where, for example, the Church of England's claim that baptism is adequately indicative is disputed on the grounds that such a figure greatly overstates the active membership of the Church of England. Similar difficulties arise over the enumeration of those who are *not* religious.

Secondly, there is no single criterion for identifying permanent representative members of faiths outside those, like the Church of England, which operate a clear, clerical and hierarchical system. The Church of

Scotland and a number of Christian denominations have only annual senior office-holders. In other cases, the Chief Rabbi, for example, does not represent all Jews, and selecting Muslims would have to negotiate differences between and within Sunni and Shia as well as other groupings. Reviewing the situation, Charlotte Smith sees not only no satisfactory calculus as to numbers but also a darker downside of the whole approach:

> It appears to be virtually impossible to make provision for the representation of religion which is truly representative of the faith communities. Further, the retreat from such provision in favour of a model of religious representation which does not aim to represent all communities, but rather to provide for a plural discourse, raises the risk of heightening the sense of exclusion and discrimination experienced by members of the smaller faith communities. (Smith 2003: 695)

Summarising, in a situation where no other sovereign democratic legislature includes religious representatives,[1] no overwhelming case appears yet to have been made for the principle in the UK. Continuing a tradition restricted to England and increasingly unrepresentative of faiths in that part of the UK would seem logically unsustainable. However, that does not of course mean that it will not continue, among other things because of the impossibility of reaching political agreement on how further reform of the second chamber should proceed. For so long as no agreement on the wider questions is reached, it is unlikely that any initiative will be taken by government to deal with the question of religious representation by itself because turmoil would be risked without conceivable gain. Provided the Church of England continues to behave reasonably, the self-appointed proxy role of the bishops – accepted and supported by the Justice Secretary (HC, 14 July 2008, col. 33) – is welcome to governments unwilling to disturb the status quo. Nonetheless, both the absence of an argued case for the inclusion of religious representatives in principle and the practical impossibility of achieving wider religious representation on any satisfactorily equitable basis lead to examining the case more particularly for the continued membership of the bishops. The next section will therefore look more closely at the case for their staying even if sheer constitutional inertia for the time being operates in their favour.

The Church of England bishops

The Church of England Synod on 14 February 2008 agreed proposals from the two archbishops to implement the Prime Minister's desire no longer to play any active role in, among other senior posts, the appointment of bishops. (The Prime Minister's wishes were set out in his July 2007 Government Paper [*The Governance of Britain*, Cm 7170], and reconfirmed in March 2008 in *The Governance of Britain – Constitutional Renewal* [Cm 7342].)

Four questions arise: the extent to which it is important that their appointment should be seen to remain in the hands of the executive; what may be the implications for the Crown of the proposed withdrawal of the Prime Minister from active involvement in their appointment; what special considerations, if any, arise from the record of their performance in the House of Lords; and how should the removal of bishops from the second chamber be effected if desired.

To repeat what the Prime Minister (Callaghan) explained in 1976, the two questions of appointment and membership of the second chamber are intimately linked:

> There are, in my view, cogent reasons why the State cannot divest itself from a concern with these appointments of the established Church. The Sovereign must be able to look for advice on a matter of this kind and that must mean, for a constitutional Sovereign, advice from ministers. The archbishops and some of the bishops sit by right in the House of Lords, and their nomination must therefore remain a matter for the Prime Minister's concern. (HC 8 June 1976, col. 613)

There are two preliminary points to make about this statement. First, it was made over thirty years ago: much water has flowed under the bridge since, including the growing sophistication of the Church of England's appointments procedures. Secondly, the statement preceded the setting up of the House of Lords Appointments Commission in 2000 which functions to recommend non-political appointments to the House of Lords. The existence of that body has rendered the second limb of the Callaghan justification redundant in so far as it had genuine force in the first place. That was because it never logically followed that, because archbishops and bishops were in the House of Lords, their nomination should have to be a specifically prime ministerial concern: the language was a rhetorical device to bolster a justification which stood or fell on the second sentence's assertion now abandoned by one of his successors.

In addition, the new appointments system raises fresh constitutional questions about the bishops' continuing membership of the House of Lords,[2] with government officials' 1975 reservations (see Chapter 12 above) continuing to have force. Despite the fig leaf of the continued involvement of a civil servant (henceforward a Cabinet Office official rather then the former Prime Minister's Appointments Secretary), the fact is that an unaccountable committee of Church of England nominees will be appointing the 26 prelates who sit ex officio in the House of Lords – 5 in right of their see (Canterbury, York, Durham, London and Winchester) and 21 in order of seniority. Their appointment will, therefore, be even more devoid of any wider, responsible and accountable public scrutiny.

Opposing direct Church of England nomination in the post-Chadwick discussions of the 1970s, the Prime Minister was quick to point out that such an arrangement could not be compared at all with the system of party leader nomination, a parallel Norman Anderson speaking for the Church had offered as justifying direct Church nomination to the sovereign:

> The Prime Minister [Wilson] said that quite different considerations applied to the nomination of the Peers recommended by Opposition Parties since this all took place within the parliamentary and political framework... Unless the Church asked for disestablishment, or renounced its special place in the Lords, the Lords consideration was basic... The church's proposal would give a lot of patronage to a small group of people and the Prime Minister wondered whether, even if broad Church opinion really wanted this, the country as a whole would be happy with it. (TNA HO 304/33, note of meeting 25 June 1975)

These arguments remain good in principle. Despite these considerations, however, there might nonetheless be a case for the bishops staying in the House of Lords ex officio if there were arguments from the record of their attendance that suggested they made a contribution that could not be made by anyone else. The fact that some bishops (for example, the former bishop of Oxford's well-regarded membership of the Science Select Committee) can make a *personal* contribution is an argument for the selection of particular personalities and expertise rather than for the automatic appointment of ecclesiastical office holders regardless of what they could individually bring to the legislature. Does the record suggest otherwise?

Episcopal performance

Reviewing the evidence does not, however, establish that the balance of argument is affected by any special considerations arising from the actual performance of bishops in the House of Lords. The available studies indicate (Drewry and Brock 1971; and Bown 1994) that bishops' diocesan duties prevent regular attendance except when on the rota for taking prayers at the beginning of each day's sittings – a fact not surprisingly highly correlated with their participation in debate. While one study asserted that the bishops' 'impact on the House is out of all proportion to their numbers' (Drewry and Brock 1971: 246), studies have also remarked that their votes rarely had any impact on outcome – one division in the eight years 1979–87 – and that the respect paid to individual bishops was not matched by a favourable opinion on their contribution to the House overall (Bown 1994: 118–19). Whereas Conservative peers might be expected to be more instinctively supportive of the bishops, Bown's Conservative ministerial interviewee was not:

They are visitors rather than contributors. If you ask me whether the work and decisions of the House would be different if they were not here, I have to say, 'No'. (Bown 1994: 106)

A more recent study which examined the period 1999–2005 (Russell and Sciara 2007) showed that bishops voted relatively little (more than five participating only on 10 occasions and more than two only on 66 occasions). In the 806 divisions over the period 1999–2005, bishops' votes made a difference on four occasions to the possible outcome, only in one instance actually leading to a government defeat. A recent defence of episcopal attendance manages no more than to say, 'It may be reasonable to complain that bishops don't attend much, but they are attending more than they used to' (Partington and Bickley 2007: 28). At the same time, bare numbers cannot tell the whole story, and there are no doubt occasions where bishops influence the behaviour of other members of the Lords. The government defeat instanced above was over an amendment to the Nationality, Immigration and Asylum Bill in 2003 where a bishop was successful in requiring that the education of detained asylum seekers' children should take place in ordinary schools rather than in detention centres.

The removal of most of the hereditary peers has, naturally, made the bishops' legitimacy more exposed. When formerly the position of the hereditaries was so much more conspicuously anomalous, the position of the bishops drew correspondingly less attention. As the Constitution Unit has pointed out before, the UK's Parliament is the only modern sovereign democratic legislature that reserves a place for explicit religious representation. While the Wakeham Royal Commission recommended

(Wakeham, recommendations 108–15) widening the basis of that representation from one particular Christian denomination, it failed to make any principled case for such unique corporatism, and nor have any of the subsequent government White Papers on further Lords reform. Finally, the fact that, as a result of the House of Commons (Removal of Clergy Disqualification) Act 2001, clergy may now sit in the Commons removes what argument there was that, since the Church of England could not be represented in the Commons, then it was right that the bishops should be able to redress the balance by virtue of their membership of the House of Lords.

If the archbishops and bishops are not altogether to be removed from the Lords, one way of conferring some credible legitimacy on their continued membership could lie in a linkage with the House of Lords Appointments Commission when that body comes to be given a statutory status. In that case, Anglican diocesans' eligibility would be judged alongside the claims of others, religious or not. Some special criteria relating to their Church's historic role in England need not be ruled out. But that sort of role is not on the cards for the Appointments Commission yet. If it were, then it is difficult to see an outcome, if the Church does not in any case voluntarily withdraw, which would not be fewer than the present 26 bishops or, indeed, the 16 spoken of by the Wakeham Commission.

In 1950 the Archbishop of York thought the number could be about nine (Garbett 1950: 125). He would have been aware of Archbishop Fisher's exchanges with the Attlee government where Fisher envisaged a representation of ten bishops – the most senior five plus five diocesans elected by their peers 'in terms of their likelihood of making a useful contribution' (Carpenter 1991: 396). Such reductions would arguably not be disproportionate in the case of a body whose active members are thought now to amount to much less than 5 per cent of the population, and would not prevent the Church from continuing to make a contribution to the national legislature.

The changes in the appointments system also have implications for the position of the Crown. While none need imperil the sovereign's role as Supreme Governor, a little constitutional reinterpretation or silent mutation will be in order. Hitherto, the strict doctrine has been that the Crown may make no executive decision other than on the advice of a responsible minister. Clearly, that view does not underpin what is envisaged by the Prime Minister in 2008. But the point of adjustment may be taken to be more in the conception of what the Crown is now asked to do than in whether it requires the endorsement of explicit ministerial engagement any more than in the case, for example, of those honours awarded by the monarch directly. From that standpoint the Supreme Governor title could remain but its holder be seen more as a sort of statutory patron who takes a serious interest in one of the larger voluntary bodies/charities which enjoys Royal patronage. The margin of difference between making appointments and approving/taking note of them can be interpreted generously. All the more would such an understanding seem desirable, defensible and indeed necessary where, as recommended in Cm 7027, the Church of England was itself allowed to decide (in an echo of the Attlee/Fisher 1949 discussions) the identity of the bishops permitted to serve in the second chamber rather than continuing with the present seniority system.

However, should anyone suggest that patrons did not themselves have to be a communicant member of the Church of England would be another matter altogether. In that case the whole of the 1689–1707 constitutional settlement would be called into question.

Removing the bishops

Removal could be achieved in one of two ways: by statute or by the bishops themselves voluntarily withdrawing – the conduct of some Law Lords who, before the new Supreme Court was invented, considered that their judicial status was incompatible with active membership of a political chamber and attended solely, therefore, for judicial business. The bishops could behave likewise, if no doubt after due notice to allow the authorities to make any necessary arrangements, for example, should it be desired to continue daily opening prayers. If Parliament decided that it wished in principle to continue with religious representation, then the two routes could be combined in an arrangement, for example, where the Church of England consented to legislation on the understanding that room would be found for a certain number less than the present 26 to be made members of the second chamber. Such a settlement might include the two archbishops and such other numbers or incumbents of other sees identified in the ways thought most appropriate. In practice, however, voluntary withdrawal might not be a deliverable part of such an equation if, for example, it is the case that bishops value Lords membership as conferring political status (Wood 2008: 65). It follows that, in the absence of any larger package of church/state realignment, voluntary withdrawal would be most unlikely to occur. That current fact does not, however, invalidate withdrawal as an option so long as doubt persists (including among the bishops themselves) about the rationale of their presence.

In addition, voluntary removal of the bishops would not by itself clear the way for the sovereign and the Prime Minister to withdraw from the appointment procedure. This is because of the constitutional doctrine – ostensibly observed in the new appointments system – that for so long as sovereigns appoint, they must do so on the advice of a responsible minister. The Church of England could be free to select its own episcopacy only where the sovereign was removed from the procedure and the need for primeministerial involvement became otiose. This could be accomplished by repeal of the 1533 and 1534 Acts governing the appointment of bishops and suffragan bishops, the abolition of the homage oath, some alteration of the Coronation Oath Act, and the repeal of the relevant parts of the various bishopric Acts limiting appointment maxima. Though there might be an expectation that all this should be dealt with by primary legislation introduced by the government of the day, achieving this effect would be within the scope of the Enabling Act and it could therefore be encompassed by Measure – a considerable advantage in parliamentary terms. Bishops would then fall to be appointed by whatever system the Church of England chose to adopt – the situation since 1871 and 1920 in Ireland and Wales and in the whole of the rest of the Anglican Communion. If there ever were doubt about the propriety of proceeding by Measure, the government has removed it by indicating in the March 2008 White Paper that that is how they expect the more limited appointment changes to be implemented (Cm 7342: para. 256).

This would be a big step but not one by itself necessarily affecting all other features of the church/state relationship. For example, there would be no need to alter the Act of Settlement, and the sovereign could remain Defender of the Faith and the Supreme Governor, though in the latter case the meaning would, as argued, in practice approximate more to the status of patron. To argue for resort to Measure is not to argue for doing so unilaterally without consultation. The point is again that the Church itself might take the initiative, here in a situation where the government, for example, would need to consider what action would need to be taken in respect of Commonwealth states under the Statute of Westminster 1931. The departure of bishops from the House of Lords would not affect the Church's continuing ability to promote legislation by Measure.

The government rightly took the view in its July 2007 Green Paper (Cm 7170) that the removal of executive government from the episcopal appointment procedure effectively removed the case for keeping the remaining ecclesiastical patronage – deans, canonries (including those associated with university posts) and benefices – in its hands. Logically, there would seem no case for doing so, and the right course would seem to be to resign all the patronage to whatever arrangements the Church of England preferred in consultation as necessary with the other interests concerned, including the personal interests of the sovereign in the case of the Royal Peculiars.

Finally, removing the bishops as ex officio members of the second chamber would not disqualify them for appointment by the Appointments Commission whether or not it be desired to have a measure of religious representation in that chamber. Anglican bishops would simply be in the same position as the representatives of any other religion and the outcome would be determined by the same principles that were applied to all other candidates. If the House so resolved, prayers could continue to be taken at the beginning of daily sittings by someone other than a bishop, though by whom exactly might well be contested (see HL, 16 July 2007, cols 4–5).

14
Towards a New Balance

This chapter starts by examining issues that at first sight seem secondary in comparison with those above. One in particular, however, could in fact have a greater impact on the organization and management of the Church of England than the others put together. Despite Chapter 13 having previously argued that there should be no representation of religion as of right in the legislature, this chapter moves to consider nonetheless whether other ways of representing religion formally in public life – 're-establishment' – might be contemplated. The chapter concludes by indicating finally how, severally, the state and the Church of England might consider approaching what the changes in their relationship might be and how they should be accomplished. It is argued that the choice is not between total disestablishment and doing nothing. Rather, it is contended that the process of mutual adjustment – not all of it disengagement – that has been occurring in the last two hundred years should be further expanded and, so far as possible, to the benefit of all the parties directly and indirectly engaged. This means reviewing not only the 'privileges' of the Church of England but also the obligations and restraints on the Church and its clergy.

Ecclesiastical law and courts

As recorded in Chapter 3, the Church of England may legislate by Measure with statutory force, and the state stands behind the ecclesiastical courts whose senior judges are appointed by the Crown and others in consultation with the Lord Chancellor. Although the 'established' Church of Scotland's 'Acts of Assembly' have statutory recognition, its courts do not have quite the same status as *part* of the judicial system.

The rationale for these arrangements is that they originate from a time when the Church of England and the state were different aspects of a joint project of governance in England and Wales. The separation between these aspects that has occurred so far remains incomplete. As to the ecclesiastical courts, apart from the considerable weight of tradition, there are no arguments which could in theory withstand others insistent on equality of treatment for all religious groups. Granted that levelling up could not be contemplated, it would in principle therefore be right to align current provision for all churches on an identical basis. That is, the Church of England should have no greater advantage in matters of law than other churches/faiths, and the Church of England's ecclesiastical courts should cease to be equivalent to all other state courts with their judges as much the Queen's judges as the judges in the ordinary civil and criminal courts. In practice, this equivalence has for long had little practical significance even if the ecclesiastical courts retain the same powers as the High Court for the attendance and examination of witnesses and the production of documents enforceable via contempt proceedings. It is difficult to see what, if any, adverse consequences for the Church of England would ensue. Its powers of internal discipline would not be eroded and it would retain the advantage (if it be one) of having its faculty jurisdiction system for heritage regulation purposes recognized by the state. Since the progressive removal in the nineteenth century of any jurisdiction affecting people other than the Church's own membership or property, the ecclesiastical courts – with the possible exception of their issuing exhumation faculties – could not be in substance distinguished from the internal tribunals of any voluntary organization.

The question now is less that of reform than of recognition of an already existing condition. For achieving such an end, the nearest and still relevant precedent is section 3 of the Welsh Disestablishment Act 1914. This declared that the relevant ecclesiastical courts should cease to have any jurisdiction and that the ecclesiastical law of the Church in Wales should cease to be law. From the date of disestablishment, the then existing law and existing 'articles, doctrines, rites, rules, discipline, and ordinances of the Church of England' should bind the members of the Church in Wales 'in the same manner as if they had mutually agreed to be so bound', the civil, temporal courts having appropriate jurisdiction. At the same time, the Church in Wales was also given the power to amend existing ecclesiastical law, including statute law. Section 3 of the Act permitted the Church in Wales to set up its own ecclesiastical courts though 'no such courts shall exercize any coercive jurisdiction and no appeal shall lie from any such court to [the Privy Council]'.

Changing the status of the Anglican courts is again a change that could be accomplished by the Church itself by Measure. It could, of course, be argued that, if the present arrangements have so little real substance beyond the appearance of privilege, then changing them would equally accomplish nothing of substance. But that argument would set at nought the presentational pretensions of the existing situation and their effete claims to a greater significance and importance than they possess. The matter is not urgent, but to leave it be would continue as a standing reproach to an institution apparently reluctant to take the steps within its power to accept the realities of its existence.

Repeal of the Enabling Act 1919

Detaching the ecclesiastical courts from the secular courts and terminating all Crown and ministerial involvement would be one thing and could stand alone. Repealing the Enabling Act 1919 would be something altogether different. Repeal would be mandatory under the fullest scheme of disestablishment but, just as the argument so far has been that disestablishment does not have to be the only alternative to establishment, so is it necessary to pause before assuming that repeal is an unavoidable concomitant of detaching the ecclesiastical courts.

It has to be assumed that repeal would not seek simply to return the situation to what obtained before the 1919 Act came into force. That is, a return to the position where the Church of England could change its law only by means of public general acts in Parliament. It follows that the object of repeal would be, while continuing in force all prior Church of England specific legislation, henceforward to give future Church of England ordinances no greater status or force than those of like civil organizations whose members agreed by mutual consent to be bound by such ordinances.

Such a deceptively simple scheme in fact hides considerable practical difficulty. While the Irish and Welsh disestablishments could never be regarded as exact precedents, they are powerfully indicative. For example, if the 1919 Act were repealed, the Church of England would be forced down similar roads of incorporation and law codification. In other words, it seems doubtful whether the Church of England could continue in its current decentralized, unstructured federalism which is the product of centuries of accumulated provision. The effects would be profound, and this likelihood raises the question whether such changes should be sought or insisted upon to the extent that creating exact correspondence with other churches implies. In other words, simple repeal by itself would not be a viable option since legislation would be needed to cater for the situation created by repeal.

Moreover, the means of legislating is also a factor in weighing this balance. Whereas it has been suggested in other cases above that there may be more room for resorting to Measure than customarily assumed and that Parliament – adequately prepared – would not resist, it is likely that parliamentary opinion in the cases here would come down fairly clearly on primary legislation as the right course despite the explicit provision in the 1919 Act that Measures may, save for the constitution of the Ecclesiastical Committee, amend or repeal any legislation.

One of the reasons would be that Parliament would be loath to give up all control, however vestigial, over what is still regarded as the national church and its assets, possibly fearful also of the consequences for the Church's management of civic religion. A fundamental change in the status of the Church of England would be entailed since legislation on these lines would convert it into a wholly voluntary body. It would in law become one denomination among others, and the common law obligations to marry and bury parishioners of whatever beliefs would disappear even if, as for the Church in Wales, the Church's status under the Marriage Acts were preserved. If so, the government would be faced with taking the initiative in the instance of a complex and possibly controversial series of issues. Granted the press of unavoidable other parliamentary business and the shortage of parliamentary time, a lack of government enthusiasm for such a project could be understood. It may, therefore, be that although much could be accomplished by Measure, proceeding to repeal the 1919 Act should be stayed even if other repeals addressed late eighteenth-/early seventeenth-century legislation.

Chaplaincies

A similar question arises whether removing present statutory provisions which make the Church of England *primus inter pares* is so important and urgent a matter that it should be pressed. It would be easier to achieve in law but the good, if in some eyes patronising, offices of the Churches of England and of Wales (Beckford and Gilliatt 1998) would have presumably to be replaced by some other organising capacity, probably secular. Especially to the government departments concerned, such a change may not be as attractive in practice – including also in Scotland – as it might seem in principle.

Legatine powers

In matters of lesser significance, the options could be as follows:

- The Church of England's connexion with <u>Notaries Public</u> is already vestigial and effectively delegated to outside authorities. The current arrangement is so obscure that it could either continue to be overlooked or tidied up in, say, a Measure which addressed the Ecclesiastical Licences Act 1533 or an available Administration of Justice Bill. (Notaries in Scotland are wholly unconnected with the Church of Scotland.)
- Special <u>marriage licences</u> – the need for these arises from the marriage responsibilities of the Church of England continued by the civil marriage Acts. Their necessity is a burden upon rather than a privilege of the Church of England. They should remain undisturbed unless and until that Church seeks to relieve itself of the duty to marry applicants for religious marriage, though because it would imply abandonment of its national role that decision will not presumably be taken lightly.
- <u>Lambeth degrees</u> – Although in practice probably conferred more scrupulously than peerages and by no means always without research and examination, in these credentialist times they are, strictly, an anomaly. While the Archbishop understandably needs means for recognising and celebrating service and Anglican merit, it could be argued that alternative private forms would be more appropriate. At the same time, the enforcement of logic could jettison something of value and abolition could result in more harm than leaving the situation alone. In the absence of abuse, the hand of logic seems best stayed.

Re-establishment

Removing, or very considerably reforming, one set of church/state relationships automatically raises the question of what, if anything, should replace them: that is, to what extent should the modern state seek to formalize its relations with religious communities of all kinds. To label the process as 're-establishment' could be seen as begging the question or conceding the kind of concurrent establishment seemingly favoured by Tariq Modood. However, as already observed, when 'establishment' is so ambiguous or capacious a term that it can simultaneously comprise the English and Scottish forms, the tent is quite large enough to comprehend very different forms of relationship in practice.

Essentially, the question here is how the state should respond to religious as opposed to Christian pluralism. One recent study distinguishes between 'principled' and 'pragmatic' pluralism (Ahdar and Leigh 2005: 84–6). In the former, where Dutch 'pillarization' is instanced as a leading example, the state deliberately structures an ostensible neutrality, which does not in practice avoid its need to make policy choices some of which will be offensive to some of the religious groups it otherwise seeks to deal with on a basis of equality. Pragmatic pluralism, in contrast, is driven not by principle but simply by an expedient recognition as even-handedly as possible of religious diversity. In a similar fashion, the authors distinguish between 'formal' and 'substantive' neutrality (Ahdar and Leigh 2005: 87–92). They prefer the latter form which (as Christian apologists) they favour because it is more likely to recognize religious views as deserving of discriminating treatment and this, of course, in a context of an argument concerned with maximising religious freedom rather than religious equality. They are also particularly concerned with what they describe as separationism.

In fact, and sometimes perhaps initially at least without consciously realising it, the state in Britain has been for some time – even before fanatics' bombs – experimenting with new forms of institutionalising state/faith relations. In England, the Inner Cities Religious Council (ICRC) – set up in 1992 and meeting three times a year under a minister's chairmanship – sought to bring representatives of all faiths together to address particular urban problems and was described as

> a forum for members of faith communities to work with the Government on issues of regeneration, neighbourhood renewal, social inclusion, and other relevant cross-departmental policies and processes. Members . . . impact on the development of Government policy and provide a channel through which Government can liaise with faith communities at a local level and build capacity. (ICRC 2008)

It was succeeded in 2006 by the Faith Communities Consultative Council, a non-statutory body still under ministerial chairmanship and aiming to provide a national forum chiefly concerned with issues related to cohesion, integration, the development of sustainable communities, neighbourhood renewal, and social inclusion plus general oversight on engagement between central government and faith communities. Its membership comprises seven Christians, three Muslims, two Hindus, two Jewish, two Sikhs, one Zoroastrian, one Buddhist, one Jain and one Baha'i. There is also a representative from the Inter Faith Network and from the Faith Based Regeneration Network. In addition, council membership includes representation from the Scottish Core Liaison Group, Inter Faith Council Wales and the Northern Ireland Interfaith body to ensure a UK-wide perspective. The council is serviced by the Neighbourhood Renewal Unit of the Department of Communities and Local Government.

Edward Norman has observed of government-funded community integration initiatives: 'These grants of public money to promote ideas held by religious groups for religious reasons are plain evidence of "Establishment" principles at work' (Norman 2008: 11). There have been several bidding rounds for grants from the Faith Communities Capacity Building Fund, the second of which shared a total of £7.5 million of government money. These grants have, since the London bombings of July 2005 particularly, been part of a government 'community cohesion' agenda which has emphasized the importance of interfaith relations. In its response of February 2008 to the report of its Commission on Integration and Cohesion, the government included a specific commitment to developing an interfaith strategy about which it launched a consultation. Its strategy would aim to

- facilitate interfaith dialogue that builds understanding and celebrates the values held in common, such as integrity in public life, care, compassion and respect;
- increase the level of collaborative social action involving different faiths;
- communities and wider civil society, where people work together to bring about positive and concrete change within their local communities;
- maintain and further develop good relations between faith communities and between faith communities and the wider civil society;
- overcome the perceived and actual barriers faced by young people and women in participating in interfaith dialogue and activity. (DCLG 2008a: 31)

The religious communities themselves have moved to elaborate their own consultative institutions at local and national levels. Churches Together in England is a Christian grouping, and there are various similar groups working across religions, such as the Churches' Legislation Advisory Service (formerly the Churches Main Committee) set up in 1941. Chaired by an Anglican bishop, it is a Judaeo-Christian ecumenical body bringing together the interests of Christian churches and the

Jewish community in their dealings with government in all its aspects (other than education). Its primary role is as a lobby group on legislation and other matters that directly affect them and likewise acting as a channel through which the government can reciprocally consult the churches as a whole. The main all-faith group is the Inter Faith Network for the UK, founded in 1987, and now with a much-expanded membership, including local affiliates. Chaired jointly by an Anglican bishop and non-Christian colleague, the network receives some government funding.

What recent years have seen are initiatives such as the Inner Cities Religious Council and the Inter Faith Network given a new impetus and status following political concerns about 'community cohesion' in the wake of riots in 2001 and, especially, the London bombings in 2005. Ministers have been experimenting pragmatically with initiatives of their own designed to address a cohesion agenda. The initiatives have, however, stopped well short of giving any permanent, high-profile status to religious organizations comparable with older forms of establishment. Although sometimes fashionable language of 'empowerment' is used, the intention has been to make that operative at local level only. At national level the mode is firmly consultative and no more. Where funds have been made available, they have been directed predominantly to local levels of action (DCLG 2008b). Within the government's 'Preventing Violent Extremism' initiative, while ministers have clearly stated that 'it is not the role of Government to seek to change any religion or religious community' (DCLG 2008b: 55), the government has nonetheless encouraged the work of the Mosques and Imams National Advisory Board, and is supporting an Oxford-and-Cambridge-led board of academics and scholars to lead the debate about Islam in the British context 'to facilitate the development of a long-term and lasting response to the false ideology promoted by violent extremists' (DCLG 2008b: 55).

While there have been proposals in favour of arrangements similar to those in Wales, such as a National Religious Council for the United Kingdom (Lamont 1989: 204), a United Kingdom Council of Faith (McLean and Linsley 2004: 21) or for a Minister for Religion actually within government (Davis, Paulhus and Bradstock 2008: 96), they do not seem to have gathered much support. Further, whereas in Wales the First Minister has himself sponsored the creation and patronage of the Inter Faith Council for Wales, in England the engagement offered is with individual government departments rather than with the government collectively at cabinet level. Some Anglicans have been critical of the government's performance outside the 'cohesion' agenda, and an exploratory study has concluded that 'when it comes to faith communities in general, and aspects of charity law and social policy in particular, the government is planning blind and failing parts of civil society' (Davis, Paulhus and Bradstock 2008: 13).

These strands apart, there appears to be no obvious, determined pressure from either the faith organizations or government for radical change in the nature of their contacts. The extent to which they are actually reinforced by Church of England representation in the House of Lords is doubtful, especially since other Christian and non-Christian believers are – less formally – also present in the House. It is significant that none of the government's White Papers on reform of the House of Lords has proposed corporate representation of non-Church of England religious organizations. The arguments against doing so are, of course, the same as those against continuing episcopal membership. In addition, as discussed above, there would be serious difficulties about identifying who was to be regarded as properly representative of which religious group even if the attendant arithmetic difficulties could be reconciled as not disproportionate to the new House's total membership.

The government's caution in these areas seems right. Re-establishment at any level above the extent of present formality does not seem either attractive or necessary. From the government's point of view, it is better that the religious groups organize themselves than that government should attempt to do it for them.

Viewing the options – the statesman

The main problem for the statesman is how to manage the adjustment away from state-backed institutions based on an exclusively Christian religious culture. These have become increasingly anomalous in a pluralized culture which includes not only non-Christian faiths but also a significant proportion of the population who have no religion and an even greater number who do not practise their nominal religion. While it could be said that the situation does not call for urgent action and the UK is a state well able to tolerate the anomalous and the asymmetric, the gap between religious theory and fact has grown, is continuing to grow and will not diminish.

Events will continue to draw attention to the anomalies. The Prime Minister's withdrawal from active involvement in the appointment of bishops and endlessly renewed discussion on Lords reform will nag away at establishment, as will the increasingly vocal divisions within the Church of England itself and its larger communion. Continuing dissatisfaction with the discriminatory aspects of the 1701 Act of Settlement will spur increasingly bold and possibly more coherent calls for reform. Recurrent unease about faith schools will call into question the rationale of government funding and the extent of government control. The ability of especially the Church of England to maintain its own buildings, so many of which have listed status, will challenge how state funding is to be channelled and on what terms. Above all, the inevitable though by no means looked for change of sovereign will precipitate a direct need to face up to questions about how the state–Crown–Church of England triangle is to be managed. While it is possible to look away from these problems, they cannot be evaded by the state. It follows that the statesman will need, in order to avoid being overwhelmed by populist agitation or clerical inertia, to engage in some contingency planning and a deal of anticipatory action. While the problem could be stated as that of converting the Church of England from a state to a national church or a church *for* the English nation, addressing that problem cannot be undertaken in isolation from possessing a clear policy in regard to all religious groupings. Among other things to be considered would be whether the Church of England would officiate at coronations or whatever events may replace them and, if so, on what basis.

The elements of a government, Cabinet Office-led review might be as follows:

1. In the context of a wider review which extends also to the non-religious aspects of the 1701 and 1707 Acts and the need to engage Commonwealth consultation, the government itself to consider
   - its policy towards *all* religious groups in a framework explicitly wider than a cohesion agenda, and the institutional forms and kinds of financial support, if any, appropriate;
   - the nature of the religious tests and oaths imposed upon the sovereign and the proper aims and means of their modification;
   - whether a House of Lords Appointments Commission could be tasked to have regard to the desirability of securing the presence of a reasonable spread of religious opinion in a statute which conferred permanent status on the Commission and also removed *automatic* Church of England representation;
   - the extent to which the state should continue to accept a liability for the maintenance of listed church buildings irrespective of denomination.
2. The government, after cross-party consultation,

- to invite the Church of England to review its own position to determine what forms of further disengagement from the state and the Crown it would prefer on the basis that disendowment comes onto the table only if the Church seeks to forego its national role; and
- to invite the Church of Scotland similarly to review whether it requires the Act of Union oath to be continued – a question on which the Scottish executive and Parliament will also have views. (If the Church of Scotland decides to withdraw from *Declaratory Article* III's requirement for universal Scottish parochial coverage, the case for retaining the oath will be substantially weakened.)

Viewing the options – the Church of England

The problem for the Church is how to develop agreement within itself about its future. The dispersed character of authority in the Church makes reaching agreement especially difficult. The Archbishop of Canterbury may lead but he cannot command. Indeed, there is great internal resistance to the creation of strong, unified executive headship.

Traditionally, the Church has responded to crises by the Archbishops setting up internal inquiries to reflect on the issues at the root of the particular crisis. In the last century, there were four such major initiatives and it is possible that a further inquiry could help clear ground and minds for the future. However, a prerequisite would have to be an initial acceptance of the case for a move to a greater level of self-government. The lesson of the Prime Minister's unilateral July 2007 initiative over episcopal appointments is that the Church cannot depend on bottomless government benignity or a willingness to continue only at a pace which suits the Church. However 'secularization' is to be understood, it is plain that the boundaries of conventional Christian belief have shifted far away from the assumptions that underpinned past and still-enduring forms of establishment.

The choice for the Church is to be either passive and allow the state to make the running or to work out its own remedies and reposition itself and the form of its service – including as to civic religion – to the English nation. In Scotland these things are different because the form of establishment effectively gives the Church of Scotland the voluntary status that the Church of England lacks. Although it is not the argument here that the Church of England should remodel itself wholly on the Church of Scotland, it is clear that there are features of the Scottish arrangements which could help point the way. But there are no easy choices and, let there be no mistake, the choices are harder for the Church than they are for the statesman.

Finally, when considering its choices (which include, of course, to do nothing), the Church of England could have regard perhaps to the fact that even purported disestablishments have affected other churches rather less than intended or supposed, the result perhaps of change being necessary to allow some things at least to stay the same. In other words, the argument is as much about repositioning as about rougher and cruder dismemberment. It could be that Lewis Dibdin, a great ecclesiastical lawyer of the past who lived through earlier, more intense and hostile arguments about establishment, was more prophetic than he could have realized:

> The Establishment has survived so many modifications that, whatever we may think, it would be rash to assert that the irreducible minimum has now nearly been reached. (Dibdin 1932: 116)

Conclusion

To help make the options discussed in this book more accessible, they are summarized in Table 14.1.

What Table 14.1 encapsulates is the extent to which, for a variety of reasons, it is becoming increasingly difficult to accept that the present forms of Church establishment can or should continue unamended. How to respond is a matter of political choice – for the churches as for governments. The problem for the churches about doing nothing or refusing to think things through is that they will be apt to be overtaken by events not of their own making. Something like that evidently happened in 2007 over the Prime Minister's decision to withdraw from active involvement in the appointment of Anglican bishops.

The aim of this book has been to help the discussion that might take place inside and outside the Churches and within the state. The fundamental point about the term 'establishment' is that while it poses as a single, coherent concept, in reality it functions as an inadequate short-hand – often lazily applied – for a complex web of relations between two particular, quite differently constituted churches (the Church of Scotland and the Church of England) and the state. Above all, the condition of uniformity of belief upon which the two churches' status was predicated, and its exclusionary character, has not only long disappeared but also been replaced by an unimagined plurality of religious belief and unbelief. Whereas statesmen of old calculated to relate only to

Table 14.1 Revising Church establishment

Topic	Issue	Aim	Action government	Action Church	Action other	Timing	Means
RC disabilities	Cannot succeed to Crown	Remove disabilities	Consult/inform Commonwealth under 1931 Act before legislation	Support consultation. Measure possible		Anytime but following accession most likely	Statute/Measure revisiting Protestant settlement
Supreme Governor	Unattainable by anyone not in communion with C of E	Remove role	Legislate	Measure		Following accession	Repeal s. 8 of the Act of Supremacy 1559 and amend Preface to Thirty-Nine Articles
Fidei Defensor	Implies exclusive Crown relationship to Christianity	Reinterpret	Nil	Nil	Declaration by sovereign after consultation with Ministers and religious interests	On accession	Public speech
Accession and coronation ceremonies	Outdated character	Modernize	Review requirement, style and cost	Review role and including options	Royal advisers to consider interests of new sovereign	Change following accession but planning to precede	Early detailed announcements to elicit public support
Oaths							
(i) Coronation	Exclusive support for C of E	Generalize	Legislate	Measure	Amend Coronation Oath Act 1689	Following accession	Statute or Measure
(ii) Church of Scotland	Whether necessary	Review in light of 1921 Act	Consult with a view to possible legislation	Nil	Scottish Executive and C of S to consider	Following accession	Possible repeal of part of Act of Union 1706/07

	Whether necessary	Review	Consult	To be consulted	Consult other Christian and non-Christian religious groups		
(iii) Accession Declaration		regardless of decision on RC disabilities				Following accession	Repeal Accession Declaration Act 1910 by statute or Measure if oath to be abolished
(iv) Bishops homage and clerical subscription	Acknowledges royal supremacy	Falls with abolition of supremacy	Legislate	Measure		Following accession	Part of Supremacy package
Appointment of diocesan bishops and suffragans	Clarify real responsibility	Direct appointment by and wholly within C of E	Nil	Measure		At any time	Repeal relevant remnant of Tudor statutes
Bishops in Lords	Indefensible exclusive anachronism	Bring within ordinary appointment arrangements	Statute to withdraw customary writs and Direction to Appointments Commission	Alternative – withdrawal from Lords on understanding of Commission's altered remit		At any time	Statute/negotiated voluntary action
Legal							
(i) Church courts	Possess exclusive public status	Relegate to voluntary sphere	Nil	Measure		At any time	Provision on lines of s. 3 Church of Wales Act 1914
(ii) 1919 Act	Exclusive privilege of C of E	No change necessary					
Public service chaplaincies	Unique statutory support in prisons but non-statutory elsewhere	No change necessary					

(Continued)

Table 14.1 Continued

Topic	Issue	Aim	Action government	Action Church	Action other	Timing	Means
Legatine remnants							
(i) Notaries public	Formally remain part of ecclesiastical system	Incorporate fully in secular jurisdiction	Legislate	Nil		At any time	Provision in convenient civil justice Bill
(ii) Special marriage licences	Part of exclusive marriage jurisdiction antedating secular marriage	No change necessary while marriage jurisdiction retained					
(iii) Lambeth degrees	Anomalous in theory	Harmless in practice, so no change					
Education: automatic membership of SACREs	Reflects parochial coverage	To remain unless coverage given up					

a single religious organization within political boundaries, the political necessity of accommodating other religious institutions and the effect of profound social changes have sapped the unique status of the 'established' churches. While their relative marginalization has helped to mask constitutional reality, their formal position – especially in England – is anomalous to the point of unsustainability. There is a limit to which such problems can be circumvented by ignoring them, especially where some of the special exclusionary protections (for example, over Roman Catholics) that do remain become increasingly exposed and repugnant to the temper of the times, and a change of sovereign will force choice.

While further adjustment is necessary, it does not require some single, climactic intervention (for example, 'disestablishment') but, rather, an intelligent process of mutual adjustment. Examined from a constitutional point of view, the ultimate boundaries of that adjustment are a matter for political choice. This book seeks to present a number of options that attempt to take account of the positions and interests respectively of the two 'established' churches, other denominations and religions, and the state. What the book does not and cannot do is claim that there must be a single, particular outcome. On the contrary, what eventuates can only be the product of the interactions in which, it is argued, all the parties should engage.

Notes

3. Monarchy and legislature

1. The Sovereign is not 'Supreme Head', an obsolete title used in the earliest Tudor legislation and long since repealed.
2. A discussion of these and related issues arising from the Fabian Society pamphlet (2003) may be found in Leigh (2004).
3. The occasions are as follows: Lord Forsyth of Drumlean, Conservative, introduced a motion (HL 2 December 1999, cols 917–19); Kevin McNamara, Labour, a Treason Felony, Act of Settlement and Parliamentary Oath Bill (HC 19 December 2001 cols 319–23); and Lord Dubs, Labour, a Succession to the Crown Bill (HL 14 January 2005, cols 495–513). In addition, Edward Leigh, Conservative, sought leave to introduce a Marriages (Freedom of Religion) Bill (HC 8 March 2005, cols 1392–4), and John Gummer, Conservative, similarly sought permission for a Catholics (Prevention of Discrimination) Bill two years later (HC 20 February 2007, cols 154–6). In addition, Jim Devine took the opportunity of a statement by the Lord Chancellor (Straw) to raise the issue and received a sympathetic response which did not, however, promise any remedial action (HC 25 March 2008, col. 27).
4. In addition to the seventeenth/eighteenth-century constitutional legislation, four other Acts are also thought relevant: Princess Sophia's Precedence Act 1711, Royal Marriages Act 1772, Union with Ireland Act 1800 and the Regency Act 1937.
5. For a recent ministerial citation of the convention, see the proceedings on the draft Civil Partnership Act 2004 (Overseas Relationships and Consequential, etc. Amendments) Order 2005 before the First Standing Committee on Delegated Legislation (HC 20 October 2005, col. 4).
6. HL 19 January 1998, cols 1282–9. For a general discussion about the religious issues raised by the Act, see Cumper (2000). For a view that the Act has the effect of moving the UK from a model of Christian toleration to one of religious pluralism, see Rivers (2000).
7. For a commentary on these recommendations, see Smith (2003).

4. Executive, Judiciary and the Legatine powers

1. The approximate annual management staff costs of this small unit's involvement with all ecclesiastical patronage amounted to about £80,000 in 2005, with an additional £60,000 attributable to support staff salary costs.
2. See press notice *Royal Peculiars*, Department for Constitutional Affairs, 9 February 2004.
3. *Select Committee on Constitutional Affairs*, oral evidence, 29 January 2004, QQ 48–95.
4. 14 February 2008, accessible at <www.cofe.org>.

5. For long in abeyance until the revival of religious communities in the nine-teenth century was a power to secularize religious (i.e. members of religious orders) at the request of their orders.

5. Financing establishment in England

1. <www.kirchensteuer.de/steuer.html>, accessed 23 September 2008.
2. MOD costings are calculated as capitation rates which are comprehensive in including, for example, employer National Insurance contributions, educa-tion support though not accommodation costs, support costs and training costs. On that basis, MOD chaplain main grade capitation rates are at £90–5k depending on the Service concerned. Assuming conservatively that the capi-tation rates of 147 Church of England chaplains run at about 85 per cent of the lowest MOD capitation rates, then the total cost would amount to about £11m.
3. The National Secular Society, however, has more recently estimated the cost to be £20 million a year, <www.secularism.org.uk/editorialbyterry-sandersonperhaps/html>, accessed 9 April 2007.
4. See, for example, <www.oxford.anglican.org/page/3371/>, accessed 9 April 2007, and Peter Luff's Parliamentary Question at HC 6 November 2006, col. 771.

6. Establishment in Scotland

1. The bewildering character of these secessions and partial unions is often rendered comprehensible by means of resort to 'wiring' diagrams. See, for example, Sjolinder (1962), Appendix 1. 'Divisions and Reunions of the Scottish Church 1690–1929'.
2. This is well understood in some modern Church of Scotland thinking: see MacLean 2004. A recent Assembly Act relating to discipline was apparently run past the Strasbourg European Human Rights Convention authorities to ensure that there was no conflict.

7. Recent developments in church/state relations in Scotland

1. The authors would like to thank Janette Wilson, Solicitor of the Church of Scotland and Law Agent of its General Assembly, for her comments on an earlier draft of this chapter; any inaccuracies remain their responsibility.
2. See for example *Logan* v. *Presbytery of Dumbarton* [1995] SLT 1228.
3. *Earl of Kinnoull and Rev R Young* v. *Presbytery of Auchterarder* (1838) 16 S 661 (1841) 3 D 778 (1843) 5D 1010 (the *Auchterarder* case); *Presbytery of Strathbogie and Rev J Cruickshank and others, suspenders, and related cases* (1839) 2D 258, 585; (1840) 2D 1047, 1380; (1840) 3D 282; (1842) 4 D 1298; (1843) 5 D 909; (1843) 15 Juris 375 (the *Strathbogie* case); *Middleton* v. *Anderson* (1842) 4 D 957 (the *Culsalmond* case); *Cuninghame* v. *Presbytery of Irvine* (1843) 3 D 427 (the *Stewarton* case).

4. Cranmer and Peterson have published an earlier and in some respects fuller version of the discussion of *Percy* (see Cranmer and Peterson 2006). We are grateful to the Editorial Board of the *Ecclesiastical Law Journal* for permission to re-use some of that material.

5. L Nicholls of Birkenhead, L Hope of Craighead, L Scott of Foscote and Bns Hale of Richmond; L Hoffman dissenting. Subsequently, the case was settled and never went back to a tribunal.

6. 'In this Act, unless the context otherwise requires ... "employment" means employment under a contract of service or of apprenticeship or a contract personally to execute any work or labour, and related expressions shall be construed accordingly ... '

7. 'Subject to the recognition of the matters dealt with in the Declaratory Articles as matters spiritual, nothing in this Act contained shall affect or prejudice the jurisdiction of the civil courts in relation to any matter of a civil nature.'

8. *Re Employment of Church of England Curates* [1912] 2 Ch 563; *Scottish Insurance Commissioners* v. *Church of Scotland* 1914 SC 16; *President of the Methodist Conference* v. *Parfitt* [1984] ICR 176; *Davies* v. *Presbyterian Church of Wales* [1986] ICR 280; *Diocese of Southwark* v. *Coker* [1998] ICR 140.

9. Citing s. 77 of the Sex Discrimination Act 1975: '(1) A term of a contract is void where–(a) its inclusion renders the making of the contract unlawful by virtue of this Act, or (b) it is included in furtherance of an act rendered unlawful by this Act, or (c) it provides for the doing of an act which would be rendered unlawful by this Act. (3) A term in a contract which purports to exclude or limit any provision of this Act or the Equal Pay Act 1970 is unenforceable by any person in whose favour the term would operate apart from this subsection.'

10. *New Testament Church of God* v. *The Rev S. Stewart* [2006] UKEAT/0293/06.

11. The full transcript is available at <http://www.bailii.org/uk/cases/UKEAT/2006/0293_06_2710.html>, accessed 15 December 2006.

12. *Parochial Church Council of the Parish of Aston Cantlow and Wilmcote with Billesley, Warwickshire* v. *Wallbank and another* [2003] UKHL 37; [2004] 1 AC 546.

13. *Helen Percy* v. *An Order and Judgment of the Employment Appeal Tribunal* (2001) 057/17/99 IH.

14. 6 March 1793 Hume Decisions 595.

15. For example, Lord Justice Clerk Moncrieff in *Wight* v. *Presbytery of Dunkeld* (1870) 8 M 921: 'If ... this were a case in which we were called upon to review the proceedings of an inferior court, I should have thought a strong case had been made out for our interference. But whatever inconsiderate *dicta* to that effect may have been thrown out, that is not the law of Scotland. The jurisdiction of the Church courts, as recognized judicatories of this realm, rests on a similar statutory foundation to that under which we administer justice within these walls ... Within their spiritual province the Church courts are as supreme as we are within the civil; and as this is a matter relating to the discipline of the Church, and solely within the cognisance of the Church courts, I think we have no power whatever to interfere.'

16. This passage was cited with approval in *Logan* v. *Presbytery of Dumbarton* 1995 SLT 1228, 1232 (Lord Osborne).

17. Hay, Craig et al. 1994, IX, para. 378, citing Sex Discrimination Act 1975 s. 65(1)(b).
18. 'I would start from the presumption – rebuttable, of course – that, where the appointment was being made to a recognised form of ministry within the Church and where the duties of that ministry would be essentially spiritual, there would be no intention that the arrangements made with the minister would give rise to obligations enforceable in the civil law': *Helen Percy* v. *An Order and Judgment of the Employment Appeal Tribunal* (2001) 057/17/99 IH at para. 13.
19. For the response, see *Equality and Diversity: Updating the Sex Discrimination Act: Government Response to Consultation* at <http://www.berr.gov.uk/consultations/page13950.html>, accessed 21 April 2008.
20. The Working Group included representatives of most of the mainstream Churches in Great Britain (though not the Orthodox) and of the Jewish, Muslim and Hindu communities, together with delegates from two trades unions: the Transport and General Workers' Union and Amicus.
21. HC 20 March 2007, cols 43–4 (emphasis added).

9. Church/state relations in Scandinavia

1: '[A]s regards whatever is on Earth and belongs to the temporal, earthly kingdom, man can have power from God. But whatever belongs to heaven and to the eternal kingdom, is subject to the Lord of heaven alone' (Luther, *Von Weltlicher Oberkeit* [On Secular Authority]). See also Melancthon's *Augsburg Confession – Article XXVIII: Of Ecclesiastical Power.*
2. In one sense, of course, this last provision is true for the United Kingdom as well; within the limits of EU law and the European Convention on Human Rights, Parliament can pass whatever laws it likes: hence the Methodist Church Act 1976 and the United Reformed Church Act 2000. But those were private Acts passed at the request of the two Churches as petitioners.
3. The first of the 'national' churches in the United Kingdom to legislate for the ordination of women was the Church of Scotland by Act XXV of 1968 [anent Admission of Women to the Ministry].
4. This has echoes of the English system of legislation by Measure: Measures must be initiated by Synod and are unamendable; but the Ecclesiastical Committee may declare them 'inexpedient' and, in any case, Parliament retains the right to enact primary legislation for the Church.
5. I am grateful to my colleague Arna Bang, of the Secretariat of *Alþingi* Secretariat, for this information.
6. The mediaeval titles of Hólar and Skálholt were fairly recently revived when it was decided to consecrate two 'ordaining bishops' – in effect, suffragans – who would be able to act during a vacancy in the See of Iceland (Österlin 1995: 279).
7. In 1994 and again in 1999 the UN Human Rights Committee concluded that Article 2.1 was in contravention of Article 18 of the UN Convention on Civil and Political Rights (Plesner 2001: 322).
8. *Folgerø and Ors* v. *Norway* [2007] ECtHR (Application Number 15472/02).

9. 'Life-stance' communities are recognized under an Act of 1981 which gives them the same right to support and funding as religious communities; the only one to have registered is the Norwegian Humanist and Ethical Association (Plesner 2001: 321).

12. The higher architecture

1. Edward Norman observes this as a function of class: 'The clergy of the Church of England have retained a deceptive proximity to public life through social class' (Norman 1994: 288).
2. At least one Anglican bishop, however, has not thought that there would be incompatibility – see speech of Bishop of Worcester, HL 14 January 2005, cols 502–3, during the debate on Lord Dubs's Succession to the Crown Bill.
3. The precise operative effect of the Statute of Westminster 1931 is ambiguous. The provision about consulting Commonwealth states is contained only in the preamble to the Act. Churchill claimed, 'The Preamble is nothing. It has no legal force' and the government of the day successfully resisted its inclusion in the body of the Act – HC 20 November 1931, cols 1195 and 1249. In 1936 the UK Parliament legislated on the abdication and the change of succession entailed before the Dominion governments. The situation appears to be one where none of the Commonwealth governments can bind any other but that there is an expectation that they will act in concert.
4. This approach seems to be favoured by the former Archbishop of Canterbury, Lord Carey – see *The Times* 5 June 2006.
5. Problems of timing could also evaporate, for example, in the event of an abdication since, for such a decision to be given legal force, legislation would be necessary, and perhaps in less hectic circumstances than in 1936.

13. The political representation of religion

1. It could be urged that the presence of the Manx bishop in Tynwald in the Isle of Man (Edge and Pearce 2004) and the non-voting presence of the Dean in the Jersey States are exceptions. However, neither of the assemblies is a sovereign legislature.
2. As Jonathan Bartley of the think tank Ekklesia has independently pointed out, and whose arguments were not, in so far as they were addressed at all, adequately countered by the Bishop of Liverpool on the BBC Radio 4's *Sunday* programme on 17 February 2008.

Bibliography

Government Papers

House of Lords: Reform (Cm 7027) February 2007.
The Governance of Britain (Cm 7170) July 2007.
The Governance of Britain – Constitutional Renewal (Cm 7342) March 2008.
An Elected Second Chamber (Cm 7438) July 2008.

Other sources

Aarflot, A. (2004), 'Safeguarding the Sacred in Society: The Future Role of the National Church – a Norwegian Perspective', *Law and Justice*, pp. 159–76.

Ahdar, R., and I. Leigh (2005), *Religious Freedom in the Liberal State* (Oxford: Oxford University Press).

Ahrén, Per-Olov (1960), 'The Church of Sweden: Organisation and Legal Status', in Robert Murray (ed.), *The Church of Sweden: Past and Present* (Malmö: Allhem), pp. 31–44.

Ashworth J., Research Matters and I. Farthing (2007), *Churchgoing in the UK* (Teddington: Tearfund).

Aurelius, C. A. (1998), 'Folk Churches of Tomorrow', paper presented to the Porvoo Communion Church Leaders' Consultation, Turku, Finland, 12–17 March 1998, <www.porvoochurches.org/archive/turkufolk.htm>, accessed 17 February 2007.

Avis, P. (2001), *Church, State and Establishment* (London: SPCK).

Bains, B. (2008), *Round Ethnic Group Populations* (London: Greater London Authority).

Barker, C. R. (2004), 'Church and State: Lessons from Germany', *Political Quarterly*, pp. 168–76.

Barley, L. (2006), *Churchgoing Today* (London: Church House).

—— (2007), 'Introduction: The Context for Churches Today', in Ashworth, Research Matters and Farthing 2007, pp. 1–2.

Beckford, J. A., R. Gale, D. Owen, C. Peach and P. Weller (2006), *Review of the Evidence Base on Faith Communities* (London: Office of the Deputy Prime Minister).

Beckford, J. A., and S. Gilliat (1998), *Religion in Prison: Equal Rites in a Multi-faith Society* (Cambridge: Cambridge University Press).

Bell, P. M. H. (1969), *Disestablishment in Ireland and Wales* (London: SPCK).

Berger, P. (ed.) (1999), *The Desacralization of the World: Resurgent Religion and World Politics* (Grand Rapids: Eerdmans).

Best, G. F. A. (1964), *Temporal Pillars* (Cambridge: Cambridge University Press).

Billing, E. (1930), *Den svenska folkkyrkan* (Stockholm: n.p.).

Blackburn, R. (2006), *King and Country: Monarchy and the Future King Charles III* (London: Politico's).

Blair, A. (2005), Press Conference 26 July 2005, <www.number-10.gov.uk/output/Page7999.asp>, accessed 1 March 2007.

Bogdanor, V. (1995), *The Monarchy and the Constitution* (Oxford: Clarendon Press).

—— (ed.) (2003), *The British Constitution in the Twentieth Century* (Oxford: British Academy/Oxford University Press).

Bowles, J. (1815), *The Claims of the Established Church, Considered as an Apostolical Institution* (London), quoted in J. C. D. Clark (2000), *English Society 1660–1832* (Cambridge: Cambridge University Press), p. 433.

Bown F. (1994), 'Influencing the House of Lords: The Role of the Lords Spiritual 1979–1987', *Political Studies*, pp. 105–19.

Brierley, P. (2006), *UK Christian Handbook: Religious Trends 6 2006/2007: Pulling out of the Nosedive – Analyses from the 2005 English Church Census* (London: Christian Research).

—— (2008), *UK Christian Handbook: Religious Trends 7 2007/2008 – British Religion in the 21st Century: What the Statistics Show* (Swindon: Christian Research).

Brown, A. (2003), 'Church of England Schools: Politics, Power and Identity', *British Journal of Religious Education*, pp. 103–16.

Brown, C. G. (2006), *Religion and Society in Twentieth Century Britain* (London: Pearson).

Brown, S. J. (2001), *The National Churches of England, Ireland and Scotland 1801–1846* (Oxford: Oxford University Press).

Bruce, S. (2002a), *God Is Dead: Secularization in the West* (Oxford, Blackwell).

—— (2002b), 'Praying Alone? Church-going in Britain and the Putnam Thesis', *Journal of Contemporary Religion*, pp. 317–28.

Bryant, C. (2008), 'A Leaky Barque: Reforming the British Constitution', in N. Yeowell and D. Bates (eds), *Powers to the People* (London: London Government Association Labour Group), pp. 84–91.

Buchanan, C. (1994), *Cut the Connexion: Disestablishment and the Church of England* (London: Darton, Longman and Todd).

Burns, A. (1999), *The Diocesan Revival in the Church of England c 1800–1870* (Oxford: Clarendon Press).

Carey, G. (2002), 'Holding Together: Church and Nation in the Twenty-first Century', Lecture at Lambeth Palace, 23 April.

Carpenter, E. (1991), *Archbishop Fisher: His Life and Times* (Norwich: Canterbury Press).

Carr, W. (1999), 'A Developing Establishment', *Theology*, pp. 2–10.

—— (2002a), 'Crown and People: Reflections on the Spiritual Dimensions of Establishment', 16 September 2002, *Jubilee Reflections at Westminster Abbey: A Series of Lectures on God, Church, Crown and State*.

—— (2002b), 'The Intimate Ritual: The Coronation Service', *Political Theology*, pp. 11–24.

Casanova, J. (2003), 'Beyond European and American Exceptionalism: Towards a Global Perspective', in Davie, Heelas and Woodhead 2003, pp. 17–29.

Cecil evidence – Oral evidence 15–17 December 1931, Church of England Record Centre, London.

Cecil of Chelwood, Lord (1936), *Church and State: Report of the Archbishops' Commission on the Relations between Church and State* (London: Church Assembly).

Chadwick, O. (1970), *Church and State: Report of the Archbishops' Commission* (London: Church Information Office).

—— (1972), *The Victorian Church*, Vols I and II (London: Black).

Church Commissioners (2008), *Annual Report for 2007* (London: Church House).

Church Heritage Forum (2004), *Building Faith in Our Future* (London: Church House).

Church News from Denmark, <www.interchurch.dk/mkreng/>, accessed as variously indicated in the text.

Church of Denmark (2008), *The Evangelical Lutheran Church in Denmark – Church and State*, <www.interchurch.dk/lutheranchurch>, accessed 14 November 2008.

Church of England (1999), *The Role of Bishops in the Second Chamber*, GS Misc 558 (London: Church House).

—— (2005), *Review of Clergy Terms of Service: Part Two*, GS 1564 (London: Church House).

—— (2006), *Church Statistics*, <http://www.cofe.anglican.org/info/statistics/churchstats2005/statisticspg30.htm>, accessed 15 July 2008.

—— (2007), *Crown Appointments in the Church of England: A Consultation Paper from the Archbishops*, October 2007.

—— (2008), *Crown Appointments: Report to the General Synod from the Archbishops*, GS 1680.

Church of Finland (2008), *Church and State*, <www.evl.fi/>, accessed 14 November 2008.

Church of Norway (n.d.), *A Thousand Years of Christianity* (Oslo: Church of Norway Information Service), <www.kirken.no/english/engelsk.cfm?artid=5730>, accessed 17 February 2007.

Church of Scotland (2008), *Report of Special Commission on Structure and Change*, <http://www.churchofscotland.org.uk/generalassembly/downloads/gareports08speccommission.doc>, accessed 14 June 2008.

Church of Sweden (2007), *Welcome to the Church of Sweden* (Uppsala: Church of Sweden Information Service), <www.svenskakyrkan.se/sprakversioner_en.asp>, accessed 17 February 2007).

Churches Conservation Trust (2007), *Annual Review for the year 2006–07*.

Cooper, T. (2004), *How Do We Keep Our Parish Churches* (London: Ecclesiological Society).

Copson, A., and D. Pollack (2008), 'Religion and the State in an Open Society', in Morris 2008a, pp. 51–8.

Cranmer F., J. Lucas and B. Morris (2006), *Church and State: A Mapping Exercise* (London: Constitution Unit UCL).

Cranmer, F., and S. Peterson (2006), 'Employment, Sex Discrimination and the Churches: The *Percy* Case', *Ecclesiastical Law Journal* 8, pp. 392–405.

Cranmer, F. A. (2000), 'The Church of Sweden and the Unravelling of Establishment', *Ecclesiastical Law Journal*, pp. 417–30.

—— (2002), 'National Churches, Territoriality and Mission', *Law and Justice* 149, pp. 157–77.

Cranz, F. E. (1959), *An Essay on the Development of Luther's Thought on Justice, Law, and Society*, Harvard Theological Studies XIX (Cambridge MA: Harvard Theological Press).

Crockett, A., and D. Voas (2006), 'Generations of Decline: Religious Change in Twentieth-century Britain', *Journal for the Scientific Study of Religion*, pp. 567–84.

Crockfords Clerical Directory (2004) (London: Church House Publishing).

Culture, Media and Sport Select Committee, House of Commons, Third Report (2006), *Protecting and Preserving Our Heritage*, HC 912-I (London: TSO).

Cumper, P. (2000), 'The Protection of Religious Rights under Section 13 of the Human Rights Act 1998', *Public Law*, pp. 254–65.

Danish Ministry of Ecclesiastical Affairs, Copenhagen (2002), *The Church in Denmark*.

—— (2006), *Freedom of Religion and Religious Communities in Denmark*, <www.kirkeministeriet.dk/fileadmin/share/Trossamfund/Freedom_of_religion.pdf>, accessed 9 July 2008.

Danish Ministry of Foreign Affairs (2008), 'Ministry of Ecclesiastical Affairs' (Copenhagen), available at <www.denmark.dk/en/menu/AboutDenmark/Government-Politics / Danish-Ministries / Ministry-Of-Ecclesiastical-Affairs/>, accessed 17 July 2008.

Davie, G. (1994), *Religion in Britain since 1945: Believing without Belonging* (Oxford: Blackwell).

—— (1999), 'Europe: The Exception that Proves the Rule?', in Berger 1999, pp. 65–83.

—— (2002a), *Europe: The Exceptional Case – Parameters of Faith in the Modern World* (London: Darton, Longman and Todd).

—— (2002b), 'Praying Alone? Church-going in Britain and Social Capital – a Reply to Steve Bruce', *Journal of Contemporary Religion*, pp. 329–34.

—— (2007), *The Sociology of Religion* (London: Sage).

Davie, M. (2008), *A Guide to the Church of England* (London: Mowbray).

Davis, F., E. Paulhus and A. Bradstock (2008), *Moral, But No Compass: Government, Church and the Future of Welfare* (Chelmsford: Matthew James).

Daw, E. D. (1977), *Church and State in the Empire: The Evolution of Imperial Policy 1846–1856* (Canberra: University of New South Wales).

Department for Communities and Local Government (DCLG) (2008a), *The Government's Response to the Commission on Integration and Cohesion* (London: DCLG).

—— (2008b), *Preventing Violent Extremism: Next Steps for Communities* (London: DCLG).

Department of Culture, Media and Sport (2005), *The Ecclesiastical Exemption: The Way Forward*.

—— (2006), *Government Response to the Culture, Media and Sport Select Committee's Report on Protecting and Preserving Our Heritage* (Cm 6947).

Derry, T. K. (1979), *A History of Scandinavia* (Minneapolis: Minnesota University Press).

Dibdin, L. T. (1932), *Establishment in England: Being Essays on Church and State* (London: Macmillan).

Doe, N. (ed.) (1992), *Essays in Canon Law: A Study of the Law of the Church in Wales* (Cardiff: University of Wales Press).

—— (1996), *The Legal Framework of the Church of England* (Oxford: Oxford University Press).

—— (2002), *The Law of the Church in Wales* (Cardiff: University of Wales Press).

Dowden, J. (1910), *The Medieval Church in Scotland: Its Constitution, Organisation and Law* (Glasgow: Maclehouse).

Drewry, G., and J. Bock (1971), 'Prelates in Parliament', *Parliamentary Affairs*, pp. 222–50.

Dübeck, I. (2005), 'State and Church in Denmark', in Robbers 2005a, pp. 55–76.

Dwyer, C. (2005), 'Royal Marriages and Human Rights', *Law and Justice*, pp. 27–30.

Edge, P. W., and C. C. A. Pearce (2004), 'Official Religious Representation in a Democratic Legislature: Lessons from the Manx Tynwald', *Journal of Church and State*, pp. 575–616.

Ellens, J. P. (1994), *Religious Routes to Gladstonian Liberalism: The Church Rate Conflict in England and Wales, 1832–1868* (Pennsylvania: Pennsylvania University Press).

English Heritage (2007), *Annual Report and Accounts 2006/07*.

English Heritage Lottery Fund (2005), *Churches, Chapels and Cathedrals: 10 Years of Heritage Lottery Funding*.

—— (2007), *Annual Report*.

Established Church Return (1840), House of Commons, *Established Church – Return to an Order dated 19 May 1840*, PP 1840 Vol. XXXIX 21.

Evangelical Alliance (2006), *Faith and Nation: Report of a Commission of Inquiry to the UK Evangelical Alliance* (London: Evangelical Alliance).

Fabian Society (2003), *The Future of the Monarchy* (London: Fabian Society).

Fell, M. (1999), *And Some Fell into Good Soil: A History of Christianity in Iceland* (New York: Peter Lang).

Fergusson, D. (2004), *Church, State and Civil Society* (Cambridge: Cambridge University Press).

Fittall, W. (2008), 'Perspectives from within the Church of England', in Morris 2008a, pp. 75–80.

Forrester, D. B. (1999), '*Ecclesia Scoticana* – Established, Free or National?', *Theology* CII.805, pp. 80–9.

Free Church of Scotland (1844), *Proceedings of General Assembly 1843* (Edinburgh: Johnstone).

Friedner, L. (2005), 'State and Church in Sweden', in Robbers 2005, pp. 537–51.

Garbett, C. (1950), *Church and State in England* (London: Hodder).

Garcia Oliva, J. (2008), 'Public Authorities and Religious Denominations in Italy and Spain', in Morris 2008a, pp. 41–50.

Gash, N. (1972), *Sir Robert Peel: The Life of Sir Robert Peel after 1830* (London: Longman).

Gill R. (2003), *The 'Empty' Church Revisited* (Aldershot; Ashgate).

Glendinning, T., and S. Bruce (2006), 'New Ways of Believing or Belonging: Is Religion Giving Way to Spirituality?', *British Journal of Sociology*, pp. 399–414.

Gore, C. (1926), *Reconstruction of Belief* (London; John Murray).

Green, C. A. H. (1937), *Disestablishment and Disendowment in Wales: A Record of 15 Years* (London: SPCK).

Green, S. J. D. (1996), *Religion in an Age of Decline: Organisation and Experience in Industrial Yorkshire* (Cambridge: Cambridge University Press).

Gustafsson, G. (1990), 'Sweden: A Folk Church under Political Influence', *Studia Theologica* 44, pp. 3–16.

—— (2003), 'Church–State Separation: Swedish Style', *West European Politics* 26.1, pp. 51–72.

Halman, L., and V. Draulans (2006), 'How Secular Is Europe?', *British Journal of Sociology*, pp. 266–88.

Harlow, A., F. Cranmer and N. Doe (2008), 'Bishops in the House of Lords: A Critical Analysis', *Public Law*, pp. 490–509.

Hastings, A. (1997), 'The Case for Retaining the Establishment', in Modood 1997, pp. 40–6.

Hay, R. C., V. C. Craig et al. (1994), 'Employment', in S. T. Smith and R. Black (eds), *The Laws of Scotland: Stair Memorial Encyclopaedia* (Edinburgh: Law Society of Scotland).

Heelas, P., and L. Woodhead (2005), *The Spiritual Revolution: Why Religion Is Giving Way to Spirituality* (Oxford: Blackwell).

Heikkilä, M., J. Knuutil and M. Scheinin (2005), 'State and Church in Finland', in Robbers 2005a, pp. 519–36.

Heino, H., K. Salonen and J. Rusama (1997), *Response to Recession: The Evangelical Lutheran Church of Finland in the Years 1992–1995* (Tampere: Research Institute of the Evangelical Lutheran Church of Finland).

Henriksen, Jan-Olav (2001), 'National Churches in a Culture of Pluralism', paper presented at a conference entitled 'The Nordic Countries and Europe' (Schœftergåden, Denmark 2001 [unpublished]).

Herbert, D. (2004), *Religion and Civil Society: Rethinking Public Religion in the Contemporary World* (Aldershot: Ashgate).

Hietakangas, Maija-Liisa (2005), 'Finances of the Finnish Evangelical Lutheran Church', in Evangelical Lutheran Church of Finland, *Church for the People* (Helsinki) e-publication available at <www.evl.fi/EVLen.nsf/Documents/162656D6533ABE72C225730F002B9F85?OpenDocument&lang=E>, accessed 17 July 2008.

Hobson, T. (2003), *Against Establishment: An Anglican Polemic* (London: Darton, Longman and Todd).

Hope, N. (1995), *German and Scandinavian Protestantism 1700–1918* (Oxford: Oxford University Press).

Höpfl, H. (1982), *The Christian Polity of John Calvin* (Cambridge: Cambridge University Press).

—— (1991), *Luther and Calvin on Secular Authority* (Cambridge: Cambridge University Press).

Howick of Glendale, Lord (1964), *Crown Appointments and the Church* (London: Church Information Office).

Hugason, H. (1990), 'The National Church of Iceland', *Studia Theologica*, pp. 51–63.

Hunt, G. L. (ed.) (1965), *Calvinism and the Political Order* (Philadelphia: Westminster Press).

Hurd, Lord (2001), *To Lead and to Serve: The Report of the Review of the See of Canterbury* (London: Church House).

Hurt, J. (1972), *Education in Evolution: Church, State, Society and Popular Education 1800–1870* (London: Paladin).

Inner Cities Religious Council (2008), <www.neighbourhood.gov.uk/page.asp?id+524>, accessed 6 April 2008.

Jahangir, A. (2008), *Freedom of Religion or Belief: Report of UN Special Rapporteur*, UN Human Rights Council (A/HRC/7/10/Add3).

Jones, K. (2003), *Education in Britain – 1944 to the Present* (Cambridge: Polity).

Jones, P. (2000), *The Governance of the Church in Wales* (Cardiff: Greenfach).

Judge, H. (2001), *Faith-based Schools and the State: Catholics in America, France and England* (Wallingford: Symposium Books).

Kemp, E. (2003), 'Legal Aspects of the History of Church and State', *Ecclesiastical Law Journal*, pp. 47–9.

King, A. (2008), *The British Constitution* (Oxford: Oxford University Press).

Lamont, S. (1989), *Church and State: Uneasy Alliances* (London: Bodley Head).

Lausten, M. S. (2002), *A Church History of Denmark* (Aldershot: Ashgate).

Leigh, I. (2004), 'By Law Established? The Crown, Constitutional Reform and the Church of England', *Public Law*, pp. 266–73.

Lodberg, P. (2000), 'Freedom of Religion and the Evangelical Lutheran Church in Denmark', *Studia Theologica*, pp. 43–54.

Mackintosh, W. H. (1972), *Disestablishment and Liberation: The Movement for the Separation of the Anglican Church from State Control* (London: Epworth).

McLean, I., and B. Linsley (2004), *The Church of England and the State: Reforming Establishment for a Multi-faith Britain* (London: New Politics Network).

MacLean, M. A. (2002), 'The Church of Scotland as a National Church', *Law and Justice*, pp. 125–33.

—— (2004), 'The Crown Rights of the Redeemer: A Reformed Approach to Sovereignty for the National Church' (PhD Thesis, University of Edinburgh).

McLeod H. (1984), *Religion and the Working Class in Nineteenth-century Britain* (Basingstoke: Macmillan).

—— (2000), *Secularism in Western Europe 1848–1914* (Basingstoke: Macmillan).

—— (2006), *North European Churches from the Cold War to Globalisation* (Tampere: Finland Church Research Institute).

—— (2007), *The Religious Crisis of the 1960s* (Oxford: Oxford University Press).

Madsen, W. Westergard (1964), 'The Danish National Church', in Poul Hartling (ed.), *The Danish Church* (Copenhagen: Den Danske Selskab), pp. 86–98.

Martin, D. (1984), 'The Church of England: From Established Church to Secular Lobby', in D. Anderson (ed.), *The Kindness That Kills: The Churches' Simplistic Response to Complex Social Issues* (London: SPCK), pp. 134–42.

—— (2002), *Pentecostalism: The World Their Parish* (Oxford: Blackwell).

—— (2005), *On Secularization: Towards a Revised General Theory* (Aldershot: Ashgate).

Marx, K., and F. Engels (1869), *Collected Works* Vol. 21 (London: International Workingmen's Association).

Methodist Church of Great Britain (2004), *Church, State and Establishment* (London: Faith and Order Committee of the Methodist Conference 2004), <www.methodist.org.uk/downloads/co_church_state_establishment0704.doc>, accessed 17 February 2007.

Moberly, W. (1952), *Church and State* (London: Church Information Board).

Modood, T. (1994), 'Establishment, Multiculturalism and Citizenship', *Political Quarterly*, pp. 53–73.

—— (1997), *Church, State and Religious Minorities* (London: Policy Studies Institute).

—— (2005), *Multicultural Politics: Racism, Ethnicity, and Muslims in Britain* (Minneapolis: Minnesota Press).

Moneypenny, W. F., and G. E. Buckle (1929), *The Life of Benjamin Disraeli, Earl of Beaconsfield*, Vol. 1 (London: Murray).

Monsma, S. V., and J. C. Soper (1997), *The Challenge of Pluralism: Church and State in Five Democracies* (Lanham and Oxford: Rowman and Littlefield).

Morgan, K. O. (1980), *Wales in British Politics 1868–1922*, 3rd edn (Cardiff: University of Wales Press).

Morris, B. (2006), 'Introduction', in Cranmer, Lucas and Morris 2006, pp. 9–12.

Morris, R. M. (ed.) (2008a), *Church and State: Some Reflections on Church Establishment in England* (London: Constitution Unit UCL).

—— (2008b), 'The Future of the Monarchy: The Reign of King Charles III', in R. Hazell (ed.), *Constitutional Futures Revisited: Britain's Constitution to 2020* (Basingstoke: Palgrave Macmillan), pp. 139–55.

Munro, C. (1997), 'Does Scotland Have an Established Church?', *Ecclesiastical Law Review*, pp. 639–45.

Murray, D. S. (2000), *Rebuilding the Kirk: Presbyterian Reunion in Scotland 1909–1929* (Edinburgh: Scottish Academic Press).

Murray, R. K. (Lord Murray) (1958), 'The Constitutional Position of the Church of Scotland', *Public Law*, pp. 155–62.

Myrhe-Nielson, D. (1990), 'Life Forms and "Folk Church": Some Aspects of Norwegian Ecclesiology', *Studia Theologica*, pp. 85–94.

National Centre for Social Research (NCSR) (2008), *British Social Attitudes 24th Report* (London: NCSR).

Norman, E. R. (1994), 'Church and State since 1800', in S. Gilley and W. J. Sheils (eds), *A History of Religion in Britain* (Oxford: Blackwell), pp. 277–90.

—— (2004), *Anglican Difficulties: A New Syllabus of Errors* (London: Morehouse Continuum).

—— (2008), 'Notes on *Church and State: A Mapping Exercise*', in Morris 2008, pp. 9–13.

Norris, P., and R. Inglehart (2004), *Sacred and Secular: Religion and Politics Worldwide* (Cambridge: CambridgeUniversity Press).

O'Beirne, M. (2004), *Religion in England and Wales: Findings from the 2001 Home Office Citizenship Survey*, Home Office Research Study 274 (London: Home Office).

Ofestad, B. (1996), 'The Collapse of the Reformation: A Perspective on the Lutheran Tradition', in J. Broadhurst (ed.), *Quo Vaditis: The State Churches of Northern Europe* (Leominster: Gracewing), pp. 18–33.

Office of National Statistics (ONS) (2007), *Social Trends* (London: Stationery Office).

Østang, Ø. (2006a), 'Commission Proposes Ending Norway's State Church System' (Oslo: Church of Norway Information Service, 2 February), <http://www.kirken.no/english/news.cfm?artid=75382>, accessed 17 February 2007.

—— (2006b), 'Church of Norway Synod Votes to Change State Relations' (Oslo: Church of Norway Information Service, 22 November), <www.kirken.no/english/news.cfm?artid=111292>, accessed 17 February 2007.

Österlin, L. (1995), *Churches of Northern Europe in Profile* (Norwich: Canterbury Press).

Parekh, B. (2000), *Report of the Commission on the Future of Multiethnic Britain* (London: Profile Books).

—— (2006), *Rethinking Multiculturalism: Cultural Diversity and Political Theory*, 2nd edn (Basingstoke: Palgrave Macmillan).

Parker-Jenkins, M. (2002), 'Equal Access to State Funding: The Case of Muslim Schools in Britain', *Race, Ethnicity and Education*, pp. 273–89.

Partington, A., and P. Bickley (2007), *Coming Off the Bench: The Past, Present and Future of Religious Representation in the House of Lords* (London: Theos).

Pearce, A. (2003), 'Aston Cantlow: Chancel Repairs and the Status of Church of England Institutions', *Law and Justice*, pp. 163–71.

Percy, M. (2001), *The Salt of the Earth* (London: Sheffield Academic Press).

Perry, Bness (2001), *Working with the Spirit: Choosing Diocesan Bishops* (London: Church House).

Persenius, R. (1996), 'Church and State in Sweden 1995', *European Journal for Church and State Research*, pp. 121–5.

—— (1999), 'The Year 2000: Disestablishment in Sweden', *Theology*, pp. 177–86.

Peterson, S., and I. McLean (2007), 'Of Wheat, the Church in Wales and the West Lothian Question', *Welsh History Review*, pp. 151–74.

Pew Forum on Religion and Public Life, US Religious Landscape Survey – <www.religions.pewforum.org/reports>, accessed 18 March 2008.

Pike L. O. (1894), *A Constitutional History of the House of Lords* (London: Macmillan).

Pilling Report (2007), *Talent and Calling*, GS 1650 (London: Church House).

Plesner, I. T. (2001), 'State and Religion in Norway', *European Journal for Church and State Research*, pp. 317–25.

—— (2002), 'State and Religion in Norway in Times of Change', *European Journal for Church and State Research*, pp. 263–70.

Podmore, C. (2005), *Aspects of Anglican Identity* (London: Church House Publishing).

Pollack, D., and G. Pickel (2007), 'Religious Individualization or Secularization? Testing Hypotheses of Religious Change: The Case of Eastern and Western Germany', *British Journal of Sociology*, pp. 603–32.

Pond, C., and O. Gay (2005), *The Act of Settlement and the Protestant Succession* (London: House of Commons Standard Note 15 March 2005).

Port, M. H. (1961), *Six Hundred New Churches: A Study of the Church Building Commission, 1818–1856, and Its Church Building Activities* (London: SPCK).

—— (ed.) (1986), *The Commission for Building Fifty New Churches* (London: London Record Society).

Protestant Dissenting Ministers Return (1840), House of Commons, *Protestant Dissenting Ministers, Regium Donum, Maynooth College, Roman Catholic Clergy, Dissenting and Roman Catholic Chapels, Return to an Order dated 19 May 1840*, PP 1840 Vol. XXXIX 71.

Public Administration Select Committee (PASC) (2002), *The Second Chamber: Continuing the Reform* (London: House of Commons).

Redfern, A. (2007), 'Establishment and Government', in C. Bryant (ed.), *Towards a New Constitutional Settlement* (London: Smith Institute), pp. 38–42.

Redgrave, S. (1852), *Murray's Official Handbook of Church and State* (London: Murray).

Religious Institutions Return (1852), House of Commons *Religious and Other Institutions, Return to an Order dated 18 March 1852*, PP 1852 Vol. XXXVIII 337.

Rivers, J. (2000), 'From Toleration to Pluralism: Religious Liberty and Religious Establishment under the United Kingdom's Human Rights Act', in Ahdar 2000, pp. 133–61.

Robbers, G. (2005a) (ed.), *State and Church in the European Union*, 2nd edn (Baden-Baden: Nomos).

—— (2005b), 'State and Church in Germany', in Robbers 2005a, pp. 77–94.

Rodger, Lord of Earlsferry (2008), *The Courts, the Church and the Constitution: Aspects of the Disruption of 1843* (Edinburgh: Edinburgh University Press).

Roper, G. (2008), 'View of a Critical Friend – from the United Reformed Church', in Morris 2008, pp. 23–32.

Russell, M. (2000), *Reforming the House of Lords: Lessons from Overseas* (Oxford: Oxford University Press).

Russell, M., and M. Sciara (2007), 'Why Does the Government Get Defeated in the House of Lords: The Lords, the Party System and British Politics', *British Politics*, pp. 299–322.

Sacks, J. (1991), The *Persistence of Faith: Religion, Morality and Society in a Secular Age*, Reith Lectures 1990 (London: Weidenfeld).

Salonen, K., K. Kääriäinen and K. Niemelä (2001), *The Church at the Turn of the Millennium: The Evangelical Lutheran Church of Finland from 1996 to 1999* (Tampere: Research Institute of the Evangelical Lutheran Church of Finland).

Savage, S., S. Collins-Mayo, B. Mayo and G. Cray (2006), *Making Sense of Generation Y: The World View of 15 to 25 Year-olds* (London: Church House).

Scottish Executive (2005), *Analysis of Religion in the 2001 Census: Summary Report* (Edinburgh).

Scottish Royal Commission on Churches (1905), Cd 2494 PP 1905 Vol. XXIII.

Selborne, 1st Earl (1887), *A Defence of the Church of England against Disestablishment* (London: MacMillan).

Selborne, 2nd Earl (1916), *Report of the Archbishops' Committee on Church and State* (London: SPCK).

Seppo, J. (2002), 'Church and State in Finland in 2001', *European Journal for Church and State Research*, pp. 145–56.

Sigurbjörnsson, K. (2000), *The Church of Iceland, Past and Present* (Reykjavik: Church of Iceland), <www.kirkjan.is/?english/church-of-iceland?kafli=1>, accessed 17 February 2007.

Simpson, C. (1931), Cecil Commission, Oral Evidence 15–17 December 1931, Church of England Records Centre, p. 509.

Sims, N. A. (2008), 'A Quaker Point of View', in Morris 2008, pp. 33–40.

Sjolinder, R. (1962), *Presbyterian Reunion in Scotland 1907–1921* (Edinburgh: T&T Clark).

Smith, C. L. (2003), 'The Place of Representatives of Religion in the Reformed Second Chamber', *Public Law*, pp. 674–96.

Smith, S. (1902), *My Life-work* (London: Hodder).

Social Security Select Committee (1996), Fifth Report, *Church of England Pensions*, HC 340.

Social Trends 2007 (London: NSO).

Sørensen, Søren Peder (1997), 'The Evangelical Lutheran Church in Denmark' (Copenhagen: Council on Inter-Church Relations 1997, available at <www.interchurch.dk/LutheranChurch/>, accessed 17 July 2008).

Stevenson, D. (1974), 'The Radical Party in the Church of Scotland, 1637–45', *Journal of Ecclesiastical History*, pp. 135–64.

—— (1988), *The Covenanters: The National Covenant and Scotland* (Edinburgh: Saltire Society).

Taylor, S. J. (2003), 'Disestablished Establishment: High and Earthed Establishment in the Church in Wales', *Journal of Contemporary Religion*, pp. 227–40.

Thompson, D. M. (1975), 'The Politics of the Enabling Act (1919)', in D. Baker (ed.), *Church, Society and Politics* (Oxford: Blackwell), pp. 383–92.

Toy, J. (1998), *Scandinavian Perspectives* (York: Dean and Chapter).

United States Department of State (2007), *International Religious Freedom Report: Denmark 2007*.

Van Straubenzee, W. (1992), *Senior Church Appointments* (London: Church House).

Voas, D. (2008), 'Foreword', in P. Brierley, *UK Christian Handbook: Religious Trends 7*, pp. 0.3–0.4.

Voas, D., and S. Bruce (2004), 'The 2001 Census and Christian Identification in Britain', *Journal of Contemporary Religion*, pp. 23–8.

Voas, D., and A. Crockett (2005), 'Religion in Britain: Neither Believing nor Belonging', *Sociology*, pp. 11–28.

Voas, D., D. V. A. Olson and A. Crockett (2002), 'Religious Pluralism and Participation: Why Previous Research Is Wrong', *American Sociological Review*, pp. 212–30.

Wakeham, Lord (2000), *A House for the Future: Report of the Royal Commission on the Reform of the House of Lords*, Cm 4534 (London: Stationery Office).

Walford, G. (2000), *Policy and Politics in Education: Sponsored Grant Maintained Schools and Religious Diversity* (Aldershot: Ashgate).

Walker, D. (1976), 'Disestablishment and Independence', in D. Walker (ed.), *A History of the Church in Wales* (Penarth: Church in Wales), pp. 164–87.

Watkin, T. G. (1992), 'Disestablishment, Self-determination and the Constitutional Development of the Church in Wales', in N. Doe (ed.), *A Study of the Law of the Church in Wales* (Cardiff: University of Wales Press), pp. 25–48.

Weller, P. (2000), 'Equity, Inclusiveness and Participation in a Plural Society: Challenging the Establishment of the Church of England', in Edge and Harvey 2000, pp. 53–67.

Weller, P., and K. Purdam (2000), *Religious Discrimination in England and Wales: Interim Report* (Derby: University of Derby).

Welsby, P. A. (1985), *How the Church of England Works* (London: Church Information Office).

Williams, R. (2004), Address at service in Westminster Abbey on 4 November 2004, to mark the 300th anniversary of Queen Anne's Bounty.

—— (2008), 'Holy Week: Faith & Politics Questions & Answers Session', 18 March, <www.archbishopofcanterbury.org/1715>, accessed 2 May 2008.

Wingren, G. F. (1969), *Einar Billing and the Development of Modern Swedish Theology*, trans. E. Wahlstrom (Philadelphia: Fortress Press).

Wood, K. P. (2008), 'The National Secular Society', in Morris 2008, pp. 59–74.

Woodhead, L., P. Heelas and D. Martin (2001), *Peter Berger and the Study of Religion* (London: Routledge).

Wright, N. G. (2008), 'A View from One of the Free Churches', in Morris 2008, pp. 14–22.

Wright, T. (2002), 'God and Caesar, Then and Now', 22 April 2002, *Jubilee Reflections at Westminster Abbey: A Series of Lectures on God, Church, Crown and State*.

Index